Understanding
Andrew Fuller

Volume 2

Andrew Fuller's frequent travels on behalf of the Baptist Missionary Society after its formation in 1792 were undertaken by means of the mail coach routes that had been developed in the 1780s at the behest of William Pitt, who was both the Prime Minister of England as well as the Chancellor of the Exchequer. There was seating both within the coach and on the outside, though the former was obviously preferable, since the latter meant that the passenger was fully exposed to the elements.

In a diary entry for September 1802, when Fuller was returning from a fund-raising and preaching trip in Scotland, he noted that he was "riding from Manchester to [Market] Harborough, in the mail [coach]." Near Loughborough in Leicestershire, a man who had been travelling in another carriage asked Fuller if he could take his place in the coach when they got to Harborough. "We dined at Leicester," Fuller continued, "and the gentleman being in the inn-yard, I went to him, and offered him my place from Leicester, proposing to ride on the outside as far as Harborough. He thanked me but declined it. He added, 'I think I have seen you, sir, before.' He dined with us; and, while at dinner, seeing my portmanteau marked A.F.K., he asked me, before our company, if my name was not Fuller. I told him it was. He then thanked me, not only for my kind offer of my place, but for a late publication, which he had read with unusual satisfaction. I made but little answer …"

The painting on the front cover, simply entitled "The Stagecoach," was painted in 1791 by the English landscape artist George Morland (1763–1804).

Volume 2

UNDERSTANDING
Andrew Fuller

Life, Thought, and Legacies

Edited by
NATHAN A. FINN,
JEFF ROBINSON SR., AND SHANE SHADDIX

Understanding Andrew Fuller: Life, Thought, and Legacies (Volume 2)
Edited by Nathan A. Finn, Jeff Robinson Sr., and Shane Shaddix

Copyright © H&E Academic 2021

Cover design by Chance Faulkner
Front cover image: The Stagecoach, George Morland, English, 1763–1804

Paperback ISBN: 978-1-989174-90-6
Ebook ISBN: 978-1-989174-91-3

Contents

Abbreviations
Acknowledgements i

Introduction 1
   Nathan A. Finn

1. An Historical and Biblical Root of the Globalization of Christianity:
The Fullerism of Andrew Fuller's *The Gospel Worthy of All Acceptation* 5
   Michael A.G. Haykin

2. "In Exhortations, Invitations, Precepts, and Threatenings":
Andrew Fuller, John Owen, and the Free Offer of the Gospel 15
   Shane Shaddix

3. "I Ever Wish to Make My Savior's Will My Own":
Andrew Fuller and the Heart of Missions 31
   Ryan West

4. "Helped on Our Way to Heaven":
The Puritan Tradition in Andrew Fuller's Theology of Marriage 45
   Matthew D. Haste

5. "A Musical Pronunciation of Affecting Truth":
The Church Music of Andrew Fuller 59
   Charles J. Bumgardner

6. Christ as the Criterion for Preaching:
Andrew Fuller and the Abrahamic Narrative 101
   David G. Norman, Jr.

7. What Contemporary Pastors Can Learn from Andrew Fuller 119
   David E. Prince

8. C.H. Spurgeon: A Fullerite? 137
   Steve Weaver

A Chronology of Andrew Fuller's Life 155
   Nathan A. Finn

Contributors 161
Scripture Index 163
Subject Index 165

Abbreviations

ABQ	*American Baptist Quarterly*
AFR	*Andrew Fuller Review*
ATR	*Anglican Theological Review*
BAR	*Baptist Annual Register*
BHH	*Baptist History and Heritage*
BQ	*Baptist Quarterly*
CBHHS	Centre for Baptist History and Heritage Studies
CTJ	*Calvin Theological Journal*
CRS	Classics of Reformed Spirituality
CWAF	Fuller, Andrew. *The Complete Works of Andrew Fuller*, 16 vols., series ed. Michael Haykin. Boston: De Gruyter, 2016–present.
DBSJ	*Detroit Baptist Seminary Journal*
FW	Fuller, Andrew. *The Complete Works of the Rev. Andrew Fuller, with a Memoir of His Life by Andrew Gunton Fuller*, 3 vols., ed. Joseph Belcher. Valley Forge, PA: American Baptist Publication Society, 1845 ed.; reprint, Harrisonburg, VA: Sprinkle Publications, 1988.
IBHSJ	*Irish Baptist Historical Society Journal*
JEH	*Journal of Ecclesiastical History*
JEH	*Journal of the Evangelical Homiletics Society*
JETS	*Journal of the Evangelical Theological Society*

JTS	*Journal of Theological Studies*
MBH	Monographs in Baptist History
MTPS	Spurgeon, Charles. *Metropolitan Tabernacle Pulpit Series*, 63 vols. London: Passmore and Alabaster, 1855–1917.
RHT	Reformed Historical Theology
PRJ	*Puritan Reformed Journal*
PRS	*Perspectives on Religious Studies*
SCJ	*The Sixteenth Century Journal*
SBET	*Scottish Bulletin of Evangelical Theology*
SBJT	*Southern Baptist Journal of Theology*
SBHT	Studies in Baptist History and Thought
SBLT	Studies in Baptist Life and Thought
SCHT	Studies in Christian History and Thought
SEHT	Studies in Evangelical History and Thought
SHT	Studies in Historical Theology
TJ	*Trinity Journal*
WAF	Fuller, Andrew. *The Works of Andrew Fuller*, ed. Andrew Gunton Fuller. 1841 ed.; reprint, Carlisle, PA: Banner of Truth, 2007.
WJE	Edwards, Jonathan. *The Works of Jonathan Edwards*, 26 vols., series eds. John E. Smith, Harry S. Stout, and Kenneth M. Minkema. New Haven, CT: Yale University Press, 1957–2008.
WJS	Stennett, Joseph. *The Works of the Reverend and Learned Mr. Joseph Stennett*, 4 vols. London, 1731.

WJO	Owen, John. *The Works of John Owen, D.D.*, 23 vols., series ed. William Goould. 1826 ed; reprint, Carlisle, PA: Banner of Truth, 1968–1991.
WJP	Priestley, Joseph. *The Theological and Miscellaneous Works of Joseph Priestley*, 26 vols., series ed. John Towill Rutt. London: Printed for G. Smallfield, 1817–32.
WTJ	*Westminster Theological Journal*
WWP	Perkins, William. *The Workes of That Famous and Worthy Minister of Christ in the Universitie of Cambridge, Mr. William Perkins*, 3 vols. London: By Io Legatt printer to the Universitie of Cambridge, 1616–1618.

Acknowledgements

Every book has a story. Some of them can be complicated. In the case of these two volumes, a story that was intended to last a couple of years has been six years in the making. Our contributors have been exceedingly gracious as the project has been delayed more than once due to a job relocation or other unforeseen complication. We trust they are pleased with the end result and that it has been worth the wait. Thanks for sticking with us, brothers.

We are grateful to our families for their patience as we have worked on these books, often frenetically and at inconvenient times. We are so blessed. We are also grateful for the support of the ministries we have served during these past six years: Union University and North Greenville University (Nathan); The Gospel Coalition, The Southern Baptist Theological Seminary, and Christ Fellowship Baptist Church (Jeff); and Southeastern Baptist Theological Seminary and Imago Dei Church (Shane). Our friend and fellow contributor, Michael Haykin, helped to rescue this project when it was sputtering at the eleventh hour. We are thankful for his kindness, as well as for his scholarship, which has influenced the way all three of us think about Andrew Fuller. Chance Faulkner and the team at H&E Publishing have been a blessing to us. We appreciate their love for Fuller and are grateful they took an interest in this project.

Several journals and publishers have kindly granted permission for previously published material to be republished or adapted for this work. Michael Haykin's chapter "Andrew Fuller and the Fading of the Trinitarian Imagination" was originally published in *A New Divinity: Transatlantic Reformed Evangelical Debates during the Long Eighteenth Century*, eds. Mark Jones and Michael A.G. Haykin (Göttingen: Vandenhoeck & Ruprecht, 2018), 193-204. David Allen's chapter "Andrew Fuller and the Extent of the Atonement" is adapted from material originally published in David L. Allen, *The Extent of the Atonement: A Historical and Critical Review* (Nashville, TN: B&H Academic, 2016), 479-497. Ian Clary's chapter "'The Centre of Christianity—the Doctrine of the Cross': Andrew Fuller as a Reformed Theologian" was originally published in *Evangelical Quarterly* 90.3 (2019): 195-212. Haykin's chapter "An

Historical and Biblical Root of the Globalization of Christianity: The Fullerism of Andrew Fuller's *The Gospel Worthy of All Acceptation*" was originally published in *The Journal of Baptist Studies* 8 (2016): 3–15. Steve Weaver's chapter "C. H. Spurgeon: A Fullerite?" was originally published in *The Journal of Baptist Studies* 8 (2016): 99–117. We appreciate permission to republish this material.

We stuck with this project in no small part because of our appreciation for Andrew Fuller. We are all three of us contemporary Fullerites in various ways. Our vision of the Christian life has been shaped by Fuller and his circle of friends. While we are scholars of Fuller and his thought, we are also Baptist ministers who wish to commend his life and thought to others. Fuller had his faults, and we disagree amongst ourselves concerning aspects of his thought, but we agree that Fuller is a giant in our tradition and that his is a legacy worth owning. We dedicate this volume to his memory.

Introduction

Nathan A. Finn

Andrew Fuller (1754-1815) is arguably one of the half dozen most important theologians in Baptist history. Fuller was in many ways the theological center of an evangelical renewal movement among the Particular Baptists during the latter half of the so-called long eighteenth century (c. 1689-1815). Fuller was not an original theologian, but rather was a creative translator of others' ideas (especially the Puritans and Jonathan Edwards) into a Particular Baptist milieu. He was so influential that the name "Fullerism" because more or less synonymous with evangelical Calvinism among the Particular Baptists, though this label was not always used in a positive way at the time. Had it not been for Fuller and other evangelicals such as Robert Hall Sr. (1728-1791), Abraham Booth (1734-1806), John Ryland Jr. (1753-1825), and William Carey (1761-1834), among others, High Calvinism may well have choked the life out of Calvinistic Baptists in the British Isles.

While Baptist historians have always appreciated Fuller and his legacy, the past forty years have witnessed what might be considered a renaissance in Fuller Studies.[1] While most of the earliest studies focused on Fuller's soteriology or his contribution to the rise of the modern missions movement, over time more attention has been given to other aspects of his thought. This is in part because Fuller wrote on so many different topics! Like Martin Luther before him, Fuller was for the most part an "occasional" theologian who wrote in response to the significant theological debates of his day. He was also a longtime pastor who reflected upon a number of themes related to pastoral ministry. Scholars still have plenty of ground to till when it comes to Fuller's life, thought, and legacy.

In North America, the "center of gravity" for Fuller Studies is the Andrew Fuller Center for Baptist Studies, founded at The Southern Baptist Theological Seminary in 2007. Roughly half of the contributors to these two volumes

---

[1] Nathan A. Finn, "The Renaissance in Andrew Fuller Studies: A Bibliographic Essay," in *SBJT* 17.2 (Summer 2013): 44-61.

are, or have been, associated with the Fuller Center. Under the directorship of Michael Haykin, the Fuller Center has hosted conferences, sponsored lectures, published scholarly journals, and facilitated the publication of books that advance our understanding of Fuller and Fullerism. The Fuller Center's work has been undertaken with an eye to both the academy and the local church. Few scholars have written dispassionate works of dry scholarship related to Fuller's life and thought. Fuller Studies has been dominated by pastor-theologians and historians for the church who are interested, not only in scholarship, but in spiritual flourishing. As such, Fuller Studies is an exercise in *ressourcement* of earlier Baptist thought for the sake of contemporary Baptist renewal.[2]

By far the most significant undertaking by the Fuller Center is *The Complete Works of Andrew Fuller*, a sixteen-volume scholarly edition of Fuller's writings published by Walter de Gruyter Press. Haykin serves as general editor of the series, and the editorial board includes John Coffey, Nathan Finn, Crawford Gribben, and Doug Sweeney. Each volume in the series provides a critical edition of the text accompanied by a scholarly introduction by the volume's editor(s). At the time of this writing, two of the volumes are in print, with two more entries forthcoming in the next twenty-four months. While non-critical reprints will continue to be the go-to resource for most pastors, *The Complete Works of Andrew Fuller* will set the standard for scholars interested in Fuller's life and thought.

The year 2015 was the bicentennial of Fuller's death. Several conferences were held to commemorate Fuller that year. In addition, two different sessions were dedicated to Fuller at the annual meeting of the Evangelical Theological Society. Almost all of the chapters in this volume originated as papers that were delivered at one or more of these conferences during 2015. Some of the contributors are seasoned scholars who have written widely on Fuller, while others are junior scholars still in the earliest stage of the career. Some hold full-time academic appointments at universities or seminaries, while others are full-time pastors who have undertaken advanced study of Fuller. Some of the contributors are primarily historians, others are systematic theologians, and still others are scholars of homiletics or spirituality. Not a few of the contributors do work in more than one of these fields. All of the contributors are convictional Baptists, with most having ties to the Southern Baptist tradition.

---

[2] For a similar initiative dedicated to retrieving the pre-modern tradition for the sake of contemporary Baptist renewal, see The Center for Baptist Renewal (http://www.centerforbaptistrenewal.com). Several contributors to this volume are fellows of the CBR.

Nathan A. Finn

As is often the case with a collection of essays, several recurring themes emerge. One such theme that is not surprising is that Fuller was dedicated to demonstrating that God's sovereignty in salvation was compatible biblically with strong appeals for sinners to repent of their sins and believe in Jesus Christ for their salvation. A related theme is Fuller's commitment to global missions, as evidenced in his longtime leadership of the Baptist Missionary Society. Another topic that recurs in multiple chapters is that Fuller was deeply concerned with the doctrine of the atonement, though the contributors disagree amongst themselves about how best to interpret Fuller's mature understanding of the cross. Still another theme returned to frequently by the contributors is Fuller's pastoral ministry, which provided the vocational context for his theological and polemical contributors. A final theme is the thoroughly Trinitarian and Christocentric aspects of Fuller's thinking.

Understanding Andrew Fuller is not a systematic study of Fuller's thought. That much-needed project has yet to be undertaken. But it is an excellent introduction to some of the elements of Fuller's life and thought that has captured the imagination of Baptist scholars in North America over the past couple of decades. We hope these volumes encourage further scholarship of the topics they address—and do not address. More importantly, our prayer is that these volumes might encourage Baptists and other evangelicals to engage deeply with Fuller's writings, learn from his insights, and embody the best of his theological vision for the glory of God, the health of the church, and the sake of the nations.

1
An Historical and Biblical Root of the Globalization of Christianity: The Fullerism of Andrew Fuller's *The Gospel Worthy of All Acceptation*

Michael A. G. Haykin

As Geoffrey F. Nuttall, the twentieth-century doyen of the study of British Nonconformity, once remarked, it has been given to few Englishmen to have a system of theological thought named after them. Andrew Fuller (1754–1815) of Kettering is among those few.[1] "Fullerism" initially appeared, it seems, as a term of reproach while Fuller was still alive. The Norfolk Baptist pastor Job Hupton (1762–1849), for instance, employed this term in an 1803 pamphlet to denote specifically the concept, erroneous in his mind, that it is "the duty of all who hear the gospel to believe it." In this pithy phrase, Hupton accurately caught an essential aspect of Fuller's thinking, though the same cannot be said for his further critique of Fuller's theology as that of a "buffoon" who regarded all "who cannot swallow his sophisms, or subscribe to his creed, as if they were not worthy to black his shoes."[2] By the time this critique and ad

---

[1] Geoffrey F. Nuttall, *Studies in English Dissent* (Weston Rhyn, Oswestry, Shropshire: Quinta Press, 2002), 207.

The classic study of Fuller's life is John Ryland, Jr., *The Work of Faith, the Labour of Love, and the Patience of Hope Illustrated; in the Life and Death of the Reverend Andrew Fuller* (London: Button & Son, 1816). The same publisher published a second edition of this biography two years later with a slightly different title: *The Work of Faith, the Labour of Love, and the Patience of Hope, illustrated; in the Life and Death of the Rev. Andrew Fuller* (London: Button & Son, 1818). It is this second edition that is used in this paper.

For two important recent studies, see Paul Brewster, *Andrew Fuller: Model Pastor-Theologian*, SBLT (Nashville, TN: B&H Academic, 2010) and Peter J. Morden, *The Life and Thought of Andrew Fuller (1754–1815)*, SEHT (Milton Keynes, UK: Paternoster, 2015). Also see the excellent study by E.F. Clipsham, "Andrew Fuller and Fullerism: A Study in Evangelical Calvinism," *BQ* 20 (1963–1964): 99–114, 146–154, 214–225, 268–276.

[2] Job Hupton, *A Blow struck at the Root of Fullerism* (London: L. J. Higham, [1803]) as cited in a review of this book in *The New Theological Repository* (1803), 116. Fuller did not reply to Hupton, though see the reply of George Stonehouse, *Fullerism Defended; or, Faith in Christ Asserted to be a*

Andrew Fuller

hominem attack appeared, though, Fuller was no stranger to theological controversy. Since the publication of *The Gospel Worthy of All Acceptation* in 1785, his rebuttal of the High Calvinism of men like Hupton,[3] he had been engaged in defending his position against various critics of his evangelical Calvinism as well as grappling in print with the heterodoxies of Socinianism and Deism. These works had brought him a measure of fame and respect as a Christian apologist.[4] Given the missional globalization of Christianity in the past two centuries, however, our attention is rightly placed upon the first of Fuller's apologies, *The Gospel Worthy of All Acceptation*, which Ernest A. Payne once described as a "book destined to effect a theological and practical revolution."[5] That revolution broke the bondage of High Calvinism that encompassed far too many British Particular Baptist communities and led directly to the formation of the Baptist Missionary Society in 1792. In Harry Boer's words: "Fuller's insistence on the duty of all men everywhere to believe the gospel ... played a determinative role in the crystallization of Carey's missionary vision."[6]

"Rest for my soul in the cross of Christ"[7]

The youngest of three brothers, Andrew Fuller was born on February 6, 1754, at Wicken, a small village now on the edge of the Cambridgeshire Fens, about six miles from the cathedral city of Ely. His parents, Robert Fuller (1723-1781) and Philippa Gunton (1726-1816), rented and worked a succession of dairy

---

Requirement of the Moral Law: in Reply to a Pamphlet, entitled, "A Blow Struck at the Root of Fullerism" (Cranbrook, [Kent]: S. Waters, 1804).

[3] For the term "High Calvinist," see Nuttall, *Studies in English Dissent*, 207 n. 4.

[4] Fuller's main refutation of Socinianism may be found Andrew Fuller, "The Calvinistic and Socinian Systems Examined and Compared, as to their Moral Tendency," in *The Complete Works of the Rev. Andrew Fuller*, vol. 2, ed. Joseph Belcher (1845 ed.; reprint, Harrisonburg, VA: Sprinkle Publications, 1988), 108-242. Hereafter *FW*. His chief response to Deism, especially that of the popularizer Thomas Paine (1737-1809), is "The Gospel Its Own Witness," in *FW*, 2:1-107. For examinations of Fuller's reply to these theological aberrations, see Michael A.G. Haykin, "'The Oracles of God': Andrew Fuller and the Scriptures," *Churchman* 103 (1989): 60-76; idem, "A Socinian and Calvinist Compared: Joseph Priestley and Andrew Fuller on the Propriety of Prayer to Christ," *Dutch Review of Church History* 73 (1993): 178-198.

[5] Ernest A. Payne, *College Street Church, Northampton 1697-1947* (London: Kingsgate Press, 1947), 22.

[6] Harry Boer, *Pentecost and Missions* (Grand Rapids, MI: Eerdmans, 1961), 24. See also Nuttall, *Studies in English Dissent*, 230; Brian Stanley, *The History of the Baptist Missionary Society 1792-1992* (Edinburgh: T&T Clark, 1992), 12-13.

[7] Andrew Fuller, Letter to Charles Stuart, 1798, in Ryland, *Life and Death of the Rev. Andrew Fuller*, 19-20.

farms.⁸ When Fuller was seven years of age, his family moved to the village of Soham, about two and a half miles from Wicken. Once settled in Soham, they joined themselves to the Calvinistic Baptist work in the village that met for worship in a rented barn.⁹ The pastor of the work was a certain John Eve (d. 1782), originally a sieve-maker from Chesterton, near the town of Cambridge. Eve had been set apart to preach the gospel by St. Andrew's Street Baptist Church, Cambridge, in 1749,¹⁰ and three years later he was ordained as the first pastor of the Baptist cause at Soham, where he ministered for nearly twenty years till his resignation in 1771.

Eve was a High Calvinist or, as Fuller later put it, one whose teaching was "tinged with false Calvinism,"¹¹ for Eve did not believe that it was the duty of the unregenerate to exercise faith in Christ. To be sure, they could be urged to attend to outward duties, such as hearing God's Word preached or being encouraged to read the Scriptures, but nothing of a spiritual nature could be required of them, since they were dead in sin and only the Spirit could make them alive to spiritual things.¹² Eve's sermons, Fuller thus noted, were "not adapted to awaken [the] conscience" and "had little or nothing to say to the unconverted."¹³

By 1767, though, Fuller had begun to read and be deeply affected by passages from John Bunyan's autobiographical *Grace Abounding to the Chief of Sinners*, as well as Bunyan's *Pilgrim's Progress* and some of the works of Ralph Erskine (1685–1752), the Scottish evangelical and Presbyterian minister. Over the next two years Fuller had a number of religious experiences accompanied by weeping and tears, but all of them ultimately proved to be transient. "The great deep of my heart's depravity had not yet been broken up," he later commented about these experiences of his mid-teens.¹⁴ It was not until November of 1769 that Fuller reckoned that he found true peace with God and, in his

---

⁸ Andrew Gunton Fuller, "Memoir," in *FW*, 1:1. For details of Fuller's family, see Ryland, *Life and Death of the Rev. Andrew Fuller*, 8–10; Andrew Gunton Fuller, *Andrew Fuller* (London: Hodder and Stoughton, 1882), 11–12.

⁹ [Ted Wilson], *Soham Baptist Church 250ᵗʰ Anniversary 1752–2002* ([Soham]: [Soham Baptist Church], 2002), [1]. This is an eight-page stapled pamphlet without pagination.

¹⁰ L.G. Champion, L.E. Addicott, and K.A.C. Parsons, *Church Book: St Andrew's Street Baptist Church, Cambridge 1720–1832* (London: Baptist Historical Society, 1991), 17.

¹¹ Fuller, "Memoir," in *FW*, 1:2, 12.

¹² Fuller, "Memoir," in *FW*, 1:12.

¹³ Fuller, "Memoir," in *FW*, 1:2.

¹⁴ Fuller, Letter to Charles Stuart, 1798, in Ryland, *Life and Death of the Rev. Andrew Fuller*, 15.

words, "rest for my soul in the cross of Christ."[15] The following spring, 1770, Fuller was baptized and joined the church at Soham.

"To feel my way out of a labyrinth"[16]

Within five years the church had called Fuller to be their pastor. Although he had personally known the deadening effect of High Calvinistic preaching, Fuller knew of no other way of dealing with non-Christians from the pulpit and initially, he said, he "durst not ... address an invitation to the unconverted to come to Jesus."[17] But as he studied the style of preaching exhibited in the Acts of the Apostles and especially in Christ's ministry, he began to see that "the Scriptures abounded with exhortations and invitations to sinners." But how was this style of preaching to be reconciled with the biblical emphasis on salvation being a sovereign work of grace?[18]

This question was not unique to Fuller, of course. It had been agitating the ranks of the Dissenters for about forty years, ever since the Congregationalist Matthias Maurice (d. 1738) had published *A Modern Question Modestly Answer'd*, in which he argued that when a person "sincerely and unfeignedly makes the Bible the rule of his faith," he cannot but conclude that "God does by his Word plainly and plentifully make it the duty of unconverted sinners, who hear the Gospel, to believe in Christ."[19] Maurice's position on this question was taken up by Abraham Taylor (fl.1727-1742), the Congregationalist minister of Little Moorfields, London, in a tract that he published anonymously in 1742, *The Modern Question concerning Repentance and Faith*.[20] What some regarded as a definitive answer to Taylor came from the doughty High Calvinist John Brine (1703-1765) in his *A Refutation of Arminian Principles, Delivered in a Pamphlet, intitled [sic], the Modern Question concerning Repentance and Faith* (1743). Brine, a confidant of his fellow London minister John Gill (1697-1771), argued that "evangelical repentance and special [saving] faith, are the duties only of such persons, to whom God reveals himself in his Word,

---

[15] Fuller, Letter to Charles Stuart, 1798, in Ryland, *Life and Death of the Rev. Andrew Fuller*, 19-20.

[16] Fuller compared his movement out of High Calvinism to the finding of a path out of a labyrinth; see Fuller, "Memoir," in *FW*, 1:13.

[17] Fuller, "Memoir," in *FW*, 1:12.

[18] Fuller, "Memoir," in *FW*, 1:15.

[19] Matthias Maurice, *A Modern Question Modestly Answer'd* (London: James Buckland, 1737), 4. See also Nuttall, *Studies in English Dissent*, 208, 215-217.

[20] Nuttall, *Studies in English Dissent*, 221-223.

as their Redeemer through Christ."[21] It is noteworthy that Gill himself did not enter directly into this controversy concerning what came to be called "the Modern Question," though it is clear that he basically stood shoulder to shoulder with Brine on the issue. As Gill wrote on one occasion, the phrase "offering Christ" is clearly unbiblical since it was "improper" and "too bold and free, for a minister of Christ to make use of."[22]

Now, important for Fuller's struggle with the "Modern Question" was Taylor's pamphlet, whom Brine had all but considered a crypto-Arminian. What especially impressed Fuller was a catena of biblical texts drawn up by Taylor that conclusively showed that "John the Baptist, Christ, the apostles, all in turn did offer grace and salvation to the unconverted."[23] By 1780 Fuller had thus come to see that his own way of preaching was unduly hampered by a concern not to urge spiritual duties upon non-believers. As he wrote in his diary for August 30 of that year:

> Surely Peter and Paul never felt such scruples in their addresses as we do. They addressed their hearers as *men*—fallen men; as we should warn and admonish persons who were blind and on the brink of some dreadful precipice. Their work seemed plain before them. Oh that mine might be so before me![24]

The "pulpit," Fuller commented a few months later,

> seems an awful place!—An opportunity for addressing a company of immortals on their eternal interests—Oh how important! We preach for eternity. We in a sense are set for the rising and falling of many in Israel. ... Oh would the Lord the Spirit lead me into the nature and importance of the work of the ministry![25]

By the time that Fuller left Soham in 1783 to take up the pastorate of the Baptist work in Kettering, Northamptonshire, he was convinced, as he told the Kettering congregation at his induction on October 7, that

---

[21] John Brine, *A Refutation of Arminian Principles, Delivered in a Pamphlet, intitled* [sic], *the Modern Question concerning Repentance and Faith* (London: A. Ward, 1743), 10.

[22] Cited in Nuttall, *Studies in English Dissent*, 220.

[23] Nuttall, *Studies in English Dissent*, 229.

[24] Fuller, "Memoir," in *FW*, 1:23.

[25] Fuller, "Memoir," in *FW*, 1:25, Diary entries for February 5 and 8, 1781.

it is the duty of every minister of Christ plainly and faithfully to preach the gospel to all who will hear it. And, as I believe the inability of men to spiritual things to be wholly of the moral, and therefore of the criminal kind—and that it is their duty to love the Lord Jesus Christ and trust in him for salvation, though they do not—I, therefore, believe free and solemn addresses, invitations, calls, and warnings to them, to be not only consistent, but directly adapted, as means in the hands of the Spirit of God to bring them to Christ. I consider it as a part of my duty, which I could not omit without being guilty of the blood of souls.[26]

Two years later, this theological revolution in Fuller's sentiments about the duty of sinners to believe the gospel and how that gospel should be preached were published for all to see and ponder in his *The Gospel of Christ Worthy of All Acceptation*.

"Cordial belief of what God says ... [is] every one's duty"[27]

Two editions of *The Gospel of Christ Worthy of All Acceptation* were issued in Fuller's lifetime. A first draft had been written by 1778, the manuscript of which is now housed in the archives of The Southern Baptist Theological Seminary. It begins thus:

> What a narrow Path is Truth! How many Extremes are there into w[h] [sic] we are liable to run! Some deny Truth; others hold it, but in Unrighteousness. O Lord, impress thy Truth upon my Heart with thine own Seal, then shall I receive it as in itself it is, "A Doctrine according to Godliness."[28]

This draft was re-written and the work was in what was roughly its final form by 1781.[29] It was another four years, however, before Fuller finally decided to publish the work. He honestly feared that it might injure the cause of Christ, and he was also afraid of the controversy that it would engender. This latter

---

[26] Andrew Fuller, *Confession of Faith* XV in Michael A.G. Haykin, ed., *The Armies of the Lamb: The Spirituality of Andrew Fuller*, CRS (Dundas, ON: Joshua Press, 2001), 279.

[27] Andrew Fuller, Preface to *The Gospel of Christ Worthy of All Acceptation*, 1st ed. (Northampton: T. Dicey and Co., 1785), iv. Subsequent references to this work are to the first edition unless otherwise noted.

[28] Andrew Fuller, "Thoughts on the Power of Men to do the Will of God, Wrote [sic] in 1777, or 1778" (Archives, The James P. Boyce Library, The Southern Baptist Theological Seminary, Louisville, KY), 1.

[29] J.W. Morris, *Memoirs of the Life and Writings of the Rev. Andrew Fuller* (London: T. Hamilton, 1816), 270.

fear was only alleviated by the conviction that his argument for the obligation of men and women to believe in Christ was indeed of vital importance. Finally, in October of 1784 Fuller took the plunge and made the decision to publish. The following month he walked the thirteen or so miles from Kettering to Northampton to deliver it into the hands of Thomas Dicey (1742–?), a wealthy Northampton printer whose father and grandfather had made the family money through the sale of ephemeral popular literature. Fuller's work was anything but ephemeral.

When the first edition appeared in May 1785, it bore a lengthy subtitle—*The Obligations of Men Fully to Credit, and Cordially to Approve, Whatever God Makes Known, Wherein is Considered the Nature of Faith in Christ, and the Duty of Those where the Gospel Comes in that Matter*. It is interesting that the advertisement of its publication in the local newspaper, the *Northampton Mercury*, cited Mark 16:15-16, and not what has come to be called the Great Commission, Matthew 28:19-20.[30] A second edition appeared in 1801 with a shortened title—*The Gospel Worthy of All Acceptation*—and simpler subtitle, *The Duty of Sinners to Believe in Jesus Christ*, which well expressed the overall theme of both editions of the book.[31] There were a number of substantial differences between the two editions, which Fuller freely admitted and which primarily related to the doctrine of particular redemption, but the major theme remained unaltered: "faith in Christ is the duty of all men who hear, or have opportunity to hear, the gospel."[32] Or as he put it in his preface to the first edition:

> true faith is nothing more nor less than an hearty or cordial belief of what God says, surely it must be every one's duty where the gospel is published, to do that. Surely no man ought to question or treat with indifference any thing which Jehovah hath said.[33]

What is quickly evident in both editions is the large amount of space given to closely reasoned exegesis. In the first edition, for example, Fuller devotes the second major part of the work to showing that "faith in Christ is

---

[30] Advertisement in *The Northampton Mercury*, May 9, 1785, 2.

[31] For the second edition, see Andrew Fuller, "The Gospel Worthy of All Acceptation," in *FW*, 2:328-416.

[32] Fuller, "The Gospel Worthy of All Acceptation," in *FW*, 2:343. Extremely helpful in tracing the differences between the two editions is Robert W. Oliver, *History of the English Calvinistic Baptists 1771-1892: From John Gill to C.H. Spurgeon* (Carlisle, PA: Banner of Truth, 2006), 156-172.

[33] Fuller, *Gospel of Christ Worthy of All Acceptation*, iv.

commanded in the Scriptures to unconverted sinners."[34] It had been his reflection on Psalm 2, for instance, that first led Fuller to doubt the High Calvinist refusal to countenance faith as the duty of the unconverted.[35] He now undertook an interpretation of this text in light of his subject, reading it, as the New Testament reads it in Acts 4, as a Messianic psalm. The command given to "the heathen" and "the people" of Israel (Ps. 2:1) as well as to "the kings of the earth" and "the rulers" (Ps. 2:2)—interpreted in Acts 4:27 as "Herod, and Pontius Pilate, with the gentiles, and the people of Israel"—is a command given to those "who were most certainly enemies to Christ, unregenerate sinners." They are commanded to "kiss the Son" (Ps. 2:12), which Fuller understood to be "a spiritual act" that from the perspective of the New Testament meant nothing less than "being reconciled to, and embracing the Son of God, which doubtless is of the very essence of true saving faith."[36] Clearly, Fuller reasoned, here was both Old and New Testament support for his position.

A number of Johannine texts also plainly revealed that "true saving faith" is "enjoined [by the New Testament] upon unregenerate sinners."[37] John 12:36, for instance, contains an exhortation of the Lord Jesus to a crowd of men and women to "believe in the light" that they might be the children of light. Working from the context, Fuller argued that Jesus was urging his hearers to put their faith in him. He is the "light" in whom faith is to be placed, that faith which issues in salvation (John 12:46). Those whom Christ commanded to exercise such faith, however, were rank unbelievers, of whom it is said earlier "they believed not on him" (John 12:37). In fact, Fuller pointed out that on the basis of the quote of Isaiah 6:10 in John 12:40, "it seems" these very same people whom Christ called to faith in him "were given over to judicial blindness, and were finally lost."[38]

Then there is John 6:29, where Jesus declares to sinners that "this is the work of God, that ye believe on him whom he hath sent." Fuller pointed out that this statement is made to men who in the context are described as following Christ simply because he gave them food to eat (John 6:26) and who are considered by Christ to be unbelievers (John 6:36). Christ rebukes them for their mercenary motives and urges them to "labour not for the meat which perisheth, but for that meat which endureth unto everlasting life" (John 6:27).

---

[34] Fuller, *Gospel of Christ Worthy of All Acceptation*, 37.
[35] Fuller, *Gospel of Christ Worthy of All Acceptation*, iii.
[36] Fuller, *Gospel of Christ Worthy of All Acceptation*, 37–39.
[37] Fuller, *Gospel of Christ Worthy of All Acceptation*, 40.
[38] Fuller, *Gospel of Christ Worthy of All Acceptation*, 40.

Their response as recorded in John 6:28 is to ask Christ, "What shall we do, that we might work the works of God?" His answer is to urge them to put their faith in him (John 6:29). It is as if, Fuller said, Christ had told them that faith in him is "the first duty incumbent" upon them "without which it will be impossible ... to please God."[39]

Again, in John 5:23 Fuller read that all men and women are to "honour the Son, even as they honour the Father." Giving honor to the Son entails, Fuller reasoned, "holy hearty love to him" and adoration of every aspect of his person. It necessarily "includes faith in him." Christ has made himself known as a supreme monarch, an advocate who pleads the cause of his people, a physician who offers health to the spiritually sick, and an infallible teacher. Therefore, honoring him in these various aspects of his ministry requires faith and trust.[40]

Among the practical conclusions that followed from such Scriptural argumentation was that preachers of the gospel must passionately exhort their hearers to repent and commit themselves to Christ.[41] In the second edition, Fuller sharpened this emphasis, for he was more than ever convinced that there was "scarcely a minister amongst us"—that is, amongst the Calvinistic Baptist denomination—"whose preaching has not been more or less influenced by the lethargic systems of the age."[42] Far too many of Fuller's fellow Baptist ministers failed to imitate the preaching of Christ and the apostles who were not afraid to exhort the unconverted to immediate repentance and faith. For a variety of reasons, these High Calvinists regarded the unconverted in their congregations as "poor, impotent ... creatures." Faith was beyond such men and women, and could not be pressed upon them as an immediate, present duty. Fuller was convinced that this way of conducting a pulpit ministry was both unbiblical and simply helped the unconverted to remain in their sin.[43]

Coda

Fuller's book was indeed an epoch-making work. It provided a theology for many others in the Calvinistic Baptist community whose thinking was moving in the same direction and developing along the same lines. Take, for instance, Thomas Steevens (1745-1802), the pastor of Colchester Baptist Church,

---

[39] Fuller, *Gospel of Christ Worthy of All Acceptation*, 40-43.
[40] Fuller, *Gospel of Christ Worthy of All Acceptation*, 43-44.
[41] Fuller, *Gospel of Christ Worthy of All Acceptation*, 163-172.
[42] Fuller, "Gospel Worthy of All Acceptation," in *FW*, 2:387.
[43] Fuller, "Gospel Worthy of All Acceptation," in *FW*, 2:387-393.

Essex, from 1774 until his death in the first decade of the next century. Steevens has in fact been described as "a 'Fullerite' before Fuller."[44] A few months after the publication of the first edition of *The Gospel Worthy of All Acceptation*, Fuller's close friend John Sutcliff (1752-1814) had written to Steevens, asking him what he thought of Fuller's work. Steevens' response reached Sutcliff on the final day of November 1785. The Colchester Baptist found much to admire in the book and admitted that since 1777 he had been coming over to Fuller's point of view, though he was unaware, he said, "that I had any partners." He was hopeful that "some who cannot fully adopt his [i.e. Fuller's] views, will yet so far profit by it as to address their fellow sinners more in the style of Scripture." He drew Sutcliff's attention, though, to the fact that many of the Baptists with whom he was personally acquainted would have nothing to do with the book. "Some of them," he further informed Sutcliff, "already deem me an Arminian,"[45] a charge also levelled against Fuller.

The counties of Suffolk and Norfolk, to the immediate north of Steevens' church in Colchester, were a bastion of High Calvinism—witness Job Hupton, the critic of Fullerism with whom this chapter began. Many of the Baptists of whom Steevens spoke in this letter to Sutcliff were almost definitely from this area of East Anglia. Theological conflict, as Fuller had foreseen, was thus inevitable. But ultimately it was a blessed conflict, for Fuller's conclusion that ministers needed to press home repentance and faith as immediate duties upon all of their hearers was foundational to William Carey's later argument that this needed to take place not only in England but throughout the world. *The Gospel Worthy of All Acceptation* thus not only answered the "Modern Question," but it also played a central role in Carey's going to India and, as such, needs to be considered as nothing less than "a missionary document."[46]

---

[44] Henry Spyvee, *Colchester Baptist Church—The First 300 Years, 1689-1989* (Colchester: Colchester Baptist Church, 1989), 31.

[45] Thomas Steevens, Letter to John Sutcliff, November 10, 1785 (JRL English Mss 369-371, John Rylands University Library, University of Manchester).

[46] A. Chadwick Mauldin, *Fullerism as Opposed to Calvinism. A Historical and Theological Comparison of the Missiology of Andrew Fuller and John Calvin* (Eugene, OR: Wipf & Stock, 2011), 60.

2
"In Exhortations, Invitations, Precepts, and Threatenings": Andrew Fuller, John Owen, and the Free Offer of the Gospel

Shane Shaddix

The emergence of the Baptist movement in England in the seventeenth century quickly developed into a mature subset of the broader English-speaking Protestant world. Here arose a movement that was dissenting in its relation to the culture, independent in its relation to other churches, and voluntary in its principle of association.[1] Despite the fact that Baptists diverged over the issue of Calvinism early on, Baptists as a whole generally considered themselves the true heirs of the Reformation. Where previous Reformers had failed to follow their principal of scriptural authority to completion, Baptists saw in the Scriptures a command that only those who had been born again of God's Spirit were truly members of God's Church, and thus only baptized believers could rightly participate in the local expression of the Church.

Despite these aims at ecclesiological purity, both Particular (Calvinistic) and General (non-Calvinistic) Baptists found their movements stalled by various heterodox or even heretical teachings within the first few generations. While many General Baptists acquiesced to the allure of the Enlightenment, falling into Deism or Unitarianism, the Particular Baptists in the eighteenth century found themselves crippled by High or Hyper-Calvinistic teachings, which precluded the free offer of the gospel to all men. Andrew Fuller, a Particular Baptist pastor who emerged in the last quarter of the eighteenth century, became a chief defender of orthodox Christianity in general and traditional Calvinism in particular while also developing a biblical defense for promiscuous appeals to the unconverted to repent and believe in Christ.

---

[1] Though he is specifically talking about Fuller's pastoral theology, I am indebted to Keith Grant's *Andrew Fuller and the Evangelical Renewal of Pastoral Theology*, SBHT (Eugene, OR.: Wipf & Stock, 2013) for these succinct categories.

Andrew Fuller

Few will deny the enormous impact that Fuller had on Particular Baptist life in England leading up to and just after the turn of the nineteenth century. Fuller did not develop and minister in a vacuum, however, and any assessment of his work must consider, among other things, his influences. Specifically, Fuller received the aid of a company of friends—fellow pastors who shared his evangelical convictions—and most importantly the friendship of good books. In these books, and in discussion with these friends, Fuller came under the influence of previous pastors, theologians, and reformers who would aid his own break with High Calvinism and his consequent embrace of evangelical convictions. Unmistakably the most significant of these influences was the New England pastor and theologian Jonathan Edwards.[2] Edwards bequeathed to Fuller and his company such foundational convictions as the centrality of the affections in true religion, the distinction between moral and natural ability, and the centrality of prayer in bringing about revival. Less documented, however, is the secondary role played by other figures, most notably the Puritan theologian John Owen. Yet, as Peter Morden has argued in his intellectual biography of Fuller, Owen's views held considerable weight to Fuller, as seen by in the prevalence and centrality of Owen quotations in Fuller's most famous and influential work, *The Gospel Worthy of All Acceptation*.[3]

This chapter examines the points of contact between Owen and Fuller regarding the free offer of the gospel and analyzes how Fuller appropriated Owen's ideas for the purpose of propagating his brand of evangelical Calvinism. It demonstrates that Owen influenced Fuller principally in three areas, namely the harmony between election and free offers of the gospel, the harmony between particular redemption and free offers of the gospel, and the proper means of freely offering the gospel to the unconverted. In each of these areas Fuller appealed to and quoted from Owen's own works and

---

[2] The impact Edwards had on Fuller is well documented, most thoroughly in the recent dissertation by Chris Chun, now published as Chris Chun, *The Legacy of Jonathan Edwards in the Theology of Andrew Fuller*, SHT (Leiden and Boston, MA: Brill, 2012).

[3] Interestingly, Fuller scholar Peter Morden, in his first monograph assessing Fuller's impact on particular Baptist life, concluded that the role played by Owen and other Puritans in shaping Fuller's convictions was primarily one of confirmation rather than development and influence. His more recent intellectual biography of Fuller, however, modifies this conclusion specifically in regards to Owen, stating, "Owen's influence on Fuller should be given more weight than I allowed." See Peter J. Morden, *Offering Christ to the World: Andrew Fuller (1754-1815) and the Revival of Eighteenth-Century Particular Baptist Life*, SBHT (Carlisle, UK/Waynesboro, GA: Paternoster, 2003), 30–33; Peter J. Morden, *The Life and Thought of Andrew Fuller*, SEHT (Milton Keynes, UK: Paternoster, 2015), 54.

controversies to show the legitimacy of his evangelical Calvinism as pertains to biblical faithfulness, theological precision, and historical continuity.

Fuller's Context

Fuller's ministry represents the convergence of several movements occurring in Europe and even America in the eighteenth century. The first, as already mentioned, was the nearly 200-year-old Baptist movement. In the early part of the eighteenth century the Calvinistic Baptists were significantly smaller in number than the General Baptists, but the latter group was largely overrun by Arianism, Deism, and Unitarianism. This inevitably contributed to a situation where the Particular Baptists represented, in their own minds at least, biblical fidelity and theological rigor over against the apostasy of their Arminian counterparts. The main torchbearer in this period was John Gill, the long-time pastor of the Horsleydown Church in London who was also a prolific author and polemicist. Gill fiercely defended Calvinistic doctrine, even as he also criticized the poor state of many Particular Baptist churches for their lack of true heart religion.[4]

The Transatlantic Awakening

Outside the Baptist strain of Protestantism, a much larger movement was taking hold in the churches of both Europe and the New World. W.R. Ward has convincingly shown that, though traditionally identified as an American phenomenon, the spiritual awakening that took hold in the American colonies in the middle of the eighteenth century was actually connected to a larger transatlantic awakening that started in Central Europe with the Silesian revivals and the emergence of German Pietism.[5] It was this movement that saw such figures as George Whitefield and John Wesley emerge as celebrities in the English-speaking world, and from this series of revivals developed the modern movement known as "evangelicalism," at least one significant feature of which was an emphasis on immediate conversion.[6]

---

[4] Curt D. Daniel, "Hyper-Calvinism and John Gill" (PhD diss., University of Edinburgh, 1983), 8–15.

[5] See W. Reginald Ward, *The Protestant Evangelical Awakening* (New York: Cambridge University Press, 1992).

[6] David Bebbington's well-known quadrilateral gives the four-fold descriptor of evangelicalism as concerned with biblicism, conversionism, crucicentrism, and activism, and is generally considered a serviceable yet debatable definition for the evangelical movement. See Bebbington, *Evangelicalism in Modern Britain: A History from the 1730s to the 1980s* (London: Routledge, 1993).

Andrew Fuller

What is most interesting about Fuller's context is that even though he was squarely situated in the temporal and geographical setting of this broad evangelical awakening, his most immediate circle of influence while growing up, and therefore the context that was most formative for his early religious experience and theological development, was not greatly affiliated with the evangelical awakening. Though Roger Hayden has effectively argued that British Baptists in the eighteenth century did receive some influence from evangelicalism, this influence was largely centered on the Bristol Baptist Academy. Further, any evangelical impulse was clearly eclipsed by the shadow left by such heavyweights as Gill. British Baptists were unmistakably more Gill-like than Bristol-like.[7] Though Fuller would find friendship among those influenced by and influential in the Bristol Academy, his own impression throughout his ministry was that British Particular Baptists were enslaved to High Calvinism for the better part of the one hundred years previous to his generation.[8]

Hyper-Calvinism and the Modern Question

Central to the system of High Calvinism was what became known as the "modern question." The issue largely concerned whether or not the unconverted have the duty to repent and believe the gospel.[9] The High Calvinists answered in the negative, supposing that total depravity, resulting from the fall of humankind, rendered all humanity completely incapable of doing any spiritual good, including responding to the gospel. Therefore, unconverted sinners could not logically be held responsible for repenting of their sins and trusting Christ for salvation. To offer the gospel to them was silly at best, if not blatantly immoral.

---

[7] Roger Hayden, *Continuity and Change: Evangelical Calvinism among Eighteenth-Century Baptist Ministers Trained at Bristol Academy, 1690–1791* (Oxfordshire, UK: Nigel Lynn and the Baptist Historical Society, 2006).

[8] Andrew Fuller, "A Defense of a Treatise Entitled *The Gospel Worthy of All Acceptation*," in *The Complete Works of the Rev. Andrew Fuller*, vol. 2, ed. Joseph Belcher (1845 ed.; reprint, Harrisonburg, VA: Sprinkle Publications, 1988), 422. Hereafter *FW*. Scholars continue to debate the extent to which High Calvinism actually dominated Particular Baptist life in the eighteenth century. These debates can be seen quite clearly in the discussion of whether or not John Gill, the most significant theologian and Bible interpreter of the first half of the century, was himself a hyper-Calvinist. Still, the material fact in understanding Fuller is that he *believed* his context to be predominantly High Calvinistic, regardless of the extent to which that was the historical reality.

[9] Morden, *Offering Christ to the World*, 36. Though working toward the end of arguing for the legitimacy and necessity of freely offering the gospel, it is worth noting that Fuller's *Gospel Worthy* is principally concerned with proving duty-faith, and thus answering the modern question.

The practical effect this conviction had on ministry was clear: pastors and preacher could not honestly and legitimately offer the gospel to unconverted persons, nor could they suggest that unconverted persons were responsible for their response to the gospel. This position was explicitly stated first by Joseph Hussey in 1707 in his work entitled *God's Operations of Grace, But No Offers of Grace*. While the contemporary debate among scholars as to whether John Gill was a Hyper-Calvinist continues, Morden suggests that in Fuller's day Gill was unmistakably associated with views similar to those of Hussey.[10]

Although such a position might seem theologically rigid and self-evidently wrongheaded, those who held to High Calvinism in the eighteenth century did not operate in a vacuum. Many were trying to protect the gospel from the prevalent errors and distortions of the day. Free offers of the gospel sounded like just anyone was able to respond to the gospel of their own ability, as though untainted by the fall. This error smacked of Arminianism to most Calvinists. To take such logic to the next level could and often did lead to the Socinian error of Universalism.[11]

Thus, even in their zeal to protect the faith, the High Calvinists could and did truly rejoice when a sinner repented and believed in the gospel. The trick was finding out who could legitimately do such a thing. This led to the idea of "warrant," by which it was meant a sinner had some stirring in their heart or a drawing to the gospel which was distinct from and prior to conversion. Warrant gave evidence that this sinner, now under conviction, might be among the elect. Often this warrant took the form of a passage of Scripture spontaneously being impressed on the unregenerate sinner's mind and heart, unable to shake the thought or principle. Through prolonged wrestling with this warrant and examination on the part of a minister, a sinner could prove herself to be among the elect and therefore an appropriate candidate for being offered the gospel.

So for the High Calvinist, the issue was not whether to offer the gospel; the issue was specifically whether to *freely* or *promiscuously* offer the gospel to all. They wondered not whether those who came under conviction ought to repent of their sins and believe, but whether *all* men and women ought to repent of their sins and believe, regardless of their present state of mind or the lack of any evidence that they were among the elect.

---

[10] Morden, *Offering Christ to the World*, 12–13.
[11] Gerald L. Priest, "Andrew Fuller, Hyper-Calvinisim, and the 'Modern Question,'" in *"At the Pure Fountain of Thy Word": Andrew Fuller as an Apologist*, ed. Michael A.G. Haykin, SBHT (Eugene, OR: Wipf and Stock, 2004), 45.

Fuller's Evangelical Conversion

Despite coming to faith by and, indeed, adopting the High Calvinist theology himself, Fuller would eventually experience a conversion, of sorts, to evangelical principles. This transformation was aided in no small measure by the influence of the New England pastor Jonathan Edwards. From Edwards Fuller learned the significant distinction between natural and moral ability in humanity, which Fuller consistently used to argue that it was the just duty of all humanity to obey the revealed will of God. In his view, the High Calvinists were correct that total depravity meant none would come to Christ outside the working of God's Spirit; they were incorrect to say that humanity was in no way able to respond to the gospel.

Edwards equipped Fuller with the understanding that men and women were naturally able to respond to the gospel, meaning they had the physical and mental capacities in place to repent and believe if they so desired.[12] On the other hand, fallen humanity was morally incapable of responding to the gospel, meaning that even though he could respond if he wanted to, no one actually wants to respond to the gospel without the working of God's Spirit. Thus, a free offer to all persons to respond to the gospel was not morally reprehensible, but the exact opposite. Ministers *must* call all people to respond because if they repent and believe, God will grant them salvation. They *can* do this because of their natural ability; they *will not* do this because of their moral inability.

Fuller's more evangelical brand of Calvinism would take root among British Baptists and would be so identified with Fuller himself that it became known as "Fullerism." The clearest and most sustained explanation Fuller gave for his system came in his most well-known work, *The Gospel Worthy of All Acceptation*.

Overview of *The Gospel Worthy*

Before examining the points of contact between Owen and Fuller, it is worth providing an overview of *The Gospel Worthy*, so as to help identify the logic of Fuller's system and how Owen fits into and helps shape it.

The Gospel Worthy develops in three parts, bookended by a preface and a conclusion. Part One introduces the subject and why it is important. Fuller

---

[12] For more thorough analysis of Fuller's appropriation of Edwards' ideas on natural and moral ability, see Chris Chun, "A Mainspring of Missionary Thought: Andrew Fuller on 'Natural and Moral Inability,'" *ABQ* 25, no. 4 (2006): 335-355. See also Thomas J. Nettles, "The Influence of Jonathan Edwards on Andrew Fuller," *Eusebeia* 9 (2008): 87-116.

here lays out some underlying assumptions he makes in the rest of his argument, particularly what he means when he talks about faith. Part Two asserts six propositions to advance his main argument. Here his main goal is to prove that faith in the gospel is a duty for all men. He wants to assert this because if all men are duty-bound to believe the gospel with true faith, then ministers may and even must freely offer it to those who ought to receive it. In Part Three, Fuller answers potential and real objections to the ideas he has put forward. It is this last section in which Fuller makes the most use of John Owen's reputation and writings.

Owen's Influence on Fuller

Upon close examination of the references Fuller makes to Owen in his writings, it becomes clear that Fuller has the utmost respect for the Puritan, and he in large part assumes that his opponents share that same respect. This makes Owen a valuable referent, and one with certain advantages even over Fuller's theological hero, Edwards. Though Edwards died a generation before Fuller, he was very much a part of the evangelical movement, providing the most robust defense in print of the evangelical awakening as well as popularizing the patron saint of evangelical activism in David Brainerd. Edwards was undoubtedly a Calvinist, but his evangelical pedigree and his association with enthusiastic revivals meant that opponents might see Fuller's reliance on Edwards as a weakness.

Indeed, Fuller's opponents did attack him at this exact point. In a letter to his brother late in his life, Fuller intimated, "We have some, who have been giving out, of late, that if 'Sutcliff, and some others, had preached more of Christ, and less of Jonathan Edwards, they would have been more useful.'" Of course, these accusations keep neither Fuller nor his friends from appealing to Edwards. Nor was he ashamed of his dedication to Edwards' system, as seen in Fuller's retort to the above:

> If those who talk thus, preached Christ half as much as Jonathan Edwards did, and were half as useful as he was, their usefulness would be double what it is. It is very singular that the Mission to the East should have originated with men of these principles; and without pretending to be a prophet, I may say, if it ever falls into the hands of men who talk in this strain, it will soon come to nothing.[13]

---

[13] Quoted in Morden, *The Life and Thought of Andrew Fuller*, 197.

Fuller was clearly neither shy about nor embarrassed of his Edwardsian pedigree, but it remained a point of attack for his opponents.

Owen, however, did not come with the same baggage. His Calvinistic résumé was indisputable, and he was widely regarded as one of the most learned, thoroughly biblical, and theologically astute Puritans of the seventeenth century. Everyone wanted Owen on their side, and therefore he made an effective authority for Fuller's arguments.

In addition to general support for Fuller's propositions regarding duty-faith, three areas in particular show Fuller's appeal to Owen. The first two are primarily theological in nature and are specifically unique to Calvinistic systems. Between the first and second editions of *The Gospel Worthy*, Fuller received objections to his system from all sides. His High Calvinist opponents, specifically, argued that Fuller had abandoned traditional Calvinism and taken a step towards the Arminian position—a step that was practically as bad as losing the gospel itself. Against these opponents, Fuller had to show that his system was consistent with traditional Calvinistic doctrine, and outside of Calvin himself, Owen was among the greatest authorities. Fuller had appealed to Owen regularly in the first edition of *The Gospel Worthy*, but by maintaining these references in the second edition Fuller tried to show that he had not switched soteriological sides.

The third category in which Owen's influence appears is more practical and pastoral in nature. Keith Grant in his recent monograph has done a superb job in showing that Fuller's evangelical Calvinism was primarily a renewal of pastoral theology, meaning Fuller was less interested in abstract theological debates detached from local church ministry than he was in discerning the proper theology to undergird his evangelistic and pastoral ministry.[14] Thus it should come as no surprise that Fuller concludes his treatise with practical instructions regarding how ministers ought to preach to the unconverted and include offers of the gospel and exhortations to all men to respond in repentance and faith.

Election

One of the objections Fuller anticipated and surely received was that the principles of election and freely offering the gospel to all could not logically or theologically be reconciled. The High Calvinists were of the mind that God has

---

[14] See Keith Grant, *Andrew Fuller and the Evangelical Renewal of Pastoral Theology*, SBHT (Milton Keynes, UK: Paternoster, 2003),

decreed in eternity past who would be saved by the death and resurrection of Jesus. These men and women, and these alone, were those who could appropriately respond to the gospel in repentance and faith. Consequently, only these elect persons ought to receive exhortations and offers to receive and believe the gospel.

Fuller's response to this objection is twofold. First, he simply notes that earlier well-respected Calvinists received a similar objection from their opponents, yet managed to unite their Reformed theology with an evangelistic thrust. In particular, he connects himself with Owen, who in advocating for the doctrine of election and particular redemption was opposed, not by High Calvinists, but by Arminians on the ground that Owen's doctrines logically meant he could not freely offer the gospel to all. Thus, Fuller turns this objection around on his accusers who say he is not Calvinistic enough. He shows that he is actually more in line with those who articulated the doctrines of grace before him, namely Owen, and that both he and Owen were able to hold together free offers of the gospel and staunch Calvinistic teaching. Ironically, he suggests that his High Calvinistic opponents are closer to Owen's Arminian opponents!

Fuller's larger argument, though, is that the High Calvinists claim too much in their objection to duty-faith. He explains that their objection is really, at bottom, an objection against using means in the temporal world to achieve what God has decreed in eternity. Taken to its logical conclusion, we are not even to work to provide food and shelter for ourselves, since these things as well are ordained by God's providence.[15] But Fuller will not allow such absurdity. He stands on the assertion that, though God has decreed that which will come to pass, including who will believe on and receive Christ, men are responsible in time and space for responding to God's revealed will.

He appeals to the Apostle Paul, who above all men "believed the doctrine of Divine decrees," yet also held men responsible for their response to the gospel in life.[16] If Paul saw no contradiction between blaming men for rejection of the gospel and likewise asserting that God in his sovereignty has chosen those who will respond in faith, then Fuller was unwilling to allow his opponents to introduce a contradiction. Fuller summarizes, "This was no other than suggesting that the doctrine of decrees must needs operate to the setting

---

[15] Fuller, "Gospel Worthy," in *FW*, 2:371. *FW* contains the second edition of *The Gospel Worthy*. Unless otherwise noted, this chapter cites from this second edition.

[16] Fuller, "Gospel Worthy," in *FW*, 2:372.

aside of the *fault* of sinners; and this is the substance of what has been alleged from that day to this."[17]

Fuller concludes with a lengthy quote from Owen's *The Death of Death in the Death of Christ*, wherein Owen explicates a helpful distinction that Fuller has been employing:

> We must exactly distinguish between man's duty and God's purpose, there being no connection between them. The purpose and decree of God is not the rule of our duty; neither is the performance of our duty in doing what we are commanded any declaration of what is God's purpose to do, or his decree that it should be done. Especially is this to be seen and considered in the duty of the ministers of the gospel, in dispensing of the word, in exhortations, invitations, precepts, and threatenings, committed unto them; all which are perpetual declaratives of our duty, and do manifest the approbation of the thing exhorted and invited to, with the truth of the connection being one thing and another, but not of the council and purpose of God, in respect of individual persons, in the ministry of the word. A minister is not to make inquiry after, nor to trouble himself about, those secrets of the eternal mind of God, namely—whom he purposeth to save, and whom he hath sent Christ to die for in particular. It is enough for them to search his revealed will, and thence take their directions, from whence they have their commissions. Wherefore, there is no sequel between the universal precepts from the word concerning the things, unto God's purpose in himself concerning persons. They command and invite all to repent and believe; but they know not in particular on whom God will bestow repentance unto salvation, nor in whom he will affect the work of faith with power.[18]

Thus, not only does Owen expose the underlying fallacy that Fuller's opponents are committing, but he likewise asserts the practical conclusion of Fuller's own position, namely that ministers of the gospel ought to make appeals—"in exhortations, invitations, precepts, and threatenings"—to the unconverted to repent and believe.

Owen's critique is that those who see a conflict in holding to the doctrine of election and freely offering the gospel are trying to do something fundamentally impossible; they are trying to operate, in their limited capacity, based on the hidden decrees of God. They devise means and methods to discern God's

---

[17] Fuller, "Gospel Worthy," in *FW*, 2:372-373.
[18] John Owen, *The Death of Death in the Death of Christ* (Carlisle, PA: Banner of Truth Trust, 2007), 187-188.

hidden will, and their aim will always be frustrated. Rather than trying to figure out those whom God has decreed to receive eternal life, ministers ought to obey the revealed will of God, which clearly demands a general call to all men.

Particular Redemption
Secondly, Fuller anticipates another objection from the High Calvinist side, similar to the one previously mentioned. Some will say, Fuller knows, that the supposition that all people are duty-bound to receive and obey the gospel contradicts the Calvinistic conviction of particular redemption, or limited atonement. This logic supposes that it cannot be one's duty to receive a gospel that is not *for them*.

In the first edition of *The Gospel Worthy*, Fuller accepts the basic logic of the atonement represented in the objection. Namely, he assumes a commercial understanding of Christ's sacrificial death whereby Jesus' death was correlated to the salvation of the elect alone, and others for whom Christ did not die had no "particular interest" in the salvation provided. In essence, there was nothing in it for them.[19] Fuller overcomes this objection by quoting from the writings of several respected Calvinists, one of whom is John Owen, to show that the Reformed tradition has been able to reconcile particular redemption with humanity's duty to believe the gospel. Through Owen he argues that rather than worrying if someone has a particular interest in Christ's sacrificial death, ministers can be assured that repentant sinners always have a duty to receive and believe whatever is true.[20] Again, Fuller's underlying view of the atonement is still commercial.[21]

Fuller's response to the same objection—the supposed incompatibility of limited atonement and the free offer—shifts in the second edition. This time, his rebuttal rests on his location of the atonement's limitation, and connected to it, the nature of the atonement itself. He argues that if the atonement is by nature something of a quantitative balancing of debts, then this objection contains some force. If the atonement works by God taking stock of all the sins of

---

[19] Andrew Fuller, *The Gospel of Christ Worthy of All Acceptation*, 1st ed. (Northampton: Thomas Dicey, 1985), 132-134.

[20] Andrew Fuller, *Gospel of Christ Worthy*, 137-138.

[21] It is worth noting that Owen's understanding of the nature of the atonement cannot neatly be categorized as commercialistic. See Edwin E.M. Tay, *The Priesthood of Christ: Atonement in the Theology of John Owen (1616-1683)*, SCHT (Milton Keynes, UK: Paternoster, 2014), 147-149. Still, Fuller is not delving into Owen's atonement theology, per se, but rather using him to show that particular redemption and duty faith can be held together—regardless of whether one has an actual "spiritual interest" in Christ.

the elect, commissioning Christ to suffer and pay sufficient penalty for that sin debt, and then crediting the elect with the payment Christ has procured, then surely Fuller's opponents have an argument.

However, Fuller comes to reject the commercial understanding of the atonement he held in the first edition. First, he argues that this creates a situation in which the elect do not come to God as sinners begging for mercy. Rather those elect persons who respond to the gospel in repentance and faith come to God as claimants of something that is owed to them.[22] This cuts against the very nature of the gospel as good news, and his assessment is that it cannot therefore rightly line up with what is in Scripture.

Second, Fuller argues that the gospel is better understood in terms of criminal debt rather than commercial debt. Here, the sacrifice of Christ is meant to express the divine displeasure of God against sin, not to line up equal measures of sin and suffering. In this sense, Christ suffered sufficiently for the entire world and all their sins. Dispelling the idea that all are saved because of this sufficient sacrifice, Fuller identifies the limitation of the atonement not in its sufficiency but in its application. He notes, "The particularity which attends it consists not in its insufficiency to save more than are saved, but in the sovereignty of its application."[23] This being the case, Christ can be said to have died for the human race in their sinfulness. Christ died for *sinners*. Therefore, there is just ground for inviting all men to believe and be saved.

Again, it is in concluding his argument that Fuller appeals to Owen's authority. Owen had discouraged preachers from trying to ascertain the secret will of God. Rather, they should take comfort in the sufficiency of Christ as they preach the gospel to all:

> That the preachers of the gospel, in their particular congregations, being really unacquainted with the purpose and secret counsel of God, being also forbidden to pry or search into it ..., may justifiably call upon every man to believe, with assurance of salvation to everyone in particular upon his so doing, knowing, and being fully persuaded of this, that there is enough in the death of Christ to save everyone that shall do so; leaving the purpose and counsel of God, on whom he will bestow faith, and for whom in particular Christ died (even as they are commanded), to himself.[24]

---

[22] Fuller, "Gospel Worthy," in *FW*, 2:373.
[23] Fuller, "Gospel Worthy," in *FW*, 2:374.
[24] Owen, *The Death of Death*, 186.

Here Fuller has in Owen a clear statement of the sufficiency of Christ to atone for all who call on him. Therefore, preachers do not need to worry that their appeals for all to call on Christ will somehow become the soteriological equivalent of checks that bounce at the bank because of insufficient funds. One can imagine a sinner calling on Christ for salvation, only to be rebuffed because Christ's death was not meant for him, and therefore Jesus' sacrifice was insufficient to save this genuinely repentant sinner. Though this is certainly a straw man argument that no one is actually supposing, Fuller indicates that it is a realistic possibility given the underlying logic of the objection. Thus, Fuller carries the objection to its conclusion, and then sets his own understanding of the atonement over against this absurd scenario.

Interestingly, the above quotation is the same one Fuller used from Owen in the first edition of *The Gospel Worthy*. Though Fuller's understanding of the atonement had changed, his reading of Owen seemed to change with him. In the first edition, Fuller appeals to this passage from Owen to show that even with an atonement limited strictly to the elect, faith is still the duty of all persons. In the second edition, Fuller uses the quotation to argue against a commercial view of the atonement altogether. Now, he sees Owen as supporting his view of Christ's all-sufficient but covenantally limited view of the atonement.[25]

Another quotation from Owen appears without comment from Fuller and adds an additional argument against the supposed contradiction between particular redemption and free offers: "When God calleth upon men to believe, he doth not, in the first place, call upon them to believe that Christ died for them, but that there is none other name under heaven given among men whereby we must be saved, but only of Jesus Christ, through whom salvation is preached."[26] Fuller's inclusion of this quote implicitly suggests that his opponents, by inquiring into the hidden decrees of God regarding who it is Christ died for, are actually leading men to trust in something other than Christ. Rather than simply looking to Jesus, Fuller suggests that the High Calvinists want repentant sinners to trust in their election and thus their having been atoned

---

[25] This shift illustrates some of why Carl Trueman argues that Fuller probably did not understand the fullness of Owen's context, and therefore Fuller may have used Owen in a way Owen would not have appreciated. Especially since Fuller's refutation of this objection involves articulating the nature of the atonement, Truman argues that in appealing to Owen to represent his agreement, Fuller is misleading, since Owen's understanding of the atonement was more nuanced than Fuller allows for here. See Carl R. Trueman, "John Owen and Andrew Fuller," *Eusebeia* 9 (2008): 53–69.

[26] Fuller, "Gospel Worthy," in *FW*, 2:375.

for. While a subtle distinction, such an implication lays a serious charge at his opponents' feet, essentially saying they are distorting the gospel itself.[27]

Appealing to the Unconverted

The final area to examine in which Fuller appropriates and appeals to Owen relates primarily to pastoral application rather than theological foundation. This passage is unique compared to the other passages, above, in that Fuller admits the personal impact it has had on him. One might wonder the extent to which Fuller has used the above passages because they have influenced him, or if he simply appeals to them to convince his hearers because they agree with his sentiments. But in his concluding remarks, Fuller confesses that this particular passage greatly influenced the nature of his own thinking regarding the free offer of the gospel. He confesses that upon reading it, it "sunk deep into my heart; and the more observation I have since made, the more just his remarks appear."[28]

The quote itself comes from Owen's classic of Reformed spirituality, *On the Mortification of Sin*, in which he instructs his readers that true repentance consists of identifying the heart of sin, rather than just the sinful manifestation. In other words, individual sins manifest because people are sinful. Therefore, when preaching to the unconverted, it is necessary to show them their sinful state. Preachers who merely call out and decry individual sins are likened to the "beating of an enemy in an open field, and driving him into him impregnable castle not to be prevailed against."[29] They may win a small victory, but they have not won the war. To truly reach the unconverted with the gospel, says Fuller, preachers must use the law of God to reveal humanity's sinful condition. Once that condition is exposed and a person's helpless estate is revealed for what it is, then the good news of the gospel may come to bear on that person's heart.

---

[27] The use of this quote from Owen bolsters Trueman's argument that Fuller either misunderstands or misuses Owen. In context, Owen is answering a similar objection to that which Fuller is addressing, yet he nowhere suggests Christ died for all "as sinners," which is Fuller's language. Instead, he provides three lines of argument: First, the elect among the nations cannot be saved without some non-elect also hearing the gospel appeal. Second, in the new covenant, it is simply God's design that the gospel be preached to all and all be called to repent. And third, that men are called to trust Christ, not that Christ died for them. Owen's answer insinuates that it would, in fact, be disingenuous to tell all men that Christ died for them, but this does not prevent preachers from calling for repentance. So, it seems Owen may concur with Fuller's application, but his reasoning would be different.

[28] Fuller, "Gospel Worthy," in *FW*, 2:390.

[29] Fuller, "Gospel Worthy," in *FW*, 2:390.

Conclusion

While these examples do not exhaust the references to Owen in Fuller's work, they provide a sufficient sample to draw some conclusions as to how Fuller appropriated Owen and was shaped by the Puritan divine in his own thought about the free offer of the gospel. First, it is clear that Fuller was in some ways indebted to Owen as a shaping influence on his evangelical thought. Early on in Fuller's ministry he was exposed to Owen's teaching, including his manner of appealing to the unconverted and his defense of the legitimacy of freely offering the gospel. At the same time, it is clear that Fuller avoided slavish obedience to Owen's convictions. For example, Fuller's articulation of the nature of the atonement in the second edition of *The Gospel Worthy* noticeably diverged from Owen's own understanding of how Christ's sacrifice brings about reconciliation.

Second, Owen served as a Calvinistic authority to whom Fuller might appeal as he defended his evangelical views against those who viewed themselves as the true and pure Calvinists. Every time Fuller was able to align himself with Owen, he showed that his views were anything but novel. It was Fuller's opponents, not Fuller himself, who had deviated from the tradition received from the Reformers.

Finally, Owen provided theological support for Fuller's arguments, often approaching the matter of the free offer from a slightly different angle. Though Fuller did not set up any developed expositions of Owen's views, his frequent citations carried a big punch, often serving to bring Fuller's own arguments to a close.

In sum, the free offer of the gospel lay at the heart of Fuller's theological, pastoral, evangelistic, and missionary enterprise. In his effort to live and serve in such a way that accorded most clearly with Scripture, Fuller sought the help of learned men who had gone before. In *The Gospel Worthy*, Fuller repeatedly appealed to the Puritan divine John Owen to help show the just harmony between strong Calvinistic soteriology and equally strong evangelistic preaching. By doing so, he found a convenient ally whose theological reputation and logical rigor helped dismantle opposing arguments and advance Fuller's brand of evangelical Calvinism towards the end of reshaping his entire denomination, and in many ways, the broader missions movement as a whole.

3
"I Ever Wish to Make My Savior's Will My Own": Andrew Fuller and the Heart of Missions

Ryan West

Andrew Fuller (1754-1815) certainly deserves the commendation given to him for his contribution to the founding and sustained effort of the Baptist Missionary Society.[1] The modern missionary movement originated within a European context of tremendous change. This setting was wrapped in religious, political, and social uncertainty as well as an attempted retention of old structures.[2] Peter Morden summarized the essence of Fuller's contribution to the BMS within this context: "His unstinting work on behalf of the BMS captures particularly well one aspect of Bebbington's 'quadrilateral' of Evangelical distinctives, namely 'activism.' Indeed, Fuller could stand as a supreme example of eighteenth- and nineteenth-century Evangelical activism, giving himself to the work of the society until his health was quite broken."[3] Well known were his editorial oversight of the *Periodical Accounts*, his numerous letters written, and the long distances travelled throughout the British Isles on behalf of the

---

[1] Hereafter referred to as BMS.

[2] Fuller served in his role as Secretary for twenty years (1793-1815). Two years before his death in 1815, Dissenters received increased freedom officially in the East India Company's 1813 charter renewal, which provided freedom for missionaries to operate in Bengal without the Company's interference. Concerning the 1813 charter renewal, see Brian Stanley, *The History of the Baptist Missionary Society, 1792-1992* (Edinburgh, UK: T&T Clark, 1992), 25-26. Morden highlights Fuller's contribution as the BMS Secretary in three categories: his theological oversight, his work as a political apologist, and his journeys to promote the cause in churches; see Peter J. Morden, *Offering Christ to the World: Andrew Fuller (1754-1815) and the Revival of Eighteenth Century Particular Baptist Life*, SBHT (Carlisle, UK/Waynesboro, GA: Paternoster, 2003), 136-155. For a nice summary of Fuller's contribution utilizing a similar categorical structure, see Paul Brewster, *Andrew Fuller: Model Pastor-Theologian*, SBLT (Nashville, TN: B&H Academic, 2010), 129-144. To understand Fuller's missional theology derived from particular Scriptural texts, see Michael A.G. Haykin, "Andrew Fuller on Mission: Text and Passion," in *Baptists and Mission: Papers from the Fourth International Conference on Baptist Studies*, SBHT, eds. Ian M. Randall and Anthony R. Cross (Colorado Springs, CO: Paternoster, 2007), 25-41.

[3] Morden, *Offering Christ to the World*, 155.

Society.⁴ Additionally, Fuller engaged reluctantly in strategic political maneuvering on behalf of the Society, a story that remains largely untold.⁵ Fuller's nurturing of the nascent missions agency has led to the justified observation that he was the central administrator of the BMS.⁶ Potentially overlooked within such efforts, however, was Fuller's deeper concern, which he understood as the basis for every other enterprise. According to his perspective, all successful missionary efforts arise from the very heart of missions: a vibrant piety derived from Scripture that created the characteristics of a true missionary as exemplified in Samuel Pearce (1766–1799).⁷

---

⁴ Fuller edited and published a newsletter, titled *Periodical Accounts Relative to the Baptist Missionary Society*, to keep the Society's supporters informed and raise funds for further missionary work.

⁵ For an introduction to Fuller's political activity, see Brewster, *Andrew Fuller*, 141–144; Morden, *Offering Christ to the World*, 143–146; and Stanley, *The History of the Baptist Missionary Society*, 20–26. For a sampling of Fuller's letters concerning a minister's involvement in politics, see Andrew Fuller to various recipients, "The Letters of Andrew Fuller," transcribed by Joyce A. Booth, gathered by Ernest A. Payne, and scanned to disc by Nigel Wheeler, Angus Library, Regents Park College, University of Oxford. All of the following references are from this collection of letters: Fuller to William Carey, January 18, 1797; Fuller to William Ward, June 13, 1800; Fuller to Ward, July 14, 1800; and Fuller to Ward, July 9, 1807. These four references are a small sampling of his numerous letters to various individuals in which he stated his position on a minister's political activity. Concerning his reluctant political maneuvering on behalf of the BMS—particularly following Ward's controversial Persian Pamphlet in 1806–1807—see this collection of letters during this timeframe. Specifically, see his letter to Ward on July 9, 1807 in which he gave a detailed account of his activity and consultation with Charles Grant (1746–1823) and Edward Parry (d. 1827), Robert Dundas (1771–1851), and the East India Company Board of Directors to defend the BMS's continued presence in India. To read the "Persian Pamphlet," see Edmonstone's transcribed copy of Carey's translation of the tract: William Ward, *An Address from the Missionaries at Serampore to all persons professing the Mohummedean religion*, IOR Home Misc. 690, British Library, London. For more concerning Ward's Persian Pamphlet, see James Ryan West, "William Carey, William Ward, and Islam: Evangelizing Bengali Muslims, 1793–1813" (PhD diss., The Southern Baptist Theological Seminary, 2014).

⁶ William Brackney identified Fuller as the central administrator of the BMS. He wrote, "The key 'executive' was undoubtedly Andrew Fuller, who became the voluntary superintendent in the operation of the society." See William H. Brackney, "The Baptist Missionary Society in Proper Context: Some Reflections on the Larger Voluntary Religious Tradition," *BQ* 34.8 (1992): 370. For similar perspectives, follow the works referenced in Brackney's article, particularly endnote 44. He cited F.A. Cox, *History of the Baptist Missionary Society of England from 1792 to 1842* (Boston, 1843), 75, and Doyle L. Young, "The Place of Andrew Fuller in the Developing Modern Mission Movement," (Ph.D. dissertation, Southwestern Baptist Theological Seminary, 1984). Brackney stated that this perspective on Fuller—as the chief executive of the BMS—was the thesis argued by Young's dissertation.

⁷ This concept comes from Michael Haykin's introduction to Andrew Fuller, *A Heart for Missions: The Classic Memoir of Samuel Pearce* (Birmingham, AL: Solid Ground Christian Books, 2006). Haykin gave this title to his reprint of Fuller's memoir of Samuel Pearce. For Fuller, Pearce served as an exemplar of missionary piety and ministerial commitments. Pearce's heart *for* missions, therefore, was what Fuller deemed to be the heart *of* missions.

Scripture and Vibrant Piety

As the foundation of Fuller's belief system, Scripture expressed a particular message—the gospel of Jesus Christ. He believed Scripture to be necessary for global missions and that a global missionary effort was the implication of correctly interpreted Scripture. For Fuller, a central commitment to the "word of God" as found in Scripture would bring about evangelical piety and a global missions effort.[8]

While Fuller was committed to the whole of Scripture, he held the gospel of Christ as more esteemed than other portions of the Bible. He wrote, "The holy Scriptures are frequently denominated the word of God, particularly in the Psalms of David. But I apprehend the term is here [Acts 12:24] used in a more specific sense; and that it is expressive strictly of the gospel of Jesus Christ, the Son of God; that gospel which the apostles were commissioned to go and preach to every creature."[9] To clarify his designation of the gospel of Christ as the "word of God," he wrote, "But why is the gospel called the word? It is sometimes denominated the word of the truth of the gospel; sometimes the word of reconciliation; sometimes the word of life. It is here emphatically called the word of God ... because it is expressive of the mind or heart of God. Words are, or should be, expressive of the heart. This word is expressive of God's heart. There is not any expression of his heart equal to it."[10] Thus, he did not disregard certain Scriptural passages but rather focused on what he perceived to be the primary message of God.

According to Fuller, one must not overlook God's other means of revelation, but they were not on par with the gospel of Christ. For example, nature displayed the wonder and character of God: "The heavens declare his power and goodness; and the firmament showeth his handy works. The providence

---

[8] Fuller's understanding of the "word of God" within Scripture should not lead one to believe that he discounted certain texts as not being revealed of God. Clearly, he believed all of Scripture to be God's revelation, but he used this phrase—as illustrated in this section of the present chapter—to denote the gospel of Jesus Christ. Fuller believed all of Scripture to express certain aspects of God's mind, but the gospel of Christ to be "expressive of his whole heart;" see Andrew Fuller, "The Progress of the Gospel," in *The Complete Works of the Rev. Andrew Fuller*, vol. 3, ed. Joseph Belcher (1845 ed.; reprint, Harrisonburg, VA: Sprinkle Publications, 1988), 833. Hereafter *FW*.

[9] Fuller, "The Progress of the Gospel," in *FW*, 3:833. In this sermon, Fuller was expounding upon Acts 12:24, which he transcribed, "But the word of God grew and multiplied." Fuller preached this sermon at the Tabernacle, Norwich on June 28, 1810. This sermon is significant because it came late in his life after having served as the BMS Secretary for seventeen years. Therefore, one can look to it as his mature thought concerning Scripture, piety, and missionary activity.

[10] Fuller, "The Progress of the Gospel," in *FW*, 3:833.

of God, and the judgments of God, which have been abroad in all ages, have been expressive of his faithfulness and righteousness. In fact, there are many things which show a part of the Divine character."[11] In addition to nature, God revealed himself in part throughout Scripture:

> There are many things expressive of the mind of God ... For instance, the holy law of God is expressive of his holiness, and of his mind in part; and the curses of that law are expressive of his displeasure against sin, and so far they are expressive of the mind or heart of God. But they do not express his final decision; because a sinner may be under the curse of the law, and yet that curse, by his fleeing to the Hope set before him in the gospel, may be removed, and turned into a blessing ... It [the gospel of Christ] is God's last decision. It is the final resolve of the eternal Jehovah.[12]

Although observers could see such revelations in nature and throughout Scripture, these modes of revelation do not depict God's fullness to the extent of the gospel of Christ.

Without discounting God's revelation as seen in nature and the whole of Scripture, he emphasized the heart of God's revelation:

> *Here* [in the gospel of Christ] all the rays of Divinity meet together, and concentrate in a focus. Here they form one general blaze. There is not an attribute in the Divine nature, or a feature in his character, but what is expressed in the gospel of salvation, in the gospel of the Son of God. This is, in a peculiar sense, called his word, because it is expressive of his whole heart.[13]

All of Scripture, according to Fuller, united to bear uniform witness to the person and work of Christ.[14]

Operating according to this hermeneutic, Fuller defined the gospel of Christ through an indirect summary when speaking of what he would say if he encountered unbelieving Hindus in India:

---

[11] Fuller, "The Progress of the Gospel," in *FW*, 3:833.
[12] Fuller, "The Progress of the Gospel," in *FW*, 3:833–834.
[13] Fuller, "The Progress of the Gospel," in *FW*, 3:833.
[14] Andrew Fuller, "The Uniform Bearing of the Scriptures on the Person and Work of Christ," in *FW*, 1:702-704.

> I would tell them there was a God in heaven—that I was a worshipper and servant of him—that idolatry, and all iniquity, was hateful in his sight—that there was an hereafter, when these things would be brought into account—that, from the love I bore to him and them, I had come amongst them to tell them of these things—that God, in love to sinners, had sent his Son to die, &c., and now commanded all men, every where, to repent; that he was able and willing to save all that returned to God by him; and that all others would everylastingly perish, &c.[15]

In another text, Fuller applied this same hermeneutic as he defined components of the gospel—the glory of the Divine character; the evil nature of sin; the lost condition of sinners; and the grace, mercy, and peace found in Christ alone—all of which centered on Christ and composed the gospel contents of the "word of God."[16]

This gospel, however, was not simply a content-rich message. It was the foundation certainly, but one that led to transformational growth in the gospel personally and involvement in global missionary activity. Fuller stated, "It [the gospel of Christ] must be planted there [in the believer] before it can grow or multiply. Brethren, this is the origin; this is the root!"[17] Fuller believed the rooting of faith was first before a blossoming evangelical piety would result in significant missionary activity.

With the sure starting point established—meaning, the gospel of Christ or the "word of God"—evangelical piety was sure to follow. First, one needed faith in this gospel, a faith from which all other spiritual disciplines begin. Describing the apostles' request for an increased faith, Fuller wrote, "[They were] asking for an increase of every other grace; this being a kind of first wheel that sets the rest in motion."[18]

Once set in motion by faith, Fuller anticipated that believers would then grow in this grace. He penned, "We proceed to notice what is said respecting its progress. It is said to grow and multiply. These terms may be said to be near

---

[15] Andrew Fuller, "The Establishment of the Glasgow Missionary Society," in *FW*, 3:825. Obviously, Fuller did not provide a systematic summary of his doctrine in this passage. Fuller intended to write a complete systematic theology. Although he did not complete this intended work, one can find the portions that he finished in Andrew Fuller, "Letters on Systematic Divinity," in *FW*, 1:684-711. For a helpful secondary source concerning Fuller's theology, see Brewster, *Andrew Fuller*, 37-64. Concerning the Glasgow Missionary Society, readers should note that it was founded in 1796.

[16] Fuller, "The Uniform Bearing of the Scriptures," in *FW*, 1:704.

[17] Fuller, "The Progress of the Gospel," in *FW*, 3:836.

[18] Andrew Fuller, "The Importance of a Lively Faith," in *FW*, 3:826.

akin, and indeed they are so; yet they do not convey precisely the same ideas. They both denote increase; but the first is increase in size; the last in number." While he expected a believer's faith to bring about growth in number—referring to evangelistic results—personal piety would come first and then materialize in several characteristics—ones that he required of all BMS missionary candidates—before resulting in numerical growth.[19]

Whereas Fuller understood piety to be the prerequisite of missionary activity, he also believed a reciprocal relationship to exist between gospel growth personally and gospel expansion globally. Without missionary activity, personal progress in the faith would be stunted. In fact, the spiritual vitality of an entire faith community depended on global missions involvement according to Fuller. He wrote,

> If the exertions of our Society have contributed to excite the public spirit which now prevails through the kingdom, it is no small reward. We have found the undertaking particularly useful in uniting and quickening us in religion; and I trust it will produce similar effects among Christians in general. Where no object of magnitude attracts our regard, we are apt to pore on our own miseries; and where nothing exists as an object in which we may all unite, we are apt to turn our attention chiefly to those things in which we differ. It is well for ourselves, therefore, to be engaged in some arduous undertaking which shall interest our hearts, bring us into contact with one another, and cause us to feel that we are brethren.[20]

Religious bodies that did not apply themselves to global missions, Fuller thought, would become inward focused and would cease being a healthy expression of Christianity. When faith communities ignored Christ's command to go make disciples, they had not the necessary object—extending God's glory into all the earth—to ensure continued unity among themselves. Instead, such self-serving Christians turned on one another and cultivated misery.

For Fuller, therefore, global missionary efforts were both a result of godliness and a necessary endeavor to assure continued spiritual health. If these

---

[19] Fuller's leadership meant that he provided authoritative guidance regarding missionaries' character, theology, and conduct. For example, when Jacob Grigg (1769–1835) became a political liability, Fuller felt it to be his responsibility to discipline Grigg and remove him as a BMS missionary.

[20] Fuller, "The Establishment of the Glasgow Missionary Society," in *FW*, 3:823.

expected results were to come about, what kind of person did he and the other BMS leaders seek to send abroad?

Characteristics of a True Missionary

When asked for advice concerning starting a missionary society, Fuller began by contrasting true and false motives. Missionaries ought to be persons of singular commitment. He said, "No man is fit to be sent, in my judgment, either as a principle [missionary] or an assistant, who does not possess a peculiar desire after the work; such a desire as would render him unhappy in any other employment."[21] When addressing William Carey (1761-1834) and John Thomas (1757-1792) during their commissioning service, he stated, "My dear brethren, let me address you in the words of our Lord Jesus to his disciples, 'Peace be unto you: as my Father sent me, so send I you!' ... Nothing could be greater for those who love Christ than to be employed by him on such an errand, and to have such an example to imitate."[22] True missionaries, in his mind, were those called by Christ to be on his errand—making the name of God great among idolaters.[23] This issue was of utmost importance for the BMS Secretary, as he understood true motives to be the missionary's sustaining power in the midst of great trials associated with the work.[24] Differentiated from true motives, Fuller perceived false intentions within certain individuals:

> It is not every person however who may possess a desire to be a missionary who ought to be accepted. You will probably find many during this great stir [i.e., the rise of the missionary movement] who will offer themselves to go, but whose desire upon examination will be found to

---

[21] Fuller, "The Establishment of the Glasgow Missionary Society," in *FW*, 3:824. In this letter, Fuller answered the question of requisite talents and character of missionaries. Fuller's position was that each mission station needed a principal missionary, one who would be the unquestioned leader in piety and ministry. Concerning secondary missionaries, he wrote, "But as to others who may accompany him, no great talents are necessary; a warm heart for Christ, an ardent love to the souls of poor heathens, an upright character, and a decent share of common sense are sufficient;" see Fuller, "The Importance of a Lively Faith," in *FW*, 3:824.

[22] Fuller, "The Nature and Encouragements of the Missionary Work," in *FW*, 1:510.

[23] The issue of the object of a missionary's ministry—rooting out idolatry among the heathen by spreading the glory of God—is discussed below in relation to Fuller's thoughts regarding a missionary's faith.

[24] He wrote, "I do not mean to plead for enthusiastical impressions; yet an impression there must be, and an abiding one too, that all the fatigues, disappointments, non-success, and discouragements of such an undertaking shall not be able to efface;" see Fuller, "The Establishment of the Glasgow Missionary Society," in *FW*, 3:824. He offered similar thoughts when commissioning Carey and Thomas; see Fuller, "The Nature and Encouragements of the Missionary Work," in *FW*, 1:512.

have originated in a dissatisfaction with something at home. They dislike the politics of their country, and therefore wish to leave it; or they have been bothered by disappointment in civil and worldly affairs; or they are vain, and conceive it to be a fine thing to attract the attention and bear a commissions from thousands; or they are idle, and wish to ramble up and down the world; or inconsiderate, and have not properly counted the cost. Even ministers will be found who are unacceptable at home, and therefore desire to change their situation. But none of these motives will bear. ... A pure, disinterested, ardent desire to serve the Lord in this work is the one thing needful.[25]

The essence of true motives within a missionary, for Fuller, was a "disinterested spirit." Without such a spirit within the missionary, other requirements—such as true doctrine and unity among the brethren—would not exist.[26] Elsewhere, he offered additional weight to his perspective: "There is, my brethren, but little expectation of the gospel's spreading, unless there be a spirit of prayer, of holy zeal, of disinterestedness; a willingness in us to lay ourselves out to the uttermost. Whenever we see this, we may hope that the word of the Lord will grow and multiply."[27] The deep impression that one could do

---

[25] Fuller, "The Establishment of the Glasgow Missionary Society," in *FW*, 3:824.

[26] The Serampore missionaries agreed with this perspective. Many years later, when defining the requirements of future missionaries and thinking through the legacy that they would leave, the missionaries expressed certain requirements for personnel that the BMS sent to Bengal. Future candidates had to be competent in Latin, Greek, and Hebrew in order to assure that their labors would not end with their own deaths. Above all, however, the missionaries wanted candidates with a disinterested spirit to preserve the unity of the mission. See William Carey, Joshua Marshman, and William Ward to the Society, Serampore, 1 November 1808, IN/21, William Carey, Joshua Marshman, William Ward, and Others to the Baptist Missionary Committee, 1800-1827 Manuscripts, Angus Library Archives, Regent's Park College, University of Oxford, Oxford. This theme dominated this letter as certain BMS missionaries "have again and again shaken the Mission to its foundation." They insisted on future missionaries being "peaceful," who are willing "to give up his own opinions and will at the voice of others."

[27] Fuller, "The Progress of the Gospel," in *FW*, 3:836. Although he did not expound upon his view of the role of prayer in missionary efforts, his perspective on this issue is well documented. For example, he appropriated Jonathan Edwards' "Call to Prayer" in response to John Sutcliff's own call to prayer for the Northampton Baptist Association; see Morden, *Offering Christ to the World*, 120-126. To read Fuller's own thoughts, see Andrew Fuller, "The Promise of the Spirit in the Grand Encouragement in Promoting the Gospel," in *FW*, 3:362. In this text, Fuller stated, "It was in prayer that the late undertakings for spreading the gospel among the heathen originated. We have seen success enough attend them to encourage us to go forward; and probably if we had been more sensible of our dependence on the Holy Spirit, and more importunate in our prayers, we should have seen much more." This statement followed his remarks that established his central principle regarding prayer—all help for the missionary task is from God and it is only by the Spirit's involvement that one can expect success. For another helpful summary of Fuller's view of prayer in relation to effective ministry, see Brewster, *Andrew Fuller*, 56-57.

nothing other than missionary work was essential to being a BMS missionary; true and false motives revealed either the existence or the lack of this deep impression. True and false motives were a first test for Fuller.

The second trait that Fuller believed a missionary should exhibit was godly character. In a letter to an inquirer, he listed five character qualities prerequisite for a true missionary: one must be upright, modest, benevolent, prudent, and patient.[28] The importance of missionary character could not be overstated in his view: "The heathen will judge of the character of your God, and of your religion, by what they see of your own character. Beware that you do not misrepresent your blessed Lord and his glorious gospel."[29] Although he believed the immutable gospel of Christ to be the same yesterday, today, and forever, the "word of God" would take root in the mind of a true missionary and continue to grow throughout the remainder of his life. This process occurred in three ways according to Fuller. First, the evidence of the truth supporting the gospel's validity increased in the believer's mind over time. He stated, "Perhaps you believe the same truths you did thirty years ago; but you believe them on very different grounds. You feel the ground on which you stand much more solid. ... It may mean seven times more than it did."[30] Second, he believed that Christians grew in their attachment to the gospel: "There is an excellency in the gospel that is to be found in nothing else. ... Is it not thus, Christians, that the more you know of Christ, the better you love him? that [sic] the more you know of the gospel, the better you love it, and the more it appears to excel all other knowledge."[31] The third way in which Fuller believed the gospel would grow within a missionary was the individual's conformity to it, which is the essence of true religion. According to him, true religion is to be of God's mind, to think as God thinks, to love what he loves, to hate what he hates.[32] Without such growth in the gospel, a missionary candidate had not the necessary character to become an ambassador of Christ.

In addition to true motives and a godly character, missionaries had to possess a lively faith.[33] Perhaps, this trait was the most essential, in Fuller's mind. He wrote, "I have been a good deal impressed with a persuasion that in our missionary undertakings, both at home and abroad, we shall not be successful,

---

[28] Fuller, "The Establishment of the Glasgow Missionary Society," in *FW*, 3:824.
[29] Fuller, "The Nature and Encouragements of the Missionary Work," in *FW*, 1:511.
[30] Fuller, "The Progress of the Gospel," in *FW*, 3:834.
[31] Fuller, "The Progress of the Gospel," in *FW*, 3:834–835.
[32] Fuller, "The Progress of the Gospel," in *FW*, 3:835.
[33] Fuller, "The Importance of a Lively Faith," in *FW*, 3:825–827.

unless we enter deeply into the spirit of the primitive Christians; particularly with respect to faith in the Divine promises."[34] He longed for BMS representatives to have such a faith. Otherwise, their efforts may prosper for a season, but would not be significant eternally if their actions were not built on God's promises.

This lively faith in God's promises—as defined by Fuller and found in Scripture—had a grand object, an authority for action, and grounds for the hope of success in missionary service. The application of a missionary's lively faith had the grand object of rooting "out idolatry, and establishing the knowledge and worship of the one living and true God."[35] This missionary objective was to follow the example of Christ and make known the glory of the Lord as his servant.[36] And the missionary accomplished this grand object through authority granted from the one true God to go and preach the gospel to every creature.[37] Success depended not on human invention or political blessing, but rather the Divine promise that he "who hath commissioned us to 'teach all nations' hath added, 'Lo, I am with you always, even to the end of the world.'"[38] A lack of this three-fold missionary faith meant that one would neither withstand expected hardships associated with missionary endeavors, nor faithfully carry out the disciplines of biblical piety or ministerial responsibility. To illustrate his assertions regarding a missionary's true motives, godly character, and lively faith, Fuller needed more than penned exhortations. He needed a model and found such a man in Samuel Pearce.

Samuel Pearce: The Exemplar

The summarized thoughts theorized in Fuller's letters found full expression in his memoir of Samuel Pearce.[39] For Fuller, Pearce served as an exemplar of his scripturally-derived ideals. His point in compiling this work was to promote

---

[34] Fuller, "The Importance of a Lively Faith," in *FW*, 3:825.
[35] Fuller, "The Importance of a Lively Faith," in *FW*, 3:826.
[36] Fuller, "The Nature and Encouragements of the Missionary Work," in *FW*, 1:512.
[37] Fuller, "The Importance of a Lively Faith," in *FW*, 3:826. Also, see his second charge to Carey and Thomas that they operated under the direction of Christ as his servants; Fuller, "The Nature and Encouragements of the Missionary Work," in *FW*, 1:512.
[38] Fuller, "The Importance of a Lively Faith," in *FW*, 3:826. Also, read his encouragement to Carey and Thomas concerning Christ's promised support in their work and their expected reward for their efforts; Fuller, "The Nature and Encouragements of the Missionary Work," in *FW*, 1:512.
[39] One can read the original version of this work in Andrew Fuller, "Memoirs of the Rev. Samuel Pearce, M.A.," in *FW*, 3:367-446. Or, an excellent—albeit revised and shortened—version is Andrew Fuller, *A Heart for Missions: The Classic Memoir of Samuel Pearce*.

true missionary piety by observing his friend's specific governing principle—a holy love to God and to others—that led to global missions.[40] Fuller summarized Pearce as having a love of the divine character as revealed in Scripture, a love of the gospel, a love for the people under his pastoral charge, and general goodwill to all mankind. This love expanded his heart and prompted him to labor in season and out of season for the salvation of sinners. Also, Fuller was quick to emphasize Pearce's expression of deep pleasure when walking closely to God.[41] Pearce's love for God cultivated the unending growth in the word of God that Fuller understood as preceding gospel multiplication.[42] All of these concerns were the result of his governing principle of holy love.

This governing principle resulted in a disinterested spirit within Pearce, which brought about the godly character Fuller believed to be essential for effective missions. In a lengthy section discussing Pearce's preaching tour in Ireland, Fuller highlighted the fact that Pearce received several appealing offers for pastorates.[43] He struggled to decline such opportunities because of his sincere desire to see the gospel proclaimed in that land. Ultimately, however, he did not accept these invitations because of his belief that God wanted him to remain in his current pastoral charge in England. He was resigned to the Lord's will and the station sovereignly ordained for him; to receive the portion God allotted for him and seek no more.[44] Additionally, his submissive spirit to his Lord was evident in his acceptance of the BMS Committee's ruling to deny his application for missionary service. He wrote, "I am disappointed, but not dismayed. I ever wish to make my Savior's will my own."[45] As a servant of Christ, what he wanted was of no consequence. Disinterested faithfulness to God's providence was key for Pearce's piety and thus significant for Fuller's end.

Finally, Fuller utilized Pearce as an example of lively faith by summarizing his character and piety in several categories. He observed in Pearce a commitment to Scripture as the source of religious truth and deep communion with

---

[40] Fuller, *A Heart for Missions*, 143.
[41] Fuller, *A Heart for Missions*, 9, 26.
[42] Fuller, *A Heart for Missions*, 13, 24, 25, 26.
[43] Fuller, *A Heart for Missions*, 81, 85. For the larger section concerning Pearce's trip to Ireland, see 72-89.
[44] Fuller, *A Heart for Missions*, 48-49, 51, 57, 64, 66. Pearce desired strongly to go to India as a BMS missionary. He stated, "My heart is at Mudnabatty, and at times I even hope to find my body there: but with the Lord I leave it"; see Fuller, *A Heart for Missions*, 81. For other helpful perspectives on Pearce's submission to God's providence, see Covington, "Swallowed Up in God: The Impact of Samuel Pearce on Modern Missions," 5-6.
[45] Fuller, *A Heart for Missions*, 48, 51.

Christ.⁴⁶ Fuller also knew Pearce to be a man who was keenly aware of his own sinfulness that brought about his great desire to approach the mercy seat of Christ through the discipline of prayer.⁴⁷ Ultimately, Fuller saw Pearce as a man who had an ever-increasing disdain for worldliness in pursuit of heavenly-mindedness.⁴⁸ Such piety contributed to Fuller's ideal of a truly pious believer with a heart for missions.⁴⁹ He was a man who illustrated a faith in Christ that was lively indeed.

Samuel Pearce thus exemplified Fuller's principles regarding the characteristics of a true missionary: the growth in the "word of God" personally that led to spreading God's glory through global evangelization. Fuller used these ideals, found in Pearce, to spur the Particular Baptist people to action and his intentions found great receptivity. For example, Richard Mardon (1775–1812) read Pearce's memoir and found great encouragement for his own missionary endeavors. Fuller included a journal entry from Mardon in the *Periodical Accounts*, in which Mardon reflected on Pearce's missionary piety:

> In the intervals of public worship I read part of the Memoir of Mr. Pearce, especially Chap. ii. "On his laborious exertions in promoting missions to the heathen, and offering himself to become a missionary." I seldom read, or hear, or talk of Pearce without feeling very peculiar sensations. I sometimes think that heaven will be the sweeter for Pearce being there. Did I feel as he felt, I should be more worthy of the name of a missionary.⁵⁰

Fuller saw typified in Pearce his own conviction that there could be no public spirituality apart from private godliness first, an opinion he stated succinctly at a later point in his career:

> We do not expect wheat, or any other grain, to multiply, till it is grown to individual maturity. We do not expect the word of God to multiply, till Christians are brought in a great degree into a likeness with God.

---

⁴⁶ Fuller, *A Heart for Missions*, 30, 56, 58, 63.

⁴⁷ Concerning Fuller's view of Pearce's awareness of his sinfulness, see Fuller, *A Heart for Missions*, 30. Concerning Fuller's summary of Pearce's discipline of prayer, see Fuller, *A Heart for Missions*, 43, 63.

⁴⁸ Fuller, *A Heart for Missions*, 55–56.

⁴⁹ Fuller, *A Heart for Missions*, 28, 36, 43, 49, 58, 61, 62.

⁵⁰ "Occurrences at Serampore, Extracted from the Journals of Brethren Ward, Moore, Marshman, and Mardon," November 9, 1806, *Periodical Accounts Relative to the Baptist Missionary Society*, vol. 3 (London: Baptist Missionary Society 1806[–1809]), 312.

There is an important connexion, I apprehend, between the growth and the multiplying of the word of God. ... [T]here is such a connexion between the progress of true religion in the soul and in the world, as to furnish abundant encouragement for us to promote religion in the heart, as the means of promoting public religion.[51]

Pearce united these two concerns perfectly in Fuller's mind. The two issues—growth in godliness and global missions—were intricately connected in the model of Pearce to bring about a particular result.

Conclusion

Certainly, Fuller has bestowed to Christ's church a theological legacy on many levels, particularly regarding global missions. For Fuller, the centrality of Scripture's unifying message—the gospel of Christ—brought about an ever-growing evangelical piety that multiplied through global missions. He perceived his role in global missions, which was spreading the gospel in the British Isles personally and overseeing the BMS global operations as its Secretary, to be the capstone of his ministry. Yet, for all of his activism in fulfilling his calling from God, the BMS Secretary believed a scripturally-derived piety among the Society's representatives to be the foundation for anything that would last. Missionaries today would be wise to follow Fuller's lead—biblical piety first before global missionary activity. Without it, one might have activity, but such effort would not represent the heart of a missionary movement.

---

[51] Fuller, "The Progress of the Gospel," in *FW*, 3:835.

4
"Helped on Our Way to Heaven":
The Puritan Tradition in Andrew Fuller's
Theology of Marriage

Matthew D. Haste

While Andrew Fuller never wrote a treatise on marriage, his views on the subject are accessible through careful study of his works. For example, in a sermon on Ephesians 5, he marveled at how "motives to the most ordinary duties are derived from the doctrine of the cross," and remarked, "Who but an apostle would have thought of enforcing affection in a husband to a wife from the love of Christ to his church?"[1] Such statements reveal that he thought of marriage through the lens of the gospel and recognized its connection to spirituality. He explained, "I am inclined to think that our personal Christianity is more manifest in this way than in any other." Character is not proven by actions on special occasions, he reasoned, but "by that which is habitual, and which, without our so much as designing it, will spontaneously appear in our language and behavior."[2] For Fuller, the doctrine of the cross lay at the heart of marriage; therefore, marriage could be helpful in appreciating the gospel. He frequently used marriage as an illustration for particular gospel truths, revealing his thoughts on matrimony in the process. By examining such references in his writings, it is possible to assemble a basic framework of Andrew Fuller's theology of marriage. The picture that emerges in this study reveals that Fuller's theology of marriage was rooted in a biblical understanding of God's plan and

---

[1] Andrew Fuller, "The Future Perfection of the Church," in *The Complete Works of the Rev. Andrew Fuller*, vol. 1, ed. Joseph Belcher (1845 ed.; reprint, Harrisonburg, VA: Sprinkle Publications, 1988), 243. Hereafter *FW*.

[2] Andrew Fuller, "The Future Perfection of the Church," in *FW*, 1:244. For an examination of Fuller's own subsequent marriages, see Matthew D. Haste, "Marriage and Family in the Life of Andrew Fuller," *SBJT* 17.1 (Spring 2013): 28-34.

purposes for the institution reminiscent of the Puritan tradition of previous generations.[3]

God's Plan for Marriage

Fuller's theology of marriage began with the recognition that God had dictated a plan for it in the Scriptures. As such, humans are accountable to their Creator and the "original law of marriage."[4] Fuller used several terms for this notion but he derived the basic concept from his reading of Genesis 2:18-25.[5]

According to Fuller, the "original design" of marriage set forth in Genesis "confines men to one wife" and "teaches them to treat her with propriety."[6] Polygamy was a significant issue in eighteenth-century England, but Fuller's positive definition of marriage here prohibited not only polygamy but other forms of fornication such as homosexuality and adultery as well. Although Fuller did not refer to homosexuality in this context, his overall theology of marriage only allowed for a heterosexual relationship. For example, in reference to Genesis 19, he referred to the acts of the Sodomites as "a species of crime too shocking and detestable to be named."[7] Fuller considered adultery

---

[3] There are numerous helpful studies on the Puritan understanding of marriage including: Edmund S. Morgan, *The Puritan Family: Religion and Domestic Relations in Seventeenth-Century New England* (New York: Harper & Row, 1966); Levin L. Schucking, *The Puritan Family: A Society Study from the Literary Sources*, trans. B. Battershaw (London: Routledge & Kegan Paul, 1969); James Turner Johnson, *A Society Ordained by God: English Puritan Marriage Doctrine in the First Half of the Seventeenth Century* (Nashville, TN: Abingdon, 1970); Leland Ryken, *Worldly Saints*, 73-90; Timothy Beougher, "The Puritan View of Marriage: The Nature of the Husband/Wife Relationship in Puritan England as Taught and Experienced by a Representative Puritan Pastor, Richard Baxter," *Trinity Journal* 10, n.s. (1989): 131-160; Daniel Doriani, "The Puritans, Sex, and Pleasure," *Westminster Theological Journal* 53 (1991): 125-143; Mark Dever, "Christian Hedonists or Religious Prudes? The Puritans on Sex," in *Sex and the Supremacy of Christ*, eds. John Piper and Justin Taylor (Wheaton, IL: Crossway, 2005), 245-270; J.I. Packer, "Marriage and Family in Puritan Thought," in *A Quest for Godliness: The Puritan Vision of the Christian Life* (Wheaton, IL: Crossway, 1990), 259-276; and Joel R. Beeke, "The Puritans on Walking Godly in the Home," in *A Puritan Theology: Doctrine for Life* (Grand Rapids, MI: Reformation Heritage Books, 2012), 859-876.

[4] Fuller, "Expository Discourses on Genesis," in *FW*, 3:66.

[5] Additional terms include "the law of nature" in Fuller, "Expository Discourses on Genesis," in *FW*, 3:10; "the Christian law" in Fuller, "Expository Discourses on Genesis," in *FW*, 3:121; and "the original simplicity" of "first principles" in Andrew Fuller, "Strictures on Sandemanianism," in *FW*, 2:633. In his discourses on the Sermon on the Mount, Fuller noted that Jesus reinstituted "the original law of creation" in regard to marriage and divorce. Andrew Fuller, "Sermon on the Mount," in *FW*, 1:571.

[6] Fuller, "Expository Discourses on Genesis," in *FW*, 3:9. Fuller's basic definition of marriage agrees with *The Second London Confession* of 1677. See William L. Lumpkin, *Baptist Confessions of Faith* (Valley Forge, PA: Judson, 1989), 284-285.

[7] Fuller, "Expository Discourses on Genesis," in *FW*, 3:77. In another work, he also referred to homosexuality as "unnatural." Andrew Fuller, "The Gospel its Own Witness," in *FW*, 2:40.

a perversion of God's plan for monogamy and recognized it as grounds for lawful divorce.[8]

In his reflections on Genesis, Fuller pointed out the failures of Lamech, Abraham, and Jacob to uphold the biblical standard of faithful monogamy. Lamech was "the first who violated the law of marriage" by taking a second wife, and Abraham followed the foolish advice of his wife into the same "deviation from the original law of marriage."[9] In regard to Abraham's choice to marry Hagar, he concluded, "There is no calculating in how many instances this ill example has been followed or how great a matter this little fire has kindled."[10] Additionally, he noted of Jacob, "The domestic discords, envies, and jealousies between Jacob's wives serve to teach the wisdom and goodness of the Christian law, that every man have his own wife, as well as every woman her own husband."[11] He considered any such form of fornication "an evil and bitter thing" because it violated God's plan for a monogamous relationship between one man and one woman.[12]

Fuller recognized that God's plan for marriage also included specific roles and responsibilities for each spouse. Consistent with the Puritan tradition of previous generations, Fuller believed that the husband was to lead his home, protecting his family from both physical and spiritual dangers.[13] In an ordination sermon preached in 1787, Fuller exhorted a young minister to pay close attention to his responsibilities as a spiritual leader in his home:

> Value [good character] at home in your family. If you walk not closely with God there, you will be ill able to work for him elsewhere. You have lately become the head of a family. Whatever charge it shall please God, in the course of your life, to place under your care, I trust it will be your concern to recommend Christ and the gospel to them, walk circumspectly before them, constantly worship God with them, offer up secret prayer for them, and exercise a proper authority over them.[14]

---

[8] See Fuller, "Sermon on the Mount," in *FW*, 1:570-571.

[9] Fuller, "Expository Discourses on Genesis," in *FW*, 3:23, 66-67.

[10] Fuller, "Expository Discourses on Genesis," in *FW*, 3:67.

[11] He continued, "No reflecting person can read this chapter without being disgusted with polygamy, and thankful for that dispensation which has restored the original law of nature, and with it, true conjugal felicity." Fuller, "Expository Discourses on Genesis," in *FW*, 3:121.

[12] Fuller, "Expository Discourses on Genesis," in *FW*, 3:137.

[13] Fuller chastised both Adam and Abraham for failing to lead their families. Fuller, "Expository Discourses on Genesis," in *FW*, 2:11, 66.

[14] Andrew Fuller, "The Qualifications and Encouragement of a Faithful Minister Illustrated by the Character and Success of Barnabas," in *FW*, 1:136. Fuller's list of fatherly responsibilities is reminiscent of Samuel Stennett's parallel consideration of the same subject. See Samuel

Fuller connected faithfulness in the home to fruitfulness in ministry, arguing that "eminent spirituality in a minister is usually attended with eminent usefulness."[15] Furthermore, as noted above, he considered a man's conduct at home to be a supreme revelation of his true character. In a sermon on false teachers, he remarked, "Men may put on the demure and the devout for mere selfish purposes, but follow them into private and domestic life, and they will ordinarily declare themselves."[16] Fuller further pointed out that a man's leadership in his home was significant because of its impact on those entrusted to his care. In a sermon entitled, "The Importance of Union of Public and Private Interests in the Service of God," Fuller again pointed out the need for men to pay attention to "the spiritual welfare of [their] families."[17] One can detect the seriousness with which he understood this responsibility from the following quote:

> Alas! How painful must be the thought, if one, or two, or more of those thus committed to our charge, be wrecked and lost! How interesting it must be to a serious mind to be able to say, at the last day, "Here am I, and the children which thou hast given me!" It is true that the parent is not accountable for the conversion of his children. He cannot change their hearts. He only that made the human mind can change it; but the means are his, the blessing is the Lord's. It is of importance that we carefully walk before our children, setting them a holy example, walking before our families and all our domestics in such a way as that we recommend them to follow us.[18]

Fuller's language of "walking" before the family as a godly model is likely rooted in the Authorized Version's rendering of Psalm 101:2, "... I will walk within my house with a perfect heart." Matthew Henry (1662-1714), the renowned Puritan commentator on the Scriptures, called this passage "The Householder's Psalm."[19] Henry called for fathers to follow the example of

---

Stennett, "Discourses on Domestic Duties," in *The Works of Samuel Stennett*, D.D., vol. 2, ed. William Jones (London: Thomas Tegg, 1824), 32-33.

[15] Fuller, "The Qualifications and Encouragement of a Faithful Minister," in *FW*, 1:143.

[16] Fuller, "Sermon on the Mount," in *FW*, 1:589.

[17] Andrew Fuller, "Importance of Union of Public and Private Interests in the Service of God," in *FW*, 1:472.

[18] Fuller, "Importance of Union of Public and Private Interests," in *FW*, 1:472.

[19] Henry's commentary was one of the most popular works of its kind in the eighteenth century. It is almost certain that Fuller would have been familiar with it. For more on Henry, see Allan M. Harman, *Matthew Henry (1661-1774): His Life and Influence* (Fearn, UK: Christian Focus, 2012).

David, who considered "not only how he would walk when he appeared in public, when he sat in the throne, but how he would *walk within his house*, where he was more out of the eye of the world, but where he still saw himself under the eye of God."[20] In this way, Fuller's understanding of the man's role in the home was consistent with Henry and others in the Puritan tradition.

Fuller also taught that God had given specific responsibilities to wives. In an address prepared for two missionaries and their wives, Fuller elaborated on some of these duties,

> My dear sisters, yours is a great work. ... It is for you to strengthen the hands of your companions, by a cheerful demeanor under their various discouragements, by conversing with the native females, by keeping order in the family, by setting an example of modesty and affection, by economy and industry.[21]

As these missionary wives followed the example of other faithful women, Fuller believed that their conduct would be "a powerful recommendation of the gospel."[22] When wives failed to fulfill their roles, their actions not only reflected poorly on the gospel but also had the potential to negatively influence their husbands. Thus, Fuller noted of the patriarch Abraham, "The father of mankind [Adam] sinned by hearkening to his wife, and now the father of the faithful follows his example [in Genesis 16]. How necessary for those who stand in the nearest relations, to take heed of being snares, instead of helps to one another!"[23]

Fuller contended that each spouse should fulfill their duties to the other out of love rather than obligation. In one sermon, he used marriage as an example of love, contending, "All the labours and journeys of a loving head of a family are directed to their comfort; and all the busy cares of an affectionate wife to the honor and happiness of her husband."[24] Similar to his Puritan predecessors, he recognized the role of affection as a motivation for fulfilling marital responsibilities.[25]

---

[20] Matthew Henry, *Commentary on the Whole Bible* (1706; repr., Peabody, MA: Hendrickson, 1991), 887.

[21] Andrew Fuller, "The Christian Ministry a Great Work," in *FW*, 1:515.

[22] Fuller, "Christian Ministry a Great Work," in *FW*, 1:515.

[23] Fuller, "Expository Discourses on Genesis," in *FW*, 3:66.

[24] Andrew Fuller, "The Nature and Importance of Love," in *FW*, 1:306.

[25] For an example of a Puritan perspective on this issue that is consistent with Fuller, see William Gouge, *Of Domesticall Duties* (London: John Haviland, 1622), 221-222.

One especially noteworthy aspect of Fuller's theology of marriage is the way he envisioned how the loving fulfillment of spousal responsibilities pointed to the power of the gospel. He contended that the husband's leadership is not to be of a tyrannical spirit as was common in pagan countries, for Christianity had restored the "woman to her original state, that of a friend and companion."[26] In a cultural context where gender inequality was assumed and accepted, Fuller considered the proper treatment of women to be one of the distinguishing marks of a truly Christian home. It would be inaccurate to cast Fuller as a revolutionary on this issue, but he did challenge men to treat their wives in a way that distinguished them from the surrounding culture. Thus, he proclaimed, "Go among the enemies of the gospel, and you shall see the woman either reduced to abject slavery, or basely flattered for the vilest purposes; but in Christian families you may see her treated with honor and respect."[27] Fuller contended that the Christian vision for marriage restored dignity to women, calling for the wife to be "treated as a friend, as naturally an equal, a soother of man's cares, a softener of his griefs, and a partner of his joys."[28] Fuller's description of marital companionship is consistent with the Puritan vision, but he expanded it by focusing on the restored dignity of women and the way in which Christian marriages ought to stand out from the culture around them.

Thus, Fuller argued that the gospel empowered Christian marriages to conform to God's original plan by restoring the ability of husbands and wives to live out their respective roles faithfully. As individual marriages attained this goal, Christian families cast a powerful vision to the watching world. Furthermore, such families provided the foundation for strong churches. Fuller's reflection on this fruit of godly families provides a helpful conclusion to this discussion and is worth quoting in full:

> A Christian family is the first nursery for the church of God. It is there that the seed of truth is ordinarily sown. It is there that the first

---

[26] Fuller, "Expository Discourses on Genesis," in *FW*, 3:16. Fuller noted that while there is "doubtless a natural subordination in innocency, through sin woman becomes comparatively a slave," especially "where sin reigns uncontrolled, as in heathen and Mahometan countries." Fuller, "Expository Discourses on Genesis," in *FW*, 2:16. Thus, Fuller agreed with his fellow eighteenth-century Baptists in grounding gender roles in the created order, even as he acknowledged how these roles had been distorted by the Fall.

[27] Fuller, "Expository Discourses on Genesis," in *FW*, 3:9. See also "The Gospel its Own Witness," in *FW*, 2:42–47.

[28] Fuller, "Expository Discourses on Genesis," in *FW*, 3:10.

principles of true religion are often instilled. The prayers, the tears, the cautions, and the example of a godly parent, who walks in the fear of God before his family, will leave effects on the mind. I have seldom known persons converted who were brought up in religious families, but they have dated their first impressions from something which took place in the family. They have dated their early convictions to what has passed in family worship, perhaps, or in the counsel and example of their friends. Thus is the church of God supplied from Christian families—thus are the lively stones furnished, by which the spiritual house is reared. Let this be an encouragement to us.[29]

God's Purposes for Marriage

Since God created marriage with a specific plan in mind, Fuller recognized the value of noting the divine purposes for the institution. Like others in the Puritan-Reformed tradition, Fuller acknowledged three primary purposes for marriage—procreation, protection, and companionship—to which he included a fourth: the display of gospel truths in reflecting the relationship of Christ and the church. In consolidating Fuller's thoughts on the subject, the following section will survey how Fuller addressed each of these purposes throughout his corpus.

First, he noted that God created marriage "for the propagation of the human race."[30] Marriage provided the proper relationship in which to obey the command to multiply and be fruitful. Fuller explained that the command "contains permission, not of promiscuous intercourse, like the brutes, but of honorable marriage."[31] Thus, one purpose for marriage is the multiplication of the human race according to God's original command in Genesis 1:26–27.

A second purpose of marriage is to make "a most distinguished provision for human happiness."[32] Fuller made this comment in relation to God's creation of Eve, noting, "The woman was made for the man; not merely for the gratification of his appetites, but of his rational and social nature."[33] In his

---

[29] Andrew Fuller, "Importance of Union of Public and Private Interests," in *FW*, 1:472. Similarly, Gouge (1575–1653) had declared nearly two centuries before: "A family is a little Church, and a little commonwealth, at least a lively representation thereof, whereby trial may be made of such as are fit for any place of authoritie, or of subjection in Church or commonwealth. Or rather it is as a school wherein the first principles and grounds of government and subjection are learned; whereby men are fitted to greater matters in Church or commonwealth." Gouge, *Domesticall Duties*, 18.

[30] Fuller, "Expository Discourses on Genesis," in *FW*, 3:9.
[31] Fuller, "Expository Discourses on Genesis," in *FW*, 3:39.
[32] Fuller, "Expository Discourses on Genesis," in *FW*, 3:9.
[33] Fuller, "Expository Discourses on Genesis," in *FW*, 3:9.

commentary on Genesis 2, he continued, "It was not good that man should be alone; and therefore a helper that should be meet, or suitable was given him."[34] In this same passage, he called Eve "a fit companion" for Adam. One way in which Fuller alluded to the centrality of companionship can be seen in the way he appealed to marriage to substantiate other points throughout his writings. For example, in arguing for the necessity of love in one's actions toward God, he reasoned, "If a wife were ever so assiduous in attending to her husband, yet if he were certain that her heart was not with him, he would abhor her endeavors to please him, and nothing that she did would be acceptable in his sight."[35] Thus, for Fuller, genuine companionship and mutual affection lay at the heart of God's purposes for marriage.

A third purpose Fuller noted for marriage was protection from sin. In his reflections on Genesis 6, he argued, "The great end of marriage, in a good man, should not be to gratify his fancy, nor to indulge his natural inclinations, but to obtain a helper; and the same in a woman."[36] Here he was not speaking of mere physical assistance, but rather moral encouragement. He continued, "We need to be helped on our way to heaven, instead of being hindered and corrupted."[37] Thus, Fuller envisioned companionship to involve both romantic affection as well as spiritual support. A century prior, the Kidderminster divine Richard Baxter (1615–1691) had acknowledged the potential for mutual encouragement in similar language: "Remember that you are hasting to the everlasting life. ... You are but to help each other in your way, that your journey may be the easier to you, and you may happily meet again in the heavenly Jerusalem."[38]

Fuller's language of being "helped on our way to heaven" may have been influenced by a popular mid-century work on marriage which he possessed in his personal library.[39] *The Advantages and Disadvantages of the Marriage-State* by John Johnson (1706–1791) was a short allegory reminiscent of John Bunyan's classic, *The Pilgrim's Progress* (1678).[40] The author recounted a dream in

---

[34] Fuller, "Expository Discourses on Genesis," in *FW*, 3:9.
[35] Andrew Fuller, "Dialogues and Letters between Crispus and Gaius," in *FW*, 2:678.
[36] Fuller, "Expository Discourses on Genesis," in *FW*, 3:26.
[37] Fuller, "Expository Discourses on Genesis," in *FW*, 3:26.
[38] Richard Baxter, "A Christian Directory," in *The Practical Works of Richard Baxter*, 3 vols. (1846; repr., Grand Rapids: Soli Deo Gloria Publications, 2008), 1:404.
[39] This work is included on the recorded list mentioned above.
[40] John Johnson, *The Advantages and Disadvantages of the Married-State* (London: George Keith, 1754). Johnson was an interesting character who started his own small sect of Dissenters. For more on John Johnson and the Johnsonian Baptists, see Kenneth Hipper, "The Johnsonian

which he witnessed four young men receiving advice from an elderly man about the importance of choosing a good companion for their journey from Babylon to Canaan. The first three men chose to ignore the man's advice and experienced various troubles as a result, with two of them being led astray to the point of falling off the way altogether. The fourth man, being wiser than the others, chose a fit companion for the journey. As the story unfolded, the two proved to be useful help-meets to one another, illustrating the blessings of a one-flesh union founded on faith, in contrast to the plight of being unequally yoked. Johnson's reflection on this happy couple may have influenced Fuller's language quoted above: "So I continued observing this united Pair advancing in their Way; for they greatly contributed to help each other forward, many Difficulties they surmounted, and many rich Blessings they enjoyed as they traveled in the Way."[41]

Fuller, of course, found his primary support for this notion in the Scriptures. The Genesis narrative provided several warnings illustrating how spouses could hinder rather than help one another in this regard. Noting how Eve led Adam astray, Fuller commented, "It was the first time, but not the last, in which Satan has made use of the nearest and tenderest parts of ourselves to draw our hearts from God."[42] Fuller recognized that the companionship of a spouse can be a source of great encouragement in sanctification or a devilish snare that leads one toward unrighteousness. In noting such dangers, Fuller pointed out the wisdom of God in prohibiting marriage with unbelievers and warned his congregation of ignoring this command.[43] The tone of his plea illustrated the high view he held of this particular function of marriage: "I would earnestly entreat serious young people, of both sexes, as they regard God's honor, their own spiritual warfare, and the welfare of the church of God, to avoid being unequally yoked together with unbelievers."[44]

In this way, Fuller argued that marriage is for the propagation of the human race, a provision for human happiness, and for protection against sin. A fourth and final purpose of marriage noted by Fuller is the picture that it provides. Fuller frequently appealed to marriage as an illustration of gospel truths and, in doing so, injected marriage with critical importance. As previously cited, he

---

Baptists of Norwich," *BQ* 38.1 (January 1999): 19–32; *History of a Forgotten Sect of Baptized Believers Heretofore Known as "Johnsonians,"* ed. Robert Dawbarn (London: Balding & Mansell, 1900).

[41] Johnson, *Advantages and Disadvantages*, 35.
[42] Fuller, "Expository Discourses on Genesis," in *FW*, 3:11.
[43] Andrew Fuller, "The Nature and Importance of Love," in *FW*, 1:306.
[44] Fuller, "Nature and Importance of Love," in *FW*, 1:306.

argued that the ultimate significance of marriage is "derived from the doctrine of the cross."[45] In a sermon entitled, "Conformity to the Death of Christ," Fuller affirmed that "the common duties of domestic life are enforced from" the principles of Christ's death.[46] As such, he employed the realities of domestic life as a means of illustrating gospel truths. With each reference to marriage in the context of the gospel, Fuller reaffirmed the necessity of doing marriage according to God's plan and purposes. Such illustrations fall into three general categories: marriage as a picture of union with Christ, marriage as a preview of eschatological hope, and marriage as a means of understanding the person of Christ.

Fuller frequently used marriage to help demonstrate the blessings of a believer's union with Christ. For example, when one of his beloved deacons died in 1792, Fuller's funeral sermon focused on the nature of this blessing for those who die in the Lord.[47] In order to explain the nature of this union, he cited the biblical comparison to marriage, as follows:

> The union between Christ and his people is frequently compared to the marriage union; as they who were twain become "one flesh, so they who are joined to the Lord are one spirit" [1 Cor 6:16-17]; and as in that case there is not only a mental, but a legal union, each becoming interested in the persons and possessions of the other, so in this we, with all we have, are Christ's, and Christ, with all he has, is ours.[48]

In another sermon, he noted, "As she that is joined to a husband becomes interested in all that he possesses, so they that are joined to Christ are, by the gracious constitution of the gospel, interested in all that he possesses."[49] Fuller considered marriage to be particularly helpful for understanding how God justifies sinners by grace through faith. He reasoned that justification is an act of grace because the sinner brings nothing into the relationship and yet, through union with Christ, the sinner becomes the recipient of all his blessings. In the same way, he pointed out that when a wife "becomes one with her husband," she becomes "legally interested in all that he possesses," regardless of her former poverty.[50] As such, Fuller concluded, "The wealth which an

---

[45] Fuller, "Future Perfection of the Church," in *FW*, 1:243.
[46] Andrew Fuller, "Conformity to the Death of Christ," in *FW*, 1:311.
[47] Andrew Fuller, "The Blessedness of the Dead Who Die in the Lord," in *FW*, 1:152-160.
[48] Fuller, "Blessedness of the Dead Who Die in the Lord," in *FW*, 1:152.
[49] Andrew Fuller, "Reception of Christ the Turning Point of Salvation," in *FW*, 1:269.
[50] Andrew Fuller, "Justification" in *FW*, 1:281.

indigent female might derive from the opulence of her husband would not be in *reward* of her having received him, so neither is justification the reward of faith."[51] In reflecting on the same illustration in *The Gospel Worthy of All Acceptation*, he remarked:

> Ask [a woman brought into an inheritance through marriage], in the height of her glory, how she became possessed of all this wealth; and, if she retain a proper spirit, she will answer in some such manner as this: It was not mine, but my deliverer's; his who rescued me from death. It is no reward of any good deeds on my part; it is by marriage; it is "of grace." ... She now enjoys those possessions by marriage; yet who would think of asserting that her consenting to be his wife was a meritorious act, and that all his possessions were given her as the reward of it?[52]

Such statements demonstrate the importance of marriage in Fuller's theology as a picture of gospel truths.[53]

In reference to the eschatological reign of Christ, Fuller declared, "The whole gospel dispensation is described as a marriage supper. What an espousal then and what a supper that will be!"[54] His sermon entitled "The Future Perfection of the Church" further drew out the implications of this imagery, demonstrating how marriage was used as a metaphor throughout Scripture to, among other things, trace the process of God perfecting his church.[55] As Fuller pointed out, in presenting the church to himself as described in Ephesians 5:25–27, Christ demonstrated both his sufficiency as a Savior and man's lowly condition in sin. Whereas the parent typically presented the bride to her groom, the church, described as an abandoned orphan in her sinful condition (cf. Ezek. 16:1–5), had no one to present her to Christ. "In this case," Fuller asserted, "the bridegroom must himself be her father, and perform the office of a father throughout, even to the presenting of her to himself. If such be the allusion, it represents in an affecting light our forlorn condition as under the fall."[56] In this passage and others, therefore, Fuller sought to explain the marriage metaphor because he considered it a means of helping believers "to

---

[51] Fuller, "Justification," in *FW*, 1:281.
[52] Andrew Fuller, "The Gospel Worthy of All Acceptation," in *FW*, 2:384.
[53] See also Fuller, "The Gospel Worthy of All Acceptation," in *FW*, 2:402.
[54] Andrew Fuller, "Expository Discourses on the Apocalypse," in *FW*, 3:286. Additional references to marriage in his exposition of Revelation include *FW*, 3:283-286, 295, 305-306.
[55] Fuller, "Future Perfection of the Church," in *FW*, 1:243-253.
[56] Fuller, "Future Perfection of the Church," in *FW*, 1:252.

heighten our love to Christ," particularly as they looked ahead to the future consummation of reconciliation to their Savior.[57]

Finally, Fuller used marriage imagery as a means of drawing attention to the person and character of Christ as the husband of the church. One such example was in an argument for the extent of the atonement, where he argued, "His death is represented as resulting from his love, which he exercises as a husband."[58] According to Fuller, Christ's conduct to the church was "the tender relation of a husband" and therefore, rooted in loving sacrifice.[59] These statements carried rhetorical power when understood with his view of the husband's role in mind. Thus, each time that Fuller appealed to marriage as a picture of biblical truths revealed not only his understanding of the gospel but also his theology of marriage.

Fuller and the Puritan Tradition

A final question remains for our present purpose: Was Andrew Fuller consciously following the Puritans on marriage or was he merely consistent with their understanding of this subject? We know that Puritan thinkers such as John Owen and Jonathan Edwards were influential in his theological development.[60] Furthermore, his personal library contained some fifteen volumes by Puritan authors and an additional fifteen works written by Edwards and the New Divinity men.[61] A number of scholars have explored the impact that these authors had on Fuller. Notwithstanding diversity within the Puritan tradition, it seems apparent that Fuller was both aware and appreciative of his indebtedness to certain Puritan thinkers.

However, none of the Puritan volumes in his library directly addressed marriage in any significant way, and Fuller himself never appealed to the

---

[57] Fuller, "Future Perfection of the Church," in *FW*, 1:253. For similar examples, see also Fuller, "The Gospel its Own Witness," in *FW*, 2:95; Andrew Fuller, "Letters to Mr. Vidler on Universal Salvation," in *FW*, 2:56, 219, 310-311, 384.

[58] Andrew Fuller, "Reply to the Observations of Philanthropos," in *FW*, 2:491.

[59] Fuller, "Reply to Philanthropos," in *FW*, 2:499.

[60] For more on how Puritan theology shaped Fuller, see Jeffrey K. Jue, "Andrew Fuller: Heir of the Reformation," *Eusebeia* 9 (Spring 2008): 27-52; Carl R. Trueman, "John Owen and Andrew Fuller," *Eusebeia* 9 (Spring 2008): 53-70; Thomas J. Nettles, "The Influence of Jonathan Edwards on Andrew Fuller," *Eusebeia* 9 (Spring 2008): 97-116; and Chris Chun, *The Legacy of Jonathan Edwards in the Theology of Andrew Fuller*, SHT (Leiden: Brill, 2012).

[61] This information is taken from Michael A.G. Haykin, "'A Great Thirst for Reading': Andrew Fuller the Theological Reader," *Eusebeia* 9 (Spring 2008): 16. For the full list of Fuller's library, see "List of Books belonging to Andrew Fuller of Kettering" (Ms. G95B, Bristol Baptist College Library, Bristol, England).

Puritans to substantiate his own arguments on the subject. This is somewhat understandable given the nature of his writings but it seems to suggest that Fuller found his doctrine of marriage in another source. Where his language is in greatest similarity to well-known Puritan phrases, it is also consistent with that of John Gill (1697–1771), whom he read thoroughly and who could be considered a conduit for Puritan thought into eighteenth-century Evangelicalism.[62] Still, Fuller never cited Gill as an authority on marriage either. It was ultimately the Bible that determined his doctrine. When one examines Fuller's comments on marriage in detail—as we have attempted to do in this chapter—it is apparent that he found his theology of marriage primarily in the pages of Scripture, even if the words and wisdom of the Puritans were perhaps echoing in his mind.

Conclusion

To summarize, Andrew Fuller considered marriage a union of one man and one woman faithfully committed to one another. He argued that God created marriage to propagate the human race, as a provision for happiness, as a means of protection against sin, and as a picture of Christ's love for the church. This vision was reminiscent of the Puritan tradition but ultimately rooted in the Scriptures. While he never focused an entire work on marriage, it is clear that Fuller saw significance in this ordinary, domestic duty, especially when viewed through the doctrine of the cross. It was at the cross that Fuller understood marriage to derive its final meaning as well as its defining mission. In emphasizing the power of marriage to proclaim the gospel, Fuller turned the minds of married believers to the watching world. Consistent with the missional focus of his larger theological scheme, Fuller considered marriage a means of pointing others to Christ, the faithful Husband of his beloved church.

---

[62] For more on Gill's theology of marriage, see Matthew D. Haste, "'A Type of the Marriage of Christ': John Gill on Marriage," *PRJ* 6.2 (July 2014): 289–302.

5
"A Musical Pronunciation of Affecting Truth": The Church Music of Andrew Fuller[1]

Charles J. Bumgardner

In his exploration of the renewed pastoral theology of Andrew Fuller (1754–1815), Keith Grant has demonstrated that this renewal was expressed in preaching that "was *plain* in composition and delivery, *evangelical* in content and concern, and *affectionate* in feeling and application." Further, Grant contends, "these expressions of Fuller's renewed pastoral theology could, also, be explored in other areas of his ministry," and suggests Fuller's leadership at the Lord's Supper and the exercise of church discipline as candidates for further study.[2] While these would doubtless be fruitful areas of inquiry, the present essay will explore Fuller's renewed pastoral theology vis-à-vis his church music. This remains an area in Fuller studies that has not been directly addressed,[3] although Fuller wrote two essays specifically on the topic.

In spite of those two essays, the limited amount of real estate occupied by the topic of church music in Fuller's extant works makes it evident that the area was not one of particular focus for him, even within the realm of his pastoral theology and ecclesiology. This is to be expected; while Fuller

---

[1] I gratefully acknowledge those who have helped me to obtain primary source material, suggested directions for research, and offered answers to questions in the course of this study: Paul Brewster, Sally Drage, Nathan Finn, Michael Haykin, Michael McMullen, Benjamin Ramsbottom, Nicholas Temperley, and Nigel Wheeler. Thanks are due as well to two of my children, Kyle and Katelyn, who assisted me by working through a large collection of Fuller's letters in search of musical references. Finally, special mention should be made of the ongoing assistance of Dr. Steve Weston, presently the music director at Fuller Baptist Church in Kettering, who with unfailing patience and grace interacted with my research and provided reproductions of primary source material archived at Kettering. While the help I have received has been invaluable, any errors in the present essay are, of course, my own responsibility.

[2] Keith Grant, *Andrew Fuller and the Evangelical Renewal of Pastoral Theology*, SBHT (Milton Keynes, UK: Paternoster, 2003), 103–104, italics his.

[3] James Leo Garrett makes passing mention in *Baptist Theology: A Four-Century Study* (Macon, GA: Mercer University Press, 2009), 186, as does Phil Roberts, "Andrew Fuller," in *Theologians of the Baptist Tradition*, eds. Timothy George and David S. Dockery (Nashville: Broadman & Holman, 2001), 366 n. 32.

appreciated verse and hymnody, and was an amateur poet himself, his writing projects were more polemical and practical than poetical, and controversies of church music in his own theological tradition had become somewhat more subdued (though not absent!) by his day.[4] All the same, the present essay will demonstrate that while church music was not of paramount importance to Fuller, he did give due attention to its role as regards his larger theological vision.

Methodologically, we will set the stage by briefly recounting the history of musical controversy and development in Fuller's ecclesiastical context up through his lifetime. With this context established, we will turn to Fuller's own thought and ministry, noting his personal interest in and use of hymnody and poetry. This will be followed by a historical investigation of the music of his church at Kettering. Finally, several brief essays of Fuller's related to church music will be summarized.

In his study of Particular Baptist ecclesiology, James Renihan notes that "at the heart of ecclesiology is the expression of worship in and by the church. The meeting of the Christian Assembly is not primarily for the transaction of church related business, but is first and foremost a meeting to worship God." He goes on to suggest that there are presently "no comprehensive investigations into the specific [worship] practices of the Particular Baptists."[5] It is hoped that the present essay, by focusing on the church music of one of the more significant Particular Baptists, will contribute to better understanding not only Andrew Fuller's ecclesiology and pastoral theology, but Particular Baptist worship more generally.

Particular Baptist Church Music through the Early Eighteenth Century
Particular Baptist church music in Britain during the century previous to Fuller's ministry at Kettering was marked by both controversy and

---

[4] As Brewster has noted, Fuller "instinctively practiced what R. Albert Mohler has recently labeled 'theological triage.' That is to say, he responded to the various theological issues of his day by devoting his greatest attention to matters of primary importance." Paul Brewster, *Andrew Fuller: Model Pastor-Theologian*, SBLT (Nashville, TN: B&H Academic, 2010), 8.

[5] James M. Renihan, *Edification and Beauty: The Practical Ecclesiology of the English Particular Baptists, 1675–1705*, SBHT (Eugene, OR: Wipf & Stock, 2009), 118. Note, however, as a recent contribution toward this end, Matthew W. Ward, *Pure Worship: The Early English Baptist Distinctive*, MBH (Eugene, OR: Pickwick, 2014). Ward argues the thesis that "pure worship was the early English Particular Baptist distinctive," contending that "their overwhelming desire to worship God purely drove the development of this group's theology and ecclesiology as well as their self-identity" (v). Ward focuses on London Particular Baptists in the mid to late seventeenth century, roughly a century before Fuller's ministry.

development, and a brief survey of its trajectory will be helpful in situating Andrew Fuller in his church-musical context.[6] Following Calvin, seventeenth-century Dissenters and Anglicans alike largely rejected "hymns of human composure" and limited their congregational singing to metrical psalms. Within the Dissent, early Baptists went so far as to disallow congregational singing altogether,[7] but while the General Baptists maintained this stance for quite some time,[8] Particular Baptists led Dissenting churches in going beyond psalms to singing hymns.[9]

The key influence toward the broad acceptance of hymn singing among Dissenters in general—and, indeed, toward the very shape of that hymnody—was Congregationalist Isaac Watts,[10] whose work in the early 1700s furthered the gains made by Benjamin Keach's arguments in the Particular Baptist

---

[6] Several works treat these musically formative years in the Baptist tradition to varying extents, but the best summary treatment is David W. Music and Paul A. Richardson, "The British Background," in *"I Will Sing the Wondrous Story": A History of Baptist Hymnody in North America* (Macon, GA: Mercer University Press, 2008), 1-70. See also the thorough Robert H. Young, "The History of Baptist Hymnody in England from 1612 to 1800" (D.M.A. diss., University of Southern California, 1959). Helpful as well are Hugh Martin, "The Baptist Contribution to Early English Hymnody," *BQ* 19 (1961-1962): 195-208, and Hugh T. McElrath, "Turning Points in the Story of Baptist Church Music," *BHH* 12 (1974): 4-13.

[7] See Young, "History of Baptist Hymnody," 14-26. This practice found support in the influential writings of John Smyth. See his *The differences of the Churches of the Seperation: containing, a description of the leitourgie and ministerie of the visible Church* (1608) and *Certayne demaundes from the auncyent brethren of the Separation*, both in *The Works of John Smyth, Fellow of Christ's College, 1594-8* (Cambridge: Cambridge University Press, 1915). Smyth took Dissenting objections to the Book of Common Prayer and logically extended them to other pre-composed forms of worship, even metrical psalmody; he contended that all such forms, whether memorized or read, stifled the free working of the Spirit.

[8] As late as 1689, their General Assembly officially condemned the practice as a "carnal formality," although doubtless not all General Baptists concurred. It was not until the end of the eighteenth century that congregational singing was everywhere accepted among General Baptists. Young, "History of Baptist Hymnody," 17-18; W.R. Stevenson, "Baptist Hymnody," in John Julian, *Dictionary of Hymnology*, 2nd rev. ed. (New York: Dover, 1907), 1:111.

[9] Congregational hymn singing was accepted at least as early as 1655 in certain Particular Baptist congregations. Renihan, *Edification and Beauty*, 146-147.

[10] "In the field of hymnography, no one held such a pioneering or chronologically decisive position as Watts. Before him attempts were tentative, and whatever may have moulded the development of later hymnographers, none of them can be said to be totally unaffected by his example, even if they did not imitate him stylistically." David J. Montgomery, "Isaac Watts and Artistic Kenosis: The Rationale behind the Work of Britain's Pioneer Hymnwriter," *SBET* 5 (1987): 174. Watts's hymnological influence is centered in his *Hymns and Spiritual Songs* (London: J. Humfreys, 1707), and *The Psalms of David Imitated in the Language of the New Testament, and apply'd to the Christian State and Worship* (London: Bible and Crown/Angel/Bible and Three Crowns, 1719).

"hymn-singing controversy" of the 1690s.[11] In Particular Baptist life, however, hymn singing received its greatest boost from the endorsement of John Gill in the late 1740s. Gill's prominence among Particular Baptists led to the widespread embrace of hymnody on principle, and thus to its flourishing within his tradition.[12] The "Golden Age of Baptist Hymnody" followed from 1760-1800 with such notable hymnists as Anne Steele, Benjamin Beddome, Samuel Stennett, and John Fawcett, and the fruit of this period enriched the Particular Baptist context in which Andrew Fuller ministered.

Looking at church music outside Fuller's Particular Baptist context, we find the Evangelical Revival in Britain both reflected and propagated in Methodist hymns.[13] From at least one perspective, Mark Noll is correct to suggest that "nothing was more central to the evangelical revival than the singing of new hymns written in praise of the goodness, mercy, and grace of God,"[14] and no one was more instrumental in providing those new hymns than Charles Wesley. Although the Wesleys' Arminian theology and their connection with the Church of England were at odds with the Calvinistic nonconformity of Particular Baptists, Charles' hymns nonetheless found their way into Particular Baptist churches, perhaps most notably through John Rippon's influential hymnal, *A Selection of Hymns*.[15]

---

[11] When it comes to the worship practices of Particular Baptists, the hymn-singing controversy has received by far the most press. See James C. Brooks, "Benjamin Keach and the Baptist Singing Controversy: Mediating Scripture, Confessional Heritage, and Christian Unity" (Ph.D. diss., The Florida State University, 2006); J. Jackson Goadby, *Bye-Paths in Baptist History: A Collection of Interesting, Instructive, and Curious Information not Generally Known Concerning the Baptist Denomination* (London: Elliot Stock, 1871), 317-349; Michael A.G. Haykin and C. Jeffrey Robinson, "Particular Baptist Debates about Communion and Hymn-Singing," in *Drawn into Controversie: Reformed Theological Diversity and Debates Within Seventeenth-Century British Puritanism*, eds. Michael A.G. Haykin and Mark Jones, RHT (Göttingen: Vandenhoeck & Ruprecht, 2011), 296-308; Renihan, *Edification and Beauty*, 146-152.

[12] See the excellent treatment of John Gill's influential teaching on singing in Deborah A. Ruhl, "Engaging the Heart: Orthodoxy and Experimentalism in William Gadsby's *A Selection of Hymns for Public Worship*" (Ph.D. diss., Ohio State University, 2013), 75-81. Gill argued that singing was an ordinance of God and the duty of all men, persuasively defending his position from Scripture.

[13] It is said of Charles Wesley, "His hymns gave wings to the doctrines of the Evangelical Revival, so that they flew everywhere." J. Ernest Rattenbury, *The Evangelical Doctrines of Charles Wesley's Hymns*, 3rd ed. (London: Epworth, 1954), 15.

[14] Mark Noll, "The Defining Role of Hymns in Early Evangelicalism," in *Wonderful Words of Life: Hymns in American Protestant History and Theology*, eds. Richard J. Mouw and Mark A. Noll (Grand Rapids, MI: Eerdmans, 2004), 3-4.

[15] John Rippon's *A Selection of Hymns, from the best authors, intended to be an appendix to Dr. Watts's Psalms and Hymns* (London: John Wilkins, 1787). For the influence of Rippon in this regard, along with that of the earlier "Bristol Collection" (John Ash and Caleb Evans, *A Collection*

Rippon's *Selection* dominated British Baptist congregational singing for forty years and may be considered the culmination of Baptist hymnody's Golden Age. In this hymnal, he collected the labors of the best Baptist hymnwriters, as well as works from outside his tradition by authors such as Philip Doddridge, John Newton, and Charles Wesley. Just as Wesley's Methodist hymns expressed and taught the doctrines of the Evangelical Revival from an Arminian perspective, so Rippon's collection expressed and taught the doctrines of the Evangelical Revival from the perspective of a Calvinism that was the same sort as Andrew Fuller's.[16] Rippon's biographer highlights the importance of the *Selection* in this regard:

> As T.G. Crippen wrote of the *Selection*: "hymns embodying the Gospel Call are as clear as any Arminian could desire." Like any good hymnbook Rippon's helped to define and interpret the Christian faith for its own generation. Not the least of the influences shaping the new evangelistic Calvinism of the Baptists was the regular singing of hymns which taught this theology. ... Sermons were expected, according to the hymns in the *Selection*, to be powerful means of bringing sinners to conversion. Hymns for the spread of the Gospel, especially in the work of foreign missions, were included in generous numbers, whilst hymns longing for revival ... were also provided. In each of these ways, the *Selection* helped advance the general spread of "Fullerism" and the genuine missionary and evangelistic concern of the Baptists.[17]

Anticipating a later discussion, we briefly note here that during Fuller's lifetime a significant shift in the music of British hymnody was afoot.[18] Routley notes the two related but divergent "lines" or "streams" of hymnody in the eighteenth century: one was grounded in historic psalmody, while the other "can trace its ancestry no further back than the music of the Restoration and is transformed by Evangelicalism into a quite new and original, but a very

---

of Hymns Adapted to Public Worship [Bristol: W. Pine, 1769]), see Ruhl, "Engaging the Heart," 83–102.

[16] It should be noted that, as in many hymnals, Rippon and others at times altered the texts of hymns (including those of Charles Wesley) to be included in the *Selection* to bring them in line with their own theology. See Ken R. Manley, *"Redeeming Love Proclaim": John Rippon and the Baptists*, SBHT (Waynesboro, GA: Paternoster, 2004), 92–98.

[17] Manley, *Redeeming Love Proclaim*, 135.

[18] "Provincial English Anglican and nonconformist church music ... underwent profound changes during the eighteenth and early nineteenth centuries." Sally Drage, "The Performance of English Provincial Psalmody *c.*1690–*c.*1840" (Ph.D. thesis, University of Leeds, 2009), ii.

influential, style."¹⁹ This musical transformation was such that "the emphasis had shifted from words to music, so that music did not now reinforce and serve the words, but often drowned them altogether."²⁰ We will see that Fuller was not in favor of this shift.

Sacred Music in the Life and Ministry of Andrew Fuller

Fuller was much more involved in missions and doctrinal debate than in church music. All the same, his hymnal collection suggests an interest in hymnody, and his occasional composition of verse strengthens that impression. Further, his journal and other writings show the impact of poetry and hymnody upon his own life,²¹ and several of his essays demonstrate the consideration that he gave to music in the church.²²

Fuller's Hymnals

In August of 1798, Fuller compiled a handwritten catalog of his books.²³ Scattered among his library of over three hundred volumes were at least six collections of hymns and/or psalms.²⁴ Two of these collections were regularly used

---

¹⁹ Erik Routley, *The Music of Christian Hymns* (Chicago, IL: G.I.A. Publications, 1981), 70. Although Methodism was a major vehicle for this sort of music, John Wesley was not himself in favor of it—he frowned on choirs, organs, vocal harmony, and some of the newer musical innovations such as fuging tunes, melismata, and polyphony—but over time "tempered his views," realizing the new music had come to stay. See Nicholas Temperley, "John Wesley, Music, and the People Called Methodists," in *Music and the Wesleys*, ed. Nicholas Temperley and Stephen Banfield (Urbana, IL: University of Illinois Press, 2010), 6-8, 17-18. See also in this regard Martin V. Clarke, "John Wesley and Methodist Music in the Eighteenth Century: Principles and Practice" (Ph.D. diss., Durham University, 2008), 137-146.

²⁰ Routley, *The Music of Christian Hymns*, 74.

²¹ Although non-hymnic poetry is not the focus of the present treatment, it may be noted in passing that Fuller most often quotes in this regard John Milton, Edward Young, and Alexander Pope.

²² Unless specified otherwise, *WAF* in this chapter references Andrew Fuller, *The Works of Andrew Fuller*, ed. Andrew Gunton Fuller (1841 ed.; reprint, Carlisle, PA: Banner of Truth, 2007). As well, unless specified otherwise, Fuller's journal entries are cited from *The Complete Works of Andrew Fuller*, vol. 1: *The Diary of Andrew Fuller, 1780-1801*, eds. Michael D. McMullen and Timothy D. Whelan (Boston: Walter de Gruyter, 2016). Hereafter *CWAF*.

²³ "List of Books Belonging to Andrew Fuller of Kettering." The catalog is archived under "Book list and other miscellaneous writings" (accession number 14500) in the Bristol Baptist College Library, Bristol, England.

²⁴ See Figure 1. Fuller compiled the list in the order that the books stood on his shelves, and the term "scattered" above reflects the disparate placement of the hymnals/psalters; they do not seem to have been shelved together. Michael A.G. Haykin mentions three of the six—Stennett, Fawcett, and Rippon—in his essay "'A Great Thirst for Reading': Andrew Fuller the Theological Reader," *Eusebeia* 9 (2008): 17. Haykin notes that if the volumes are still extant, their whereabouts is unfortunately unknown (personal correspondence, 1 October 2013).

in the congregation at Kettering: Isaac Watts's *Psalms and Hymns* and John Rippon's above-mentioned *Selection*.[25] In addition, Fuller owned volumes by Barton, Stennett, Erskine, and Fawcett.[26] We will look briefly at each in order of their original publication date.

FIGURE 1
THE HYMNALS/PSALTERS OF FULLER'S LIBRARY CATALOG
(Reproduced with the permission of Bristol Baptist College)

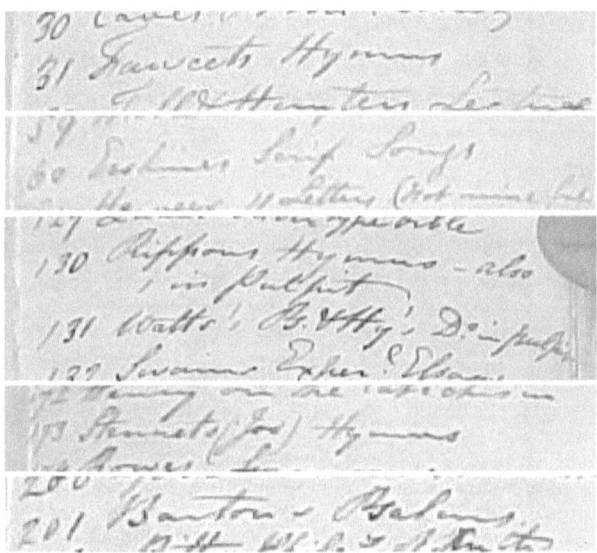

"*Bartons Psalms.*" A friend of Richard Baxter's, William Barton (1597/8–1678) first published his versified psalter in 1644.[27] He revised and reprinted

---

[25] Rippon's work is catalogued as no. 130, listed as "Rippons Hymns." Watts's hymnal is no. 131, noted as "Watts's Ps. & Hy's." The notation for Rippon is followed by "also 1 in pulpit," and Watts similarly has "D° [ditto] in pulpit" immediately following; this alone strongly suggests their use in congregational worship, which is made certain in Fuller's biography written by his son. See Andrew Gunton Fuller, *Andrew Fuller* (London: Hodder and Stoughton, 1882), 78.

[26] "Bartons Psalms" (no. 201); "Stennets (Jos) Hymns" (no. 173); "Erskines Scrip Songs" (no. 60); "Fawcets Hymns" (no. 31). The "(Jos)" in the Stennett title stands for "Joseph" and is likely included to distinguish Joseph Stennett from his grandson Samuel Stennett (1727-1795) who was also a hymnwriter. In addition to these six hymnals/psalters, Fuller indicates his familiarity with the Bristol Collection (journal entry for 2 January 1785) and John Mason's *Spiritual Songs, or Songs of Praise to Almighty God* (journal entry for 25 July 1785).

[27] On Barton, see James Love, *Scottish Church Music: Its Composers and Sources* (Edinburgh: William Blackwood and Sons, 1891), 72-73; Elizabeth Clarke, "Hymns, Psalms, and Controversy in the Seventeenth Century," in *Dissenting Praise: Religious Dissent and the Hymn in England and Wales*, eds. Isabel Rivers and David L. Wykes (Oxford: Oxford University Press, 2011), 16-19.

this work a number of times, with the last of his revisions published posthumously in 1682.[28] In at least his last revision, the collection of psalms is preceded by eighteen various tunes with which to sing them. In his preface, Barton provides a brief apologia for psalm-singing against those who disallowed congregational singing altogether.[29] Baptist minister Robert Robinson produced an edition of Barton's *Psalms* in 1768, and given the publication date of Barton's original editions, it is likely that Fuller owned Robinson's edition rather than one published by Barton himself.[30]

"*Stennets (Jos) Hymns.*" Joseph Stennett (1663-1713) was a Seventh-Day Baptist,[31] and is generally considered to be the first Baptist hymnist of note.[32] The hymnal of Stennett's owned by Fuller was likely the slender volume *Hymns in Commemoration of the Sufferings of Our Blessed Saviour Jesus Christ*.[33] Stennett strove for a care and sobriety in his poetic composition; this is both noted in the preface and evident throughout the work.[34] He also anticipated Isaac Watts's hymnological program in aiming for maximum accessibility to the volume's typical user.[35] In Young's estimation, Stennett's hymnal

---

[28] William Barton, *The Book of Psalms in Metre. Close and Proper to the Hebrew: Smooth and Pleasant for the Metre* (London: Printed for the Company of Stationers, 1682).

[29] Barton speaks of "the express command of God (who hath given all men voices) injoining all to sing his praise aloud, Psal. 66.1,2 especially his professed people to do this duty jointly and together, Psal. 34.3. 111.1 149.1)." *The Book of Psalms*, A2-A3. One of the arguments Barton was fighting was that congregational singing was inappropriate because unbelievers present in "mixt congregations" would then be singing songs meant only for Christians.

[30] No copies of Robinson's edition are extant. Music and Richardson, "*I Will Sing,*" 34.

[31] On Stennett, see "Some Account of the Life of the Reverend and Learned Joseph Stennett," in *The Works of the late Reverend and Learned Mr. Joseph Stennett* (London: Printed for J. Darby et al., 1732), 1:3-36; Clarke, "Hymns, Psalms, and Controversy," 28-31; Benjamin A. Ramsbottom, "The Stennets," in *The British Particular Baptists, 1638-1910*, ed. Michael A.G. Haykin (Springfield, MO: Particular Baptist Press, 1998), 1:136-138.

[32] Julian, *Dictionary of Hymnology*, 2:1091. Julian's estimation is justified by Virginia Ann Cross in her analysis of Stennett's hymns: "Joseph Stennett (1663-1713) and the Development of English Hymnody" (M.C.M. thesis, Southwestern Baptist Theological Seminary, 1974).

[33] Joseph Stennett, *Hymns in Commemoration of the Sufferings of Our Blessed Saviour Jesus Christ. Compos'd for the Celebration of his Holy Supper* (London: J. Darby, 1697); expanded editions were published in 1705 and 1712. Fuller's notation "Stennets (Jos) Hymns" might instead reference Stennett's later *Hymns compos'd for the Celebration of the Holy Ordinance of Baptism* (London: J. Darby, 1712), but *Hymns in Commemoration* seems to have been more popular. Both collections are found in Joseph Stennett, *The Works of the Reverend and Learned Mr. Joseph Stennett*, vol. 4 (London, 1731), 49-170. Hereafter *WJS*.

[34] "I have carefully avoided those very bold flights and those heathenish phrases which some have indulged even in divine poesy; for I cannot think them consistent with the gravity, purity, and perspicuity which ought to be preserv'd in hymns calculated for the immediate service of God, and for the common edification of christians [sic]." Stennett, *WJS*, 4:55.

[35] Note the concern for "perspicuity" in the previous quotation. Stennett also included a table of "The more difficult Words explained," and marginal Scripture references "by which means

"probably aided the cause of singing among Baptists more than all the pamphlets of the [hymn-singing] controversy combined,"[36] and the third edition (1713) includes an anonymous ("by another hand") apology for hymn-singing in Christian worship.

"*Watts's Ps. & Hy's.*" Isaac Watts (1674-1748) published his *Hymns and Spiritual Songs* in 1707 and his *Psalms of David Imitated* in 1719.[37] The two works went through many editions; they were revised, reprinted, and variously combined with each other, with hymns from other writers, with an appendix of various tunes, and so forth. When joined with each other, the result was known simply as *Watts's Psalms and Hymns*—or more colloquially, "Watts Entire"—and it was a combined edition of this sort that was used at Kettering.[38] Andrew Gunton Fuller gives a detailed description: it "consisted first of a metrical version of the Psalms, followed by first, second, and third books of hymns, to which were appended several newer hymns as supplementary to the 'first book.'"[39] Watts's work was an attempt to remedy the poor quality of the singing in nonconformist churches.[40] His compositions were published at a time when many Dissenting congregations sang psalms exclusively,[41] and they were instrumental in the transition from this practice to the inclusion of "hymns of human composure."[42] In using the *Psalms and Hymns* of Watts—

---

the reader, if he is pleased to turn to the passages refered to, may easily explain to himself those phrases and allusions, which at the first glance appear somewhat hard and obscure." Stennett, *WJS*, 4:54-55, 84.

[36] Young, "History of Baptist Hymnody," 60.

[37] Isaac Watts, *Hymns and Spiritual Songs* (London: J. Humfreys, 1707); *The Psalms of David Imitated in the Language of the New Testament, and apply'd to the Christian State and Worship* (London: Bible and Crown et al., 1719). Treatments of Watts and his hymnody are legion, but see especially J.R. Watson, *The English Hymn: A Critical and Historical Study* (Oxford: Clarendon Press, 1997), 133-70.

[38] Fuller, *Andrew Fuller*, 78.

[39] A number of publishers produced editions of *Psalms and Hymns* that fit this description, and the specific edition to which A.G. Fuller refers is not clear.

[40] In the preface of *Hymns and Spiritual Songs*, Watts spoke of his work as an "attempt for the Reformation of Psalmody amongst the Churches" (xiii).

[41] Watts included in the first edition of *Hymns and Spiritual Songs* an essay justifying the use of such "evangelical Hymns," and gave indication therein that "many Christians" were already singing them (266).

[42] Indeed, while Jonathan Edwards was on a journey in 1742, his congregation at Northampton had Watts's hymns introduced to them by visiting preacher Samuel Buell. In a later letter to Benjamin Colman, Edwards noted that upon his return he found that the people (with at least one exception) were so taken with the hymns that they "sang nothing else, and neglected the Psalms wholly." Edwards accepted and defended the use of the hymns, but not to the exclusion of psalmody; he reinstituted psalm-singing, limiting the use of Watts's compositions. Jonathan Edwards to the Rev. Benjamin Colman, 22 May 1744, in *Letters and Personal Writings*, Works of Jonathan Edwards, vol. 16, ed. George S. Claghorn (New Haven, CT: Yale University Press, 1998), 144. On

who was, of course, a Dissenter himself—the Kettering congregation was in line with the vast majority of Dissenting churches by Fuller's time.

"Erskines Scrip Songs." Ralph Erskine (1685-1752) was a Scottish churchman,[43] most widely known for his *Gospel Sonnets*, a collection of theological poems. According to his catalog, Fuller does not seem to have owned this popular volume (although he quotes from it in his memoirs), but did have a copy of Erskine's *Scripture Songs*.[44] Consisting of six "books," *Scripture Songs* was published piecemeal from 1750-1754,[45] and later as a single volume. As its title implies, this work consists of metricized versions of all of the "scriptural songs" outside of the book of Psalms, such as Hannah's and Mary's songs, along with poetic versions of other significant passages. Fuller might have this volume in mind when he says in one of his essays, "I have sometimes had my doubts whether we ought not to sing the poetical parts of Scripture set to sacred music. I should rejoice to see a book of such Divine hymns introduced into all our churches, taking place of a vast load of trash and insipidity."[46]

"Fawcets Hymns." John Fawcett (1739-1817)[47] was a British Baptist minister in northern England, roughly 150 miles distant from Kettering. Best known for the hymn now called "Blest Be the Tie that Binds," Fawcett was converted under the ministry of George Whitefield and produced his *Hymns* in 1782.[48] He was a correspondent of Fuller's and even gave a small measure of assistance with Fuller's treatise against Socinianism.[49] He declined both the prestigious pastorate at Carter Lane in London, as well as the presidency of the Baptist Academy at Bristol, in order to remain with his congregation in

---

Edwards's church music in connection with his theology and larger pastoral task, see Ronald Story, *Jonathan Edwards and the Gospel of Love* (Amherst, MA: University of Massachusetts Press, 2012), 40-45.

[43] On Erskine, see Donald Fraser, *The Life and Diary of the Reverend Ralph Erskine, A.M.* (Edinburgh: William Oliphant & Son, 1834); A.R. MacEwen, *The Erskines* (Edinburgh: Oliphant Anderson & Ferrier, 1900).

[44] *The Sermons, and Other Practical Works, of the Late Reverend Ralph Erskine, Minister of the Gospel in Dunfermline* (Glasgow: William Smith, 1778) contains both *Gospel Sonnets* (10:47-307) and *Scripture Songs* (10:421-676). *Gospel Sonnets* has recently been reprinted as *Gospel Sonnets: Or Spiritual Songs*, ed. Mike Renihan (Pelham, AL: Solid Ground Christian Books, 2010).

[45] Julian, *Dictionary of Hymnology*, 1:353.

[46] Andrew Fuller, "On Instrumental Music in Christian Worship," in *WAF*, 858.

[47] On Fawcett, see Josiah Miller, *Singers and Songs of the Church*, 2nd ed. (London: Longman, Green, and Co., 1869), 271-274; Henry S. Burrage, *Baptist Hymn Writers and Their Hymns* (Portland, ME: Brown Thurston & Company, 1888), 79-84.

[48] *Hymns: Adapted to the Circumstances of Public Worship and Private Devotion* (Leeds: G. Wright and Son, 1782).

[49] J.W. Morris, *Memoirs of the Life and Writings of the Rev. Andrew Fuller*, ed. Rufus Babcock, Jr. (Boston: Lincoln & Edmands, 1830), 226.

Yorkshire. His hymns were typically homiletical in nature, meant for use in association with particular sermons, and they provided some small measure of competition in northern England with Rippon's slightly later collection—to which we now turn.

"*Rippons Hymns.*" The newest hymnal in Fuller's collection was the already-mentioned *Selection of Hymns* compiled by his acquaintance John Rippon in 1787. The Kettering congregation was using Watts when Fuller became the minister there, but while Watts was a nonconformist, he was not a Baptist. Rippon, however, was the quintessential eighteenth-century Baptist,[50] and his hymnal reflects his convictions by including a number of hymns specifically related to believer's baptism.[51] Perhaps more significantly for Fuller, Rippon was an evangelical Calvinist, a stance firmly reflected in his hymnal.[52] Originally published in 1787 with 588 hymns, Rippon's *Selection* was unquestionably the hymnological masterwork of his day; it had no serious competitor.[53] It culled the best from over ninety American and English hymnbooks in addition to introducing over three hundred compositions that had never been printed in a compilation hymnal. Given the date of publication, it must have been Fuller who introduced Rippon's *Selection* to the church at Kettering; by doing so, Fuller engaged a hymnological resource that furthered his own theological program.

Fuller's Personal Use of Poetry and Hymnody

Fuller's son, Andrew Gunton Fuller, noted that his father "had an ear for music," and at least once attempted the composition of a hymn tune.[54] Indeed,

---

[50] In *Redeeming Love Proclaim*, Manley thoroughly demonstrates the thesis that Rippon significantly influenced nearly every major aspect of the renewal and expansion experienced by Particular Baptists in the late eighteenth and early nineteenth centuries.

[51] A first edition of Rippon's *Selection* was unavailable for this study, but the essentially identical fourth edition (1792; the first major revision came with the tenth edition of 1800) contained seventeen hymns and a number of single stanzas in the section entitled "Baptism." Not all of these speak directly of baptism; several set forth more generally the need to identify with Christ, the hardships of following Christ, and so forth.

[52] Ian Bradley rightly speaks of "a strong tendency within Nonconformist hymnody, and not least within Baptist ranks, for hymnals to be produced along clearly drawn theological lines." Ian Bradley, "Nonconformist Hymnody," in *T&T Clark Companion to Nonconformity*, ed. Robert Pope, T&T Clark Companions in Theology and Biblical Studies (New York: Bloomsbury T&T Clark, 2013), 239.

[53] This accolade reflects the judgment of Young, "History of Baptist Hymnody," 126. The "Bristol Collection" was the closest contender, but even this relatively popular hymnal fell short of Rippon's work, as detailed in Manley, *Redeeming Love Proclaim*, 87.

[54] Fuller, *Andrew Fuller*, 79. "Taking it to a musical friend who remarked that it was in a 'flat key,' 'very likely,' said [Fuller], 'I think I was born in a flat key.'"

while not known as a hymnwriter,⁵⁵ Fuller composed verse throughout his ministry. Of his efforts we know of at least the following: a poem dedicating his daughter to Christ (1779), another poem upon the occasion of her early death (1786), verse composed after the death of his friend Joseph Diver (1780), verse composed in memory of Robert Hall (1791), an epitaph for Kettering deacon Beeby Wallis (1792), another for his first wife Sarah (1792), some free verse in memory of his deceased first wife (1793), and two published passages in blank verse (1802).⁵⁶ Clearly, his compositions tended to be occasional in nature and were usually associated with the death of those close to him.⁵⁷

While not especially frequent, it was not unusual for Fuller to refer to hymns or other verse in his various writings.⁵⁸ Recollecting his pre-conversion days, he spoke of a time when, despairing of acceptance by God, he considered giving himself wholly over to sin. A passage from Ralph Erskine's *Gospel Sonnets* came to mind, arresting him:

> But say, if all the gusts
> And grains of love be spent,
> Say, Farewell, Christ, and welcome lusts—
> Stop, stop: I melt, I faint!⁵⁹

---

⁵⁵ He noted once, "I never had any talent for composing hymns." A. Fuller to T. Steevens, Olney, 5 October 1793, *Baptist Magazine* 8 (1816): 494.

⁵⁶ Morris, *Memoirs*, 37–43; John Ryland, *The Work of Faith, the Labour of Love, and the Patience of Hope, illustrated; in the Life and Death of the Rev. Andrew Fuller* (Charlestown: Samuel Etheridge, 1818), 78, 256-263; Thomas Ekins Fuller, *A Memoir of the Life and Writings of Andrew Fuller* (London: J. Heaton & Son, 1863), 157-158. The two 1802 passages are recorded in Ryland's catalog of Fuller's publications thus: "The Life of Faith Exemplified, by an anecdote and two passages versified in the Life of Miss Anthony, entitled 'Devotedness to God in Easy Circumstances.' Ditto 'under Dark and Threatening Providences'—both in blank verse." Fuller was also apparently the composer of certain passages of verse which he records in his diary, for which he names no author; internet searches do not connect these passages with anyone but Fuller. See entries recorded in Ryland, *The Work of Faith*, for July 7, 1780 (p. 64); July 17, 1780 (p. 78); Sep 23, 1780 (p. 69); Jan 29, 1781 (p. 77).

⁵⁷ In his journal entry for Oct 31, 1784, he records hearing that "Mr G is dying." His response: "I was much affected with this news. Sung Psa. xc." Doubtless, this psalm was from Watts, who wrote five different pieces based on Psalm 90 in his *Psalms of David Imitated*, one of which is now sung as "O God, Our Help in Ages Past."

⁵⁸ It should be noted here that the large unpublished collection of Fuller's letters (1788-1815)—nearly 850 typewritten pages—copied by Joyce A. Booth, transcribed by Ernest Payne, and presently archived at the Angus Library in Oxford, generally contain only passing and very occasional references to Fuller's music. The single item of value in this regard is a transcription of Fuller's missionary hymn "Farewell, beloved friends," noted below.

⁵⁹ Ryland, *The Work of Faith*, 13. The lines are from Ralph Erskine, *Gospel Sonnets, or Spiritual Songs*, first published in 1720. Note that this is a different (and much more popular) work than the *Scriptural Songs* found in Fuller's library. In his memoir of Fuller's life, Charles Stuart testified that "Fuller never forgot the impact this passage made on him. Stuart said he had heard Fuller

Fuller dates this incident to the autumn of 1769. Around a year previous, he had taken up the volume and had "read, and as I read, I wept. Indeed, I was almost overcome with weeping, so interesting did the doctrine of eternal salvation appear to me."[60] The content of Erskine's work no doubt affected him more than the form, but it well may be that the poetic shape of *Gospel Sonnets* contributed toward his response.

When Fuller quotes an identifiable hymn, he almost invariably quotes Watts, whether in his journal,[61] his polemical works,[62] his sermons,[63] or other works.[64] Fuller no doubt had a particular affinity for this hymnological giant,[65] whom he spoke of as "the sweet singer of our Israel."[66] All the same, Watts was ubiquitous: during Fuller's lifetime, if a Dissenting church sang psalms or hymns (as opposed to not singing at all), they would more than likely be using Watts. Since the Baptist church at Soham that Fuller attended—and

---

repeat this passage 'with great emotion, and strong emphasis.'" Michael A.G. Haykin, *The Armies of the Lamb: The Spirituality of Andrew Fuller*, PRS (Dundas, ON: Joshua Press, 2001), 74.

[60] Ryland, *The Work of Faith*, 8-9. The portion that brought Fuller to tears was "The Redeemer's Work; Or, Christ all in all, and our complete Redemption. A Gospel-Catechism for Young Christians." See Ralph Erskine, *The Sermons and Other Practical Works, of the Late Reverend and Learned Mr. Ralph Erskine*, vol. 10 (Falkirk: Printed by Patrick Mair, 1796), 253-257.

[61] Note his journal entries for 1 July 1780 ("Why does your face, ye humble souls"); 31 October 1784 ("O for this love, let rocks and hills"); 31 December 1784 ("Now to the Lord a noble song"); 10 February 1785 ("Hush, my dear; lie still and slumber"). As well, A.G. Fuller notes that a month before his death, his father quoted Watts's "Jesus is gone above the skies" with particular emphasis in celebrating the Lord's Supper, and shortly thereafter, in contemplating his impending death, mentioned a couplet from Watts's "God, my supporter and my hope." Andrew Gunton Fuller, "Memoirs of the Rev. Andrew Fuller," in *WAF*, lxxxiii-lxxxiv.

[62] See Andrew Fuller, "The Gospel Worthy of All Acceptation," in *WAF*, 168 ("Election sovereign and free").

[63] *WAF*, 466 ("Now from the roaring lion's rage"), 474 ("'I lift my banner,' saith the Lord"), 669 ("Let others boast how strong they be"). Note as well the citation of Cowper's "Oh for a closer walk with God" (*WAF*, 357), and Toplady's "Awake! sweet gratitude, and sing" (*WAF*, 616).

[64] *WAF*, 860 ("Sweet is the work, my God, my King"), 942 ("Ere the blue heavens were stretch'd abroad"). Note also his citation of John Mason, "Ah Lord, ah Lord, what have I done?" (*WAF*, 875-876).

[65] All the same, Fuller's admiration was not uncritical. In his "Remarks on the Indwelling Scheme," he contrasts Watts's present theological position with an earlier and more orthodox position as expressed in one of his hymns, noting of Watts, "How are the mighty fallen!" *WAF*, 942.

It may be noted here that Fuller's daughter, who at nineteen years old died only thirteen months after her father, is said to have taken particular delight in Watts's *Psalms and Hymns* as well as his *Divine Songs for Children* during her last illness. Ryland, *The Work of Faith*, 292.

[66] "Remarks on the Indwelling Scheme," in *WAF*, 942.

eventually pastored—was a "singing" church, it is probable that Watts shaped Fuller during his formative years.[67]

Along with quoting hymns in his works, Fuller speaks of his own singing. Witness his journal:

> Preached this afternoon on the *breadth*, and *length*, and *depth*, and *height* of Christ's love. Some sweet pleasure at the Lord's Supper. O to know more of Christ, and live upon him! I feel very happy tonight: can hardly forbear singing, as I go about, [here follows a hymn by Watts].[68]

> An affecting meeting of prayer, this evening, for the revival of real religion: found much pleasure in singing, and freedom with God in prayer.[69]

> A dull and heavy state of mind the chief part of the day. Somewhat revived in singing some cheerful hymns at evening meeting.[70]

With his fellow committee members for the Baptist Missionary Society, he often sang William Williams' missionary hymn "O'er the gloomy hills of darkness."[71] Fuller knew from experience the affective power of hymnody in his own life,[72] and recognized its potential to affect others. He once hatched a plan to communicate gospel truth to the young lacemakers in Kettering by printing short hymns on the paper that wrapped the lace-thread they purchased, hymns he described as "the most impressive that I can either find or make."[73]

As an example of Fuller's occasional efforts at verse, his hymn addressed to a group of Baptist Missionary Society missionaries to India may here be set forth:[74]

---

[67] For Soham as a "singing" church, see the incidental references in Fuller's memoirs in Ryland, *The Work of Faith*, 22-23, 34; Fuller, "Memoirs of the Rev. Andrew Fuller," in *WAF*, xxii. Fuller's family moved to Soham in 1761 when Fuller was seven or eight.

[68] 31 October 1784, emphasis his.

[69] 6 December 1784.

[70] 18 July 1785.

[71] Andrew Fuller, "Memoirs of the Rev. Samuel Pearce," in *WAF*, 767.

[72] "I had an affecting day, especially in singing and prayer. The revival of nature at this season of the year, seemed to kindle an earnest desire for the revival of religion." Journal entry for 11 March 1781.

[73] Morris, *Memoirs*, 55.

[74] Originally set down in correspondence to the missionaries, the hymn may also be found in a letter of June 7, 1899 to William Carey (*The Letters of Andrew Fuller* [unpaginated], copied by Joyce A. Booth and transcribed by Ernest Payne); in W. Staughton, *The Baptist Mission in India* (Philadelphia: Hellings and Aitken, 1811), 308-309; and in T.E. Fuller, *Memoir*, 120-121. Technically, the hymn is anonymous, but Fuller intimates that it is his; in connection with watching the

Farewell, beloved friends, once more, farewell!
For you our hearts have felt, and still shall feel:
Of late we've cared, and some attention given;
Now we must leave you to the care of heaven.

If we should ever wickedly omit
To aid, or offer up our strong desire,
Let our right hands their wonted[75] skill forget,
And all our hopes and joys in death expire!

Go then, dear friends, in your Redeemer's cause,
Go plough the briny wave, and brave the deep:
Mercy and truth be with you as you pass;
Preserve your souls, your lives in safety keep.

Go join those much-loved names on yonder shores;
Go share their ardent, honourable toil;
Mingle your tears[76] with theirs—with theirs your joys,
And bear to them the blessings of your native isle.[77]

Go teach the nations, sound the Saviour's name:
As he was sent of God, he doth you send;
His word of promise still remains the same,
"Lo! I am with you always to the end!"

Reading Fuller's verse reveals that he was no Watts, and certainly no Wesley; his finest talents lay elsewhere. That being said, the number of hymns in his library,[78] combined with his propensity to quote hymns in his writings,

---

missionaries' ship sail into the distance, he notes, "The following lines are expressive of what were of one, & I believe of all at and since that time."

[75] Staughton gives "wanted," but "wonted" (i.e., "customary") in T.E. Fuller and Booth/Payne is doubtless correct.

[76] Staughton gives "souls," against "tears" in T.E. Fuller and Booth/Payne.

[77] In Booth/Payne, "isle" is capitalized.

[78] More research remains to be done, but it is interesting that while Fuller had at least six hymnals or psalters in his personal library, there appear to be *none* in the personal and still-extant library of Fuller's contemporary Benjamin Beddome (a noted hymnwriter himself). Beddome's library was roughly the same size as Fuller's. Thanks are due to Emily Burgoyne of the Angus Library who, in connection with the present project, manually searched the card catalog of Beddome's library for roughly 35 various hymnwriters (the Baptist writers listed in Young, "History of Baptist Hymnody," as well as Watts, Whitefield, Wesley, the Countess of Huntingdon, and Newton). In considering the apparent disparity between Fuller's and Beddome's libraries, noted hymnologist Benjamin Ramsbottom suggested that Beddome may have dispersed any hymnals he owned to others before his death, or was just not that interested in hymnody *as such* (i.e., not a "poet" like Anne Steele) in that his hymns were typically *ad hoc* compositions written to be sung

indicates a lifelong interest in hymnody that was not merely academic or polemic in nature.[79] This may be most directly evidenced in a 1793 letter to Thomas Steevens, Baptist pastor in Colchester, worth quoting at length:[80]

> I never had any talent for composing hymns, yet I read the hymns of others with much pleasure. How often have I, of late, wept, in reading, or singing over the 324th hymn of Rippon's Selection, written by my dear friend Fawcett.—Also the 254th of the same selection, and composed by the same hand.[81] Do read and sing it over, and think of me, and others. I have been ready to shed tears of joy while I have been singing it, in thinking of those whom I love, not only at and about Kettering, but in Yorkshire, in Birmingham, in Bristol, in Hampshire, in Cambridgeshire, in London, in Essex, and (I hope by this time, nearly) in Indostan!
>
> You have indulged yourself in many a solitary hour in composing hymns.—You have volumes of them.—Probably some of the notes of your plaintive soul might sound in unison with my feelings.—Would it be too much to ask you to send me a volume of them, by Mr. Perkins? I will peruse them about a year, and then return them.[82]

When he lay dying, he caught sound of his congregation singing in the chapel, and asked to be raised up in bed to join them, and thus passed into eternity.[83]

Church Music at Kettering

The Baptist church at Kettering was founded in 1696.[84] This was just as the Particular Baptist hymn-singing controversy was most prominent, but it is not known what position the Kettering congregation took.[85] Indeed, little is known about church music at Kettering until Andrew Fuller's time. As mentioned above, Fuller's library catalog suggests that by 1798, the church was using

---

after his sermons (personal correspondence, 22 October 2013). In personal conversation, Michael Haykin opined that Ramsbottom's first suggestion is more likely.

[79] A list of hymns either referenced by Fuller, or which evidence shows him to have known, is given in a table at the close of this essay.

[80] On Steevens, see "Memoir of the Rev. Thomas Steevens, late pastor of the Baptist church at Colchester," *Baptist Magazine* 9 (1817): 81–88.

[81] The two hymns to which Fuller refers are headed "Thus far my God hath led me on" (324) and "Blest be the tie that binds" (254).

[82] A. Fuller to T. Steevens, Olney, 5 October 1793, in *Baptist Magazine* 8, 495.

[83] T.E. Fuller, *Memoirs*, 309–310.

[84] See the account of its origin and its pastors before Fuller in Ryland, *The Work of Faith*, 349–351.

[85] Stephen J. Weston, *As of Old, Hosannas Sing: A History of Music at Fuller Baptist Church, Kettering* (Kettering, UK: printed by author, 1996), 1. Thanks are due to Dr. Weston for providing a gratis copy of his work for this study.

Watts's *Psalms and Hymns* in conjunction with Rippon's *Selection*. Also noted earlier, Particular Baptists in Fuller's day had as a rule accepted the use of "hymns of human composure" for worship, and Fuller's churches in Soham and Kettering were no exception. Fuller's diary entry from January 2, 1785, a Sunday, notes that before he preached to the young people of the church in an afternoon service, "one of the Bristol new year's hymns was sung."[86] If hymn singing was acceptable less than two years after Fuller's arrival, it was doubtless acceptable before he came; this becomes even more likely given the absence of any mention of instituting hymn singing at Kettering after Fuller arrived. It is probable that Kettering was already using Watts as its standard hymnal when Fuller arrived, given its prevalence among Dissenting churches.[87]

Unusually, we have a detailed description of the music at Kettering during Fuller's ministry there, thanks to his son. However, while Fuller speaks of "much pleasure in singing" on a particular occasion at the church, his son's opinion of the music at Kettering was somewhat less positive. As the single substantive testimony in this regard, outside of occasional references in Fuller's writings,[88] it is worth quoting at length:

> The public worship of the church at Kettering was characterized by great seriousness and solemnity, but there was little of life in the singing, whilst the arrangement of one "long" prayer, instead of its division into two or more parts as in modern usage, was wearying, especially as it was

---

[86] Journal entry for 2 January 1785.

[87] This is the case even given Fuller's mention of the Bristol Collection, and the contribution it evidently made to the church's song. It might have been that the Kettering church regularly used the Bristol Collection alongside Watts, replacing it with the similar but superior work of Rippon after 1787. The hymn Fuller mentions was a hymn for the new year, and this sort of hymn may not have been forthcoming from Watts's collection, while the Bristol Collection (at least in the fourth edition of 1781) contains four specifically labeled "For New-Year's Day" (#73-#76). In considering which hymnal(s) Kettering *regularly* and *most commonly* used, it must be realized that because songs were "lined out" to the congregation—a practice we will discuss momentarily—churches could and did draw from various sources for their hymnody; in the preface to his *Selection*, Rippon cites this practice as rationale for producing his compilation hymnal.

[88] There is a single reference to music at Kettering in the memoirs of George Wallis, deacon at Kettering during Fuller's tenure, who provides this entry regarding the funeral of his father:

Funeral text, 8th John v51st. 1st noticed the promise held out in the text and then 2dly the characters to whom it was made.

Hymns - the 44th in Dr Watts's Sermons, viz The death of Saints & Sinners improv'd - 104th Doddridge

Newton or Olney Hymns.

George Wallis, entry for 7 October 1810, in manuscript diary (15 March 1805 - 1 June 1817), Fuller Baptist Church, Kettering, UK. Special thanks are due to Steve Weston for his personal search of Wallis's memoirs for this project.

offered in a standing position, sitting being reserved for singing. ... The *machinery* of the psalmody was something ludicrous. ... There was invariably a clerk or precentor, who would announce the hymn thus: 116th hymn, first book, long metre; or 119th psalm, eighteenth part, long metre: read several verses, and then, with due regard for the natural obfuscation of the people's intellects, *parcel it out two lines at a time.* The singing of a line occupied nearly double the time that is usual in modern practice. There was in use at Kettering a larger proportion than in some other places of the staid old tunes, such as *Bedford, Abridge,* &c. There was, nevertheless, an itching among the singers for a class of tunes with fugues and endless repetitions, which were applied indiscriminately to all kinds of words; repetitions of two lines, repetitions of one line, repetitions of half a line, repetitions of half a word, repetitions of such words as "blast them in everlasting death,"[89] without any apparent thought of their awful meaning.[90]

Due to differences between modern congregational singing practices and those in Fuller's day and tradition, some of A.G. Fuller's testimony requires further explanation.

---

[89] This phrase is found in Watts's "Sweet is the work, my God, my King," drawn from Psalm 92, and would have been found in Kettering's Watts hymnal. The pertinent stanza reads,
Fools never raise their thoughts so high;
Like brutes they live, like brutes they die;
Like grass they flourish, till thy breath
Blast them in everlasting death.
See in Figure 4 two examples of tunes in which the offending phrase would have been repeated.
[90] A.G. Fuller, *Andrew Fuller*, 76–78, italics his.

FIGURE 2
MUSICAL EXAMPLES

A.G. Fuller objected to unnecessary repetition in songs at Kettering, and highlights "repetitions of such words as 'blast them in everlasting death,' without any apparent thought of their awful meaning." The text is from Watts's "Sweet is the work, my God, my King," but the particular tune he had in mind is unknown;[91] two possibilities are KETTERING (note the repetition in the text of the last line)[92] and BROMLEY.[93]

---

[91] Nicholas Temperley's online Hymn Tune Index (hymntune.library.uiuc.edu) lists over 90 tunes that were associated with this text prior to 1815. KETTERING is here chosen because of the connection of the tune name with Fuller's town, although it is not known whether it is associated with Fuller's church. BROMLEY is chosen in that (1) it was the most commonly printed fuging tune in long meter in Britain before 1801 (Temperley, *Fuging Tunes*, 18-19), and (2) it is included in Rippon's *Tune Book*, although it is not known whether the church at Kettering had a copy of that volume.

[92] Here taken from Samuel Holyoke, *The Columbian Repository of Sacred Harmony* (Exeter, NH: Henry Rantlet, [1803]).

[93] Here taken from Rippon's *Tune Book*.

Manley brushes broadly but is likely right to note that as a general rule during the late eighteenth century, "singing among dissenters was uniformly poor."[94] At least two factors contributed toward the low quality of music in the Dissenting churches of Fuller's day. First, the use of instruments in worship was taboo; singing was generally *a capella*.[95] The second factor was the commonplace practice of "lining out" the songs, in which the music was "parceled out" (to use A.G. Fuller's term) either by the pastor or by a clerk ("precentor").[96] The hymn was generally first read in its entirety, then it would be sung a line or two at a time by the leader with the congregation responding in repetition. This method of singing had been introduced in England long before Fuller's day in order to facilitate congregational singing even by those who were without a hymnbook due either to illiteracy or poverty.[97] Without instruments to provide tempo or pitch, and especially with a leader who had little

---

[94] Ken R. Manley, "John Rippon and Baptist Hymnody," in *Dissenting Praise*, 114; see also Kenneth R. Long, *The Music of the English Church* (New York: St. Martins, 1971), 325. The quality of Dissenting music is an area of further exploration and would depend at least in part on the standard for comparison. Jonathan Edwards noted that his congregation was in times of worship "generally carrying regularly and well three parts of music, and the women a part by themselves," although he does note that they "excelled all that ever I knew in the external part of the duty before." Jonathan Edwards, *The Great Awakening*, ed. C.C. Goen, Works of Jonathan Edwards 4 (New Haven: Yale University Press, 1998), 144. Temperley contends that "by 1790 dissenters had gained a high reputation for singing," and "by 1800 dissenters had made great strides in the quality of their music" ("The Music of Dissent," in *Dissenting Praise*, 210, 218).

[95] This prohibition was shifting in Dissenting churches toward the end of Fuller's ministry, with the introduction of stringed instruments and, somewhat later, organs; Fuller himself, however, argued against instrumental music in divine worship.

[96] The practice of "lining out" was introduced by the Westminster Assembly of Divines in *A Directory for the Publique Worship of God* in 1644. The section "Of Singing of Psalms" recommended that ideally, all who could read should have their own psalter, and the rest should be "exhorted to learn to reade." Given that a number of people were illiterate in the congregation, however, the Assembly recommended that the leader "do reade the Psalme, line by line, before the singing thereof." Although he recognized it as a necessary evil and made allowance for it in his hymns, Watts in the prefatory material of his *Psalms of David Imitated* considered the practice an "unhappy Manner of Singing." Rippon was able by the late 1700s to note in his *Selection* that singing without lining out the songs was "gaining ground in some congregations of the first note in London, at Bristol, and elsewhere," but the change apparently had not yet been embraced at Kettering. Temperley rightly notes that "lining out, whatever its practical benefits, tended to have a dispiriting effect on psalmody and to place a recurring check on any accumulation of devotional feeling that the music might promote" ("The Music of Dissent," 199). See also K.H. MacDermott, *The Old Church Gallery Minstrels* (London: S.P.C.K., 1948), 61.

[97] After her death in 1812, it was found that Martha Wallis—the wife of Fuller's deacon and loyal friend Beeby Wallis—had left money in her will toward hymnbooks for the poor of the church. F.W. Bull and William Page, "Kettering," in *The Victoria History of the Counties of England, Volume III, A History of Northamptonshire*, ed. William Page (1930; repr., Folkestone, UK: Dawsons of Pall Mall, 1970), 226.

musical talent or training, the singing would as a rule be extremely slow,[98] with dissonance caused by voices moving from one note to the next at different times.[99] As well, the Kettering congregation sat while singing, a less than ideal posture for excellent vocalization.[100]

In spite of certain detriments to the music at Kettering, however, there is some indication that not all was negative. First, in the midst of A.G. Fuller's litany of the shortcomings of the services at Kettering (which extended well beyond the singing), he notes,

> Notwithstanding these, and perhaps other usages on which modern appointments are an improvement, *there was a quiet power* which hardly consists with the restless transit from scene to scene of the present day. There seems hardly time to digest, still less to assimilate our spiritual ailment. It is like a continental *table d'hôte*, where you have not time to see what one course is made of, before it is whipped away and another thrust before you.[101]

A second indication that not all was negative is that during Andrew Fuller's tenure there was likely a choir at Kettering which had a decent level of musical ability. The evidence, while somewhat mixed, leans more heavily toward affirming the presence of such a choir during Fuller's ministry.[102] Positive evidence is found in A.G. Fuller's description of Kettering's music already cited; he references the desire of the "singers" for a different sort of tune, and this was the standard term for a voluntary choir.[103] Further, in speaking about a

---

[98] Weston indicates that each note would have lasted two to three, even four, seconds. Stephen J. Weston, "The Instrumentation and Music of the Choir Church-Band in Eastern England, with Particular Reference to Northamptonshire, during the Late Eighteenth and Early Nineteenth Centuries" (Ph.D. diss., University of Leicester, 1995), 16.

[99] A very complete description and explanation is provided in Nicholas Temperley, "The Old Way of Singing," in *Studies in English Church Music, 1550-1900*, Variorum Collected Studies Series CS926 (Farnham, UK: Ashgate, 2009), 69-102.

[100] Although there were questions about the propriety of standing while singing to God, John Rippon argued for the upright position as part of his ongoing campaign to improve congregational hymnody among Dissenters. Manley, *Redeeming Love Proclaim*, 124-125. John Wesley speaks of "the indecent posture of sitting" contrasted with "standing before God" while singing. *Selected Letters of John Wesley*, ed. Frederick C. Gill (New York: Philosophical Library, 1956), 103-104.

[101] A.G. Fuller, *Andrew Fuller*, 77-78, italics mine.

[102] A choir was certainly in place by 1829, at which time it sang an anthem at the funeral of Fuller's successor John Keen Hall. Weston, *As of Old, Hosannas Sing*, 4.

[103] Nicholas Temperley, personal correspondence, 25 November 2013. See also Weston's survey of Northamptonshire churchwardens' accounts for music-related expenses from 1760-1870, which almost invariably uses this terminology ("Instrumentation and Music," 285-348).

farmer who was a member of Fuller's church, and who seems to have regularly hosted a sort of annual harvest banquet, A.G. Fuller relates,

> At the close of supper, which would be at an early hour of the evening, commenced the singing of hymns, followed by more elaborate sacred music, for which purpose a staff of "singing men and singing women" was especially invited, being the choir of singers at the Meeting House at Kettering.[104]

Presumably, the "Meeting House at Kettering" is Fuller's church, although the reference is slightly ambiguous.[105] If Fuller's church is indeed in view, A.G. Fuller's description indicates a choir there that was perhaps more accomplished than average.[106]

Against A.G. Fuller's testimony, however, may stand an account book of pew rents from Fuller's day, still archived at the present-day Fuller Baptist Church and recently unearthed by Keith Grant. A seating plan is included, and entries in the book indicate that the sections toward the front of the rear gallery were for "singers";[107] this location is consistent with the typical rural church choir in Fuller's day.[108] While the pew rent book testifies to the presence of a choir, it indicates the pews are occupied by congregants through 1815, at which time they seem to have been preempted for the "singers."[109] This evidence suggests that *something* happened vis-à-vis a choir at the Kettering church in

---

[104] A.G. Fuller, *Andrew Fuller*, 85–86.

[105] On the one hand, this is the sole use of "Meeting House" in the biography; Fuller's church is often referenced simply as "the church at Kettering." On the other hand, "the church at Kettering" is parallel to "the Meeting House at Kettering," and while "meeting house" was a generic term for a church building, there are some contemporary references that clearly refer to Fuller's church with that terminology; see "Some Account of a Discourse by Mr A. Fuller," *The Missionary Magazine* 8 (October 17, 1803): 457; "Epitaph on the Late Rev. Andrew Fuller," *The Baptist Magazine* 9 (April 1817): 160.

[106] Although A.G. Fuller presumably continued to attend his father's church with his mother after his father's death, his description of the church's musical life may be presumed to correlate with his father's tenure; he closes his description of it by noting his father's disapproval of instruments. His description of the farmer's harvest feast does not specifically involve Andrew Fuller, but may also be presumed to have occurred during his father's ministry at Kettering. On balance, it seems best to understand A.G. Fuller as describing the church music—and thus the presence of a choir—*during* Andrew Fuller's ministry, not *after* it, even where his father is not specifically mentioned; his biography, after all, centers on his father, not the church at Kettering *per se*.

[107] See Figure 3 for the seating plan. Sincere thanks are due to Keith Grant for providing this seating chart, and to Steve Weston who provided pictures of the pertinent pages of the account book. The original is located at Fuller Baptist Church in Kettering.

[108] See the discussion in Weston, "Instrumentation and Music," 24–29.

[109] See an example of the relevant entries in Figure 4.

the year of Andrew Fuller's death, but if A.G. Fuller's testimony is being understood correctly here, does not necessarily indicate its formation.

FIGURE 3
SEATING PLAN OF THE BAPTIST CHURCH AT KETTERING
(Reproduced by permission of the archivists of Fuller Baptist Church, Kettering, UK)

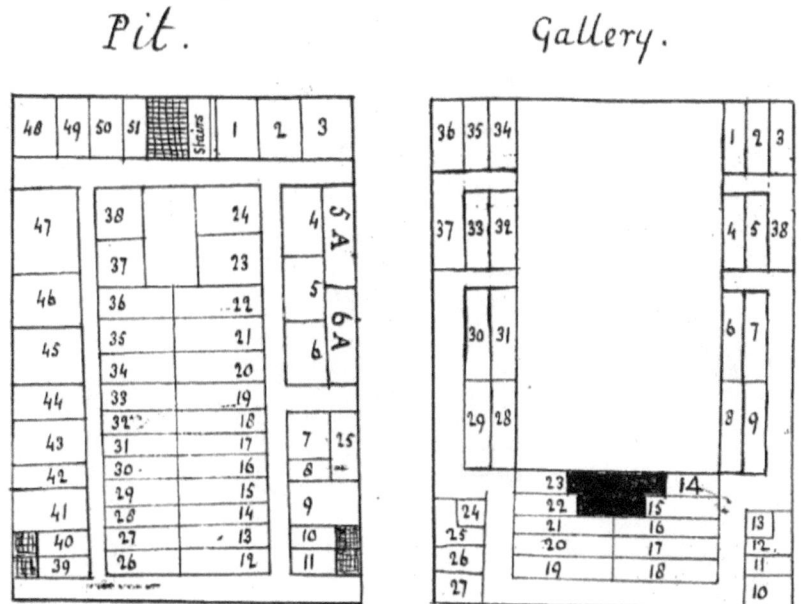

This seating plan was found by Keith Grant in an account book of pew rents that is part of the archival material stored at Fuller Baptist Church in Kettering. The front of the auditorium is at the top of the plan. The accounts of pew rents in the book suggest that sections 21–23 at the front of the gallery were preempted for "singers," or a voluntary choir, in 1815; section 14 seems to have been preempted for the same purpose in 1817.

FIGURE 4
BOOK OF PEW RENTS FROM THE BAPTIST CHURCH AT KETTERING
(Reproduced by permission of the archivists of Fuller Baptist Church, Kettering, UK)

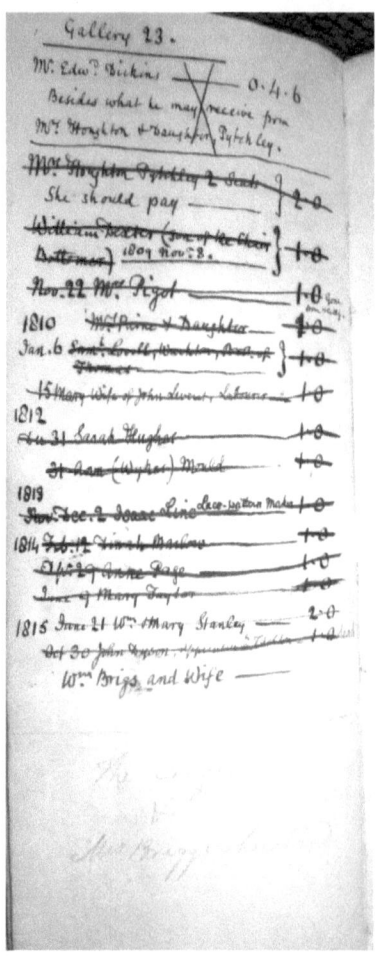

Note at the bottom of the page, the addition in pencil of "The Singers & Mrs. Briggs & husband." Similar additions are found for gallery pews 14 ("Hennell & Singers"), 21 ("The Singers // Sam[l] Chaten[?]"), 22 ("The Singers & Mr. Goode & Wife").

Although the choir, such as it was, no doubt added some measure of musical stability to the singing at Kettering, it might have had some detrimental effect as well.[110] A.G. Fuller indicates that while "staid old tunes" were typically used in the services,[111] the "singers" had an "itching ... for a class of tunes with fugues and endless repetitions." This account reflects the already mentioned shift in church music which was occurring in Fuller's time and tradition.[112] Beginning in the late seventeenth century in Britain, there was a sharp increase in the production of new church music among Anglicans, involving many new tunes,[113] harmonized psalmody, and choir anthems. Music instructors moved about the countryside to instruct students in the art of singing and to peddle their own books of church music. As voluntary choirs grew in skill, they progressed from merely providing musical leadership for the congregational singing, to singing anthems at the end of services and introducing more complicated and elaborate tunes for the church's psalmody. Their elaborations included innovations such as melisma and repeating lines,[114] and culminated in the 1740s with "fuging tunes" involving imitative counterpoint where various vocal parts sang different words simultaneously. This development was earliest in parish churches,[115] but the second half of the eighteenth century

---

[110] See Weston, "Instrumentation and Music," 89-90.

[111] The examples given are the tunes ABRIDGE, first published in 1770, and BEDFORD, first published around 1732. Weston notes that ABRIDGE seems to be miscategorized in this account; its composer Isaac Smith was "one of the new school of tune writers" (*As of Old, Hosannas Sing*, 3).

[112] The description of this shift here is drawn from Nicholas Temperley and Charles G. Manns, *Fuging Tunes in the Eighteenth Century*, Detroit Studies in Music Bibliography 49 (Detroit: Information Coordinators, 1983), 3-22, 25-31.

[113] Only an extremely limited number of hymn tunes were used among British churches prior to this period. See Young, "History of Baptist Hymnody," 93-95.

[114] An early example of hymnic melisma is found in EASTER HYMN (tightly connected with "Christ the Lord Is Risen Today") with its moving "Alleluias," produced in 1708. A familiar repeating tune is ADESTE FIDELES, composed around the 1740s and generally sung with "O Come, All Ye Faithful," with its echoing "O come, let us adore him" in the refrain. But all was not this pleasant, as A.G. Fuller intimates; MacDermott indicates that "the words of the Psalms were frequently 'mangled and mauled' in a most absurd way to make them fit the tunes. Long runs in the music would have single syllables, repeated several times, to make them suit, however ridiculous the effect." MacDermott, *The Old Church Gallery Minstrels*, 61.

[115] Note also that this was the musical flavor of early Methodism. Regarding tunes of the "Old Methodist" style, Adams noted their character as "florid tunes, with repeating-texts, and sometimes with 'hallelujah choruses,' and melismas that often stretch into more than one measure." Nelson F. Adams, "The Musical Sources for John Wesley's Tune-Books: The Genealogy of 148 Tunes" (S.M.D. diss., Union Theological Seminary, 1973), 126.

saw decided trends among Dissenters which "favoured harmony and repeated refrains and increasingly tolerated anthems and fuging tunes."[116]

These musical shifts did not come without opposition, however. Average congregants who were left behind as the music grew more complex could become disgruntled. As well, the singing of choirs tended to become "a performance for its own sake rather than an aid to worship," and clergy naturally opposed this.[117] Even with a self-effacing choir, however, the more complicated fuging tunes, with their overlapping parts, tended to obscure the text being sung. As Temperley rightly notes, music "which not only discouraged congregational participation but often made it difficult for listeners to understand the text" was "hardly compatible with most dissenters' views."[118] This general incompatibility is reflected in some Dissenters' refusal to utilize such tunes.[119] Additionally, Dissenters that did use them tended toward tunes with a less pronounced fugal quality, generally utilizing distinct repetition more than overlapping texts.

Where did Andrew Fuller stand on the matter? We will turn in a moment to Fuller's formal works on church music, but here may be highlighted his criticism of some music done in the newer style. Thomas Jarman, a composer who lived about fifteen miles away from Kettering in neighboring Clipston,[120] composed for the opening of a chapel an anthem titled "Enrobed in Light," with words by Frank Cox of Hackney.[121] A brief, intriguing reference to this piece was published in *The Northampton Mercury* in 1880, in which the anonymous author indicates Fuller's strong disapproval of the composition:

> A copy of verses, to which a certain historic value attaches, has just been brought to light. The words, by Mr. Frank (afterwards Dr.) Cox, were

---

[116] Temperley, "The Music of Dissent," 212. Within the Particular Baptist tradition, for instance, we find twenty fuging tunes included in Rippon's influential *Tune Book* (c. 1791) intended to accompany his *Selection*.

[117] Temperley, *Fuging Tunes*, 5. See also Weston, "Instrumentation and Music," 89-90.

[118] Temperley, "The Music of Dissent," 206.

[119] See examples in Temperley, *Fuging Tunes*, 28.

[120] On Jarman, see Stephen J. Weston, "A Northamptonshire Composer—Thomas Jarman of Clipston," in *Northamptonshire Past and Present* 8.5 (1993-1994): 385-391; Hilary Davidson, *Choirs, Bands and Organs: A History of Church Music in Northamptonshire and Rutland* (Oxford: Positif, 2003), 222-223, 240-242.

[121] The piece was published in Jarman's collection titled *Sacred Music, comprising select Hymns adapted to Public Worship together with two anthems, the last of which was expressly composed for the opening of Clipston New Chapel by Thomas Jarman* (London: For the author by Henry Thompson, [c. 1803-1805]). Only two copies are known to be extant, one in the British Library, and one in the Northamptonshire Records Office.

set to music by Jarman, of Clipstone, for the important event stated hereunder ["the opening of Clipstone New Meeting, Oct. 12th, 1803"]. Andrew Fuller was the preacher, and when the words were handed to him in the pulpit, he naturally enough frowned at the display—a flagrant departure from the stern spirit of Baptist worship in those days, and, after scowling for awhile at the verses, said, "Let us sing to the praise and glory of Mr. Cox and Thomas Jarman."[122]

"Enrobed in Light" may be described as "a *verse anthem*, set for chorus with sections for solo voices" and it contained a separate instrumental part which could have been played by a cello (bass viol) or bassoon. The generally florid style of the piece involves aspects to which Fuller would have objected on principle: imitative fuging sections and melisma, which could obscure the text, and potentially self-glorifying solo parts.[123]

It is difficult to ascertain the extent to which the newer music was used as Kettering. Given Fuller's stance, one might think it was disallowed altogether. This would be a hasty conclusion, however, and here we must revisit A.G. Fuller's testimony:

> There was in use at Kettering a larger proportion than in some other places of the staid old tunes. ... There was, nevertheless, an itching among the singers for a class of tunes with fugues and endless repetitions, which were applied indiscriminately to all kinds of words; repetitions of two lines, repetitions of one line, repetitions of half a line, repetitions of half a word, repetitions of such words as "blast them in everlasting death," without any apparent thought of their awful meaning.

The "larger proportion" of old tunes indicates that there was at least a small proportion of new tunes, and the remarks on the newer "class of tunes" sounds more descriptive of reality than mere yearning on the part of the "singers." Further, given A.G. Fuller's testimony elsewhere that the "choir of singers" was able to transcend mere hymn singing and produce "more elaborate sacred music," we may assume that anthems were within their grasp and their

---

[122] *The Northamptonshire Mercury*, 17 January 1880, p. 3, col. 1. See Figure 5. The author's source for this information must remain conjectural; since the incident described was 77 years prior to the article's publication, it is only just possible that the source was an eyewitness. This report of Fuller's response may very well be exaggerated, but the piece is unquestionably one to which he would have objected, given his writings elsewhere.

[123] I am indebted to Steve Weston for his evaluation of Jarman's composition (personal correspondence, 3 April 2014).

repertoire. But would they have sung them in the Sunday services?[124] In his writings, Fuller expresses mixed feelings toward anthems. On the one hand, he saw them as "nearest to the Scriptural way of singing" because they conformed the music to the text, not the text to the music; on the other hand, though, he considered the anthems of the day to "possess too much levity for worship, and abound with a number of unnecessary, because unmeaning, repeats."[125] Given his perspective, it seems that on balance, anthems would only have been used very selectively, if at all, in worship services at Fuller's church, although the choir's proficiency in them suggests they were used on other occasions.

---

[124] It may be asked when such music would be used, if not when the church gathered for worship. A distinction was often made, however, between the formal time of assembled worship, and other devotional occasions, such as the harvest banquet mentioned above; note as well the distinction the Sandemanians made, as discussed below. See Temperley, "The Music of Dissent," 206.

[125] Andrew Fuller, "Thoughts on Singing," in *WAF*, 862.

FIGURE 5
FULLER'S OBJECTION TO "ENROBED IN LIGHT"

A COPY OF VERSES, to which a certain historic value attaches, has just been brought to light. The words, by Mr. Frank (afterwards Dr.) Cox, were set to music by Jarman, of Clipstone, for the important event stated hereunder. Andrew Fuller was the preacher, and when the words were handed to him in the pulpit, he naturally enough frowned at the display—a flagrant departure from the stern spirit of B ptist worship in those days, and, after scowling for awhile at the verses, said. "Let us sing to the praise and glory of Mr. Cox and Thomas Jarman." The following are the lines:—

A HYMN
Written for the opening of Clipstone New Meeting, Oct. 12th, 1803, by F. A. Cox, M.A.

TRIO.
 Enrobed in light, the Holy One
 Dwells on His high and sapphire throne;
 While gath'ring round the' eternal blaze,
 Archangels tremble as they gaze.

CHORUS.
 Hark! how the heavenly temple rings,
 While soaring on their golden wings
 They chant the' immortal anthem round;
 O could we catch the tuneful sound!

DUET.
 O could we imitate their lays,
 Like them the King of Glory praise;
 This clay-built synagogue of prayer
 Should echo like the temple there.

CHORUS.
 Within these walls we long to see
 Ten thousand converts born to thee;
 And those whose tongues were dumb before,
 Sing of Thy love, and grace, and power.

TRIO.
 Here may the lame, with joyful heart
 Leap like the young and bounding hart!
 Here may the blind have eyes to see:
 The deaf, dear Saviour, hear of Thee!

DUET.
 O may this desert-place be found
 Replete with springs to cheer the ground!
 And the dry soil productive prove
 Of all the fruits of peace and love.

TRIO.
 Here may we dwell in concord sweet!
 And here each circling Sabbath meet;
 That day the best of all the seven,
 T' enjoy the antepast of heaven!
 So may our unborn children rise
 To trace our footsteps to the skies;
 And when this house no longer stands
 Praise Thee in one not made with hands.

The Northamptonshire Mercury (17 January 1880), p. 3, col. 1.

Andrew Fuller

Fuller's Thought on Church Music

Although a number of Fuller's sermons and essays might be brought to bear upon the use of music in the church,[126] we will limit ourselves to three that focus more or less particularly on the topic. More general in nature, the first is the tenth letter in *Strictures on Sandemanianism*, titled "An Inquiry into the Principles on which the Apostles Proceeded in Forming and Organizing Christian Churches." Two other essays address more specific topics: "On instrumental music in Christian worship" and "Thoughts on singing."[127]

"An Inquiry into the Principles ... "

In 1810, Fuller composed *Strictures on Sandemanianism*, comprised of twelve letters, to speak to some distinctive beliefs and practices to be found among certain Dissenting churches in Scotland. He was responding most directly to Alexander McLean and the Scotch Baptists, but aimed at least part of his response directly toward the popularizer of these distinctive practices and views, Robert Sandeman. Churches who followed the teachings of John Glas and Robert Sandeman, respectively the theological genius and evangelist of Sandemanianism, were restorationist in nature. As such, "in public worship they were Psalm singers, but for their fellowship meetings were composed *Christian Songs*,"[128] most of which were composed by Glas and his disciple Robert

---

[126] For instance, Fuller's thought on worship in the second chapter of Andrew Fuller, "The Gospel Its Own Witness" (*WAF*, 7), or in his remarks on "public worship" from Psalm 68:26-28 (*WAF*, 665).

[127] While not attaining the prominence of his other writings, Fuller's opinions on church music did have influence through the nineteenth century. See especially something of an attempt to follow his musical ideal in Thomas Binney, *Psalms and Hymns from Holy Scripture: Selected and Arranged for Chanting*, 3rd ed. (London: Ward and Co., 1855). See also references to Fuller's musical thought in J.G. Fuller, *The Rise and Progress of Dissent in Bristol; chiefly in relation to the Broadmead Church, etc.* (London: Hamilton, Adams, and Co., 1840), 61-62; Gilbert M'Master, *An Apology for the Book of Psalms, in Five Letters; Addressed to the Friends of Union in the Church of God*, 4th ed. (Philadelphia: Daniels & Smith, 1852), 135-136; Joseph Belcher, *Historical Sketches of Hymns, their Writers, and their Influence* (Philadelphia: Lindsay & Blakiston, 1859), 68-69; J. Spencer Pearsall, *Public Worship: The best methods of conducting it*, 2nd ed. (London: Jackson, Walford, and Hodder, 1867), 90. Charles Spurgeon refers to Fuller's opinion on instrumental music (with which he largely agreed) in *The Treasury of David*, 2nd ed. (New York: Funk & Wagnalls, 1892), 4:272.

[128] Louis F. Benson, "The Hymnody of the Evangelical Revival," *Princeton Theological Review* 12 (1914): 70, referring to John Glas [?], ed., *Christian Songs. To which is prefixed, the evidence and import of Christ's Resurrection versified, for the help of the memory* (Edinburgh, 1749). The first edition, with 38 songs, was expanded through numerous later editions. Note the detailed description of editions and the list of Glasite hymns that had passed into more common usage under "Scottish Hymnody," in Julian, *Dictionary of Hymnology*, 2:1030-1031.

Sandeman.[129] The Scotch Baptists were not Sandemanian, strictly speaking,[130] but very similar in their primitivism. As to their church music, McLean notes that the Scotch Baptists engaged in "singing of psalms, hymns, and spiritual songs,"[131] which may indicate an acceptance of hymnody *in public worship*, contrary to Sandemanian practices.[132]

Fuller does not specifically speak against the practices of church music of either the Sandemanians or the Scotch Baptists in *Strictures on Sandemanianism*. In the tenth letter, however, he does object to their deriving positive commands about all the minutiae of the "order, government, and discipline of gospel churches" from the New Testament; such an endeavor, Fuller contends, is "impracticable."[133] Only a fairly general outline of such matters has been preserved in Scripture, although where it does speak at times to particulars, it should be followed.

Church music in particular does not come up for detailed discussion, but Fuller does use it as an example to support his larger point about Scripture's ecclesial guidance being fairly general. Specifically, he notes that in the New Testament we have no "formula of worship," and while we are "taught to sing praises to God in psalms, hymns, and spiritual songs," we "have no inspired tunes."[134]

Later in the tenth letter, Fuller notes some proper and improper applications of his larger point. The general nature of ecclesial guidance in Scripture does not mean "that all forms of worship and of church government are indifferent, and left to be accommodated to times, places, and circumstances." No, instead, "we are not at liberty to deviate" from the general principles we do have; we must "fill up" these general contours "by a pure desire of carrying them into effect according to their true intent." Further, if these general principles do happen to be exemplified in the New Testament, we are obliged to

---

[129] Douglas J. Maclagan, *The Scottish Paraphrases* (Edinburgh: Andrew Elliot, 1889), 26–27.

[130] McLean strongly repudiated this identification in "The Scotch Baptists not Sandemanians," in *The Works of Mr. Archibald M'Lean*, vol. 6, ed. William Jones (London: Printed for William Jones, 1823), xxxiii–li.

[131] Quoted in William Jones, "Memoir of the Life, Ministry, and Writings of the Author," in *The Works of Mr. Archibald M'Lean*, l:xxvii.

[132] It is not clear whether the Scotch Baptists used the Sandemanian *Christian Songs*. Julian does make passing reference to a collection of "12 hymns" published as *A Collection of Hymns and Spiritual Songs* by "A. McLean" in Glasgow in 1755. *Dictionary of Hymnology*, 2:1032.

[133] The tenth letter, from which this section is derived, is found in Fuller, "Strictures on Sandemanianism," in *WAF*, 286–289.

[134] Note the use of the same language as McLean engages to describe Scotch Baptist congregational music practices, which makes Fuller's illustration more pointed.

follow that example *in similar cases*. Caution must be exercised, however, not to view Scripture as binding in the matter of "accidental circumstances" associated with positive institutions of worship practices; so, for instance, Jesus and his disciples reclined at table to eat when the Lord's Supper was instituted, but this is not intrinsic to the observance and need not be duplicated.

"On Instrumental Music in Christian Worship"[135]
Everett Ferguson's summary is helpful as broad historical background to this essay of Fuller's:

> When the Reformation came, the Lutheran and Anglican churches continued instrumental music from their Catholic past. The Reformed and Anabaptist branches of Protestantism eliminated the instrument as a Catholic corruption and only came to reaccept it (and then not uniformly) about the 18th and 19th centuries. Zwingli eliminated singing along with the organ in his reformation of Zurich. Some of the early Anabaptists at Zurich followed his lead and interpreted the New Testament texts as permitting only a "singing in the heart." The major influence on Reformed churches came to be that of John Calvin, and the singing of the Psalms without instrumental accompaniment was the prevailing practice in these churches for many years. Instrumental music was re-introduced only in the face of opposition.[136]

In his remarks, Fuller contends that instrumental music was merely an accouterment of Old Testament worship and is "utterly unsuited to the genius of the gospel dispensation," and therefore unacceptable in Christian worship.[137] Assuming the regulative principle, he makes several arguments to support his contention. Instrumental music in worship is not merely a circumstance left to one's discretion, an assertion supported by the fact that it was "from the first a subject of *Divine injunction*," as when God commanded instrumental music in association with temple worship in 2 Chronicles 29:25-29. All the same, since this command was not a *moral* command ("commanded because it is

---

[135] Andrew Fuller, "On Instrumental Music in Christian Worship," in *WAF*, 859-861. Note that this essay was also included in J.W. Morris, ed., *Miscellaneous pieces on various religious subjects, being the last remains of the Rev. Andrew Fuller* (London: Wightman and Cramp, 1826), 17-28, and at the end of the piece, Morris includes remarks by Fuller's successor John Keen Hall, whose position differed significantly from Fuller's in this matter.

[136] Everett Ferguson, *A Capella Music in the Public Worship of the Church*, 1st ed. (Abilene, TX: Biblical Research Press, 1972), 82-83.

[137] Fuller, "On Instrumental Music in Christian Worship," in *WAF*, 860.

right" and binding for "all ages and nations") but a *positive* command ("right because it is commanded" and "binding only at those places to which the appointment extends"), Christians are not morally obligated to observe it in that the ceremonial law has been abolished by the gospel.[138]

Further, if instrumental music were a moral duty and thus obligatory for Christian worship, "we should have read of it, as I think we do of every moral duty, in the New Testament."[139] The worship of heaven, portrayed in Revelation as involving harps, does not support instrumental music in Christian worship, because "the heavenly employments and enjoyments are frequently illustrated by things borrowed from the Jewish ceremonial [law]" without intending those things to be a part of Christian worship (e.g., priests, temples, altars).[140]

For sake of argument, even if instruments in worship were a matter of discretion in the present dispensation, "the use of them occasions offence to many serious minds," and the principle of abstention set forth in 1 Corinthians 8:13 would come into play.[141] However, Fuller contends, instrumental music in worship is indeed not a matter of discretion, for in the former dispensation, instrumental music was either "for the purpose of promoting civil joy" (and in these cases not part of worship) or "when employed in Divine worship, authorized by Divine appointment."[142] Finally, the first three centuries of church history afford no examples of instrumental music as part of the church's worship. The practice seems to have "originated in the dark ages of popery, when almost every other superstition was introduced under the plea of its according with the worship of the Old Testament."[143]

---

[138] Fuller, "On Instrumental Music in Christian Worship," in *WAF*, 859.

[139] Fuller, "On Instrumental Music in Christian Worship," in *WAF*, 859.

[140] Fuller, "On Instrumental Music in Christian Worship," in *WAF*, 859-860.

[141] Fuller, "On Instrumental Music in Christian Worship," in *WAF*, 860.

[142] Fuller, "On Instrumental Music in Christian Worship," in *WAF*, 860. Key to Fuller's argument here is that divine authorization for particular examples of instrumental music as part of worship in the OT need not be "express," but could occur without explicit divine command by "being ordered or done by *men who were Divinely inspired*." Further, because David's instrumental worship in 2 Samuel 6 was accepted by God, it may be inferred that "it was performed in obedience to the Divine will."

[143] Fuller, "On Instrumental Music in Christian Worship," in *WAF*, 861.

"Thoughts on Singing"[144]

While Fuller's "On instrumental music" is technical and involved, his "Thoughts on singing" is broad, sweeping, and visionary.[145] Importantly, Fuller opens the essay with this programmatic statement: "The intent of singing is by a musical pronunciation of affecting truth to render it still more affecting. To accomplish this end, the music ought, at all events, to be adapted to the sentiments."[146] Given this understanding, Fuller objects to the common practice of composing tunes, then conforming a hymn-text to the tune. The biblical pattern, he avers, was just the opposite: David would compose a song, then submit it to the "chief musician," who would "set it to sacred music."[147] Fuller argues that this Davidic model should be employed in church music: the music should conform to the text, because the text has precedence. In this connection, he finds the anthems of his day to "approach the nearest to the Scriptural way of singing," but still finds them possessing "too much levity for worship," and deficient due to their unnecessary (and thus unmeaning) repetition.[148]

Fuller briefly sets forth his vision for congregational singing: "*a selection of divine hymns or songs, taking place of all human compositions.*"[149] By this, he explains, he means "the pure word of God translated without any respect to rhyme or number [i.e., meter], after the manner of Lowth's Isaiah,[150] and set

---

[144] Fuller, "Thoughts on Singing," in *WAF*, 861-862. The New Haven edition of Fuller's works indicates this essay was originally published in *The Theological and Biblical Magazine* in 1805; this attribution is apparently incorrect, as a search of the 1801-1807 issues of that periodical did not yield the essay. The essay was reprinted in *The Christian Magazine* 4.6 (June 1835): 186-190, with what appear to be both intentional and unintentional (and unnoted) variations from the *Works*.

[145] Fuller's son said of this piece, "His ideas of psalmody ... are singular and not unworthy of attention." A.G. Fuller, *Memoirs*, in Fuller, *Works*, xc. Note many of the same ideas in William Cole, *A View of Modern Psalmody, being an Attempt to Reform the Practice of Singing in the Worship of God* (Colchester: J. Chaplin, 1819). Cole argues *for* the use of instruments but shares many of Fuller's specific concerns regarding singing. He does not reference Fuller in his work, thus any direct dependence upon Fuller is not clear.

[146] Fuller, "Thoughts on Singing," in *WAF*, 861. This directive is built upon Fuller's understanding that "as in common speaking there is a sound or modulation of the voice adapted to convey every sentiment or passion of which the human soul is at any time possessed, so I conceive it is in a considerable degree with regard to singing; there are certain airs or tones which are naturally expressive of joy, sorrow, pity, indignation, &c."

[147] Fuller, "Thoughts on Singing," in *WAF*, 861.

[148] Fuller, "Thoughts on Singing," in *WAF*, 862.

[149] Fuller, "Thoughts on Singing," in *WAF*, 862, italics his.

[150] Robert Lowth, *Isaiah. A new translation; with a preliminary dissertation, and notes critical, philological, and explanatory* (London: J. Nichols, 1778). Fuller lists a copy of this work in his library catalog (no. 115). See Figure 6 for an example of Lowth's work in *Isaiah*.

to plain, serious, and solemn music, adapted to the sentiments." His goal, clearly, is to emphasize the Scripture, not the setting.[151] To illustrate this, he highlights the power of Handel's *Messiah* (while noting that its ostentatious setting makes it unsuitable for worship), noting that there one finds "the Scriptures appearing in their native majesty, without being tortured into rhyme and number [i.e., meter], and set to music adapted to the sentiments."[152]

---

[151] While the Wesleys' hymnological program was doubtless not intended to shortchange the text, it seems to be the consistent opinion of music historians that they did in fact embrace music that took a step further toward the dominance of the tune over the text. See, e.g., Martin V. Clarke, "John Frederick Lampe's *Hymns on the Great Festivals and Other Occasions*," in *Music and the Wesleys*, ed. Nicholas Temperley and Stephen Banfield (Urbana, IL: University of Illinois Press, 2010), 18; "John Wesley and Methodist Music in the Eighteenth Century: Principles and Practice" (Ph.D. diss., Durham University, 2008), 137-146. More generally, see Nicholas Temperley, "John Wesley, Music, and the People Called Methodists," in idem, 3-25. While Fuller did not necessarily reject Charles Wesley's hymns on musical grounds, the direction they were going does not seem to be one of which he approved.

[152] Fuller, "Thoughts on Singing," in *WAF*, 862.

FIGURE 6
LOWTH'S *ISAIAH*

> *Andrew Fuller*
>
> 216 ISAIAH. Chap. XL.
> 4 Every valley shall be exalted, and every mountain and hill be brought low;
> And the crooked shall become strait, and the rough places a smooth plain:
> 5 And the glory of JEHOVAH shall be revealed;
> And all flesh shall see together the salvation of our God:
> For the mouth of JEHOVAH hath spoken it.
> 6 A voice sayeth: Proclaim? And I said, What shall I proclaim!
> All flesh is grass, and all its glory like the flower of the field:
> 7 The grass withereth, the flower fadeth;
> When the wind of JEHOVAH bloweth upon it.
> Verily this people is grass.
> 8 The grass withereth, the flower fadeth;
> But the word of our God shall stand for ever.
> 9 Get thee up upon a high mountain, O daughter that bringest glad tidings to Sion:
> Exalt thy voice with strength, O daughter that bringest glad tidings to Jerusalem.
> Exalt it; be not afraid:
> Say to the cities of Judah, Behold your God!
> 10 Behold, the Lord JEHOVAH shall come against the strong one,
> And his arm shall prevail over him.
> Behold, his reward his with him, and the recompense of his work before him.
> 11 Like a shepherd shall he feed his flock;
> In his arm shall he gather up the lambs,
> And
>
> Chap. XL. ISAIAH. 217
> And shall bear them in his bosom; the nursing ewes shall he gently lead.
> 12 Who hath measured the waters in the hollow of his hand;
> And hath meted out the heavens by his span;
> And hath comprehended the dust of the earth in a tierce,
> And hath weighed in scales the mountains, and the hills in a balance?
> 13 Who hath directed the spirit of JEHOVAH;
> And, as one of his counsel, hath informed him?
> 14 Whom hath he consulted, that he should instruct him,
> And teach him the path of judgement;
> That he should impart to him science,
> And inform him in the way of understanding?
> 15 Behold, the nations are as a drop from the bucket;
> As the small dust of the balance shall they be accounted:
> Behold, the islands he taketh up as an atom.
> 16 And Lebanon is not sufficient for the fire;
> Nor his beasts sufficient for the burnt-offering.
> 17 All the nations are as nothing before him;
> They are esteemed by him as less than nought, and vanity.
>
> 18 To

"It has been observed by some of the ablest critics that the spirit of David's psalms (and the same would hold true of the other poetic parts of Scripture) can never be preserved in a translation of them into modern verse; but in a translation like our common Bibles, or that of Lowth's Isaiah, it is generally allowed, I believe, that the spirit of them is well preserved. Why then do we not set them as they are to sacred music? It is of a thousand times more importance to preserve the spirit of a psalm or scripture song than to have it in numbers [i.e., meter], even supposing a uniformity in numbers were of advantage."[153]

---

[153] Fuller, "Thoughts on Singing," in *WAF*, 862.

Conclusion and Directions for Further Study

While Fuller's thought on church music is not nearly as well developed as his response to many of the teachings he wrote against—Arminianism, Unitarianism, Socinianism, High Calvinism, Sandemanianism—it is evident that he has opinions on the matter. It will be recalled from the beginning of the present essay that Fuller's renewed pastoral theology was expressed in preaching that "was *plain* in composition and delivery, *evangelical* in content and concern, and *affectionate* in feeling and application." Something similar may be argued for his church music as a reflection of his pastoral theology.

First, Fuller argued for and used church music that was *plain*, and he did this for the good of his congregation. In discussing Fuller's preaching, Keith Grant notes,

> It may, also, be instructive to compare the "plain style" of preaching, and Fuller's intentional accounting for the capacities of illiterate hearers, with the principles of hymnody espoused by Isaac Watts, in his *Hymns and Spiritual Songs*: "The Metaphors are generally sunk to the Level of vulgar Capacities, I have aim'd at Ease of Numbers and Smoothness of Sound, and endeavored to make the Sense plain and obvious."[154]

Fuller's strong affinity for Watts will, of course, be immediately recalled, and if the plainness of Watts's hymnody is comparable to Fuller's preaching, how much more to Fuller's Watts-centered church music? Indeed, Fuller himself draws a connection between preaching and suitable congregational song:

> The criterion of a good tune is, not its pleasing a scientific ear, but its being quickly caught by a congregation. *It is, I think, by singing, as it is by preaching*: a fine judge of composition will admire a sermon which yet makes no manner of impression upon the public mind, and therefore cannot be a good one. That is the best sermon which is adapted to produce the best effects; and the same may be said of a tune.[155]

Fuller's "plainness" in church music, it can be seen, is calculated to provide the greatest benefit for those singing.

Along with congregational edification, however, Fuller was duly concerned—and arguably, more concerned—with the *suitability* of congregational

---

[154] Grant, *Andrew Fuller and the Evangelical Renewal of Pastoral Theology*, 83.
[155] Fuller, "Thoughts on Singing," in *WAF*, 862, italics mine.

music for the worship of God,¹⁵⁶ and in his understanding, suitable music was *plain* music. So, for instance, Fuller argued against the use of instruments in worship, and in this connection Andrew Gunton Fuller notes that "Mr. Fuller disapproved of the use of 'things without life-giving sound,' considering their use in worship as not in harmony with the *simplicity* of the Christian dispensation."¹⁵⁷ Further, in his "Thoughts on singing," Fuller objects to all that is flashy about music such as that of Handel's *Messiah*, which music is "not designed for [Divine worship], but rather for a company of musicians who should display their skill."¹⁵⁸ The right path, Fuller argues, is to take the unadorned scriptural text of Handel's Messiah and set it "*to plain music* without any of those trappings which recommend it to the attention of a merely musical audience."¹⁵⁹

Second, Fuller's church music was *evangelical*. By this descriptor is meant, not all that the term involves in the present day, but the more limited notion of a willingness to call the unconverted to faith in Christ. The evangelical nature of Fuller's church music is reflected in his interest in Watts,¹⁶⁰ but noticeable as well in the fact that it was Fuller who introduced Rippon's *Selection of Hymns* to the church at Kettering during his tenure there.¹⁶¹ As Deborah Ruhl rightly notes, "The most important legacy of Rippon's hymnbook ... is its function in teaching and promoting evangelical Calvinism."¹⁶² Fuller's plan to distribute hymns among the young lacemakers of Kettering, mentioned above, also reflects his conception of church music as evangelical.

Third, Fuller's church music was *concerned with the affections*.¹⁶³ In this regard, Fuller's programmatic statement at the beginning of his "Thoughts on

---

¹⁵⁶ Note that although Fuller wanted music that was "adapted to the sentiments," this was not his only criterion; in the same breath, he spoke of such music as being "plain, serious, and solemn." Fuller, "Thoughts on Singing," in *WAF*, 862.

¹⁵⁷ A.G. Fuller, *Andrew Fuller*, 78.

¹⁵⁸ Fuller, "Thoughts on Singing," in *WAF*, 862.

¹⁵⁹ Fuller, "Thoughts on Singing," in *WAF*, 862, italics mine.

¹⁶⁰ Indeed, Watts was evangelical enough that High Calvinist William Gadsby—an opponent of Fullerism—felt the need in his 1814 hymnal to pass over or to edit certain of Watts's texts in order to conform his hymnal to High Calvinist theology. See Ruhl, "Engaging the Heart," 69-70 (Watts's embrace of "free offer" evangelism), 111-122 (Gadsby's selective use of Watts's hymns). See also Ruhl's summary treatment in "'Feeling Religion': High Calvinism, Experimentalism and Evangelism in William Gadsby's *A Selection of Hymns for Public Worship*," *The Hymn* 65.2 (2014): 14-22.

¹⁶¹ Fuller became pastor at Kettering in 1782, and Rippon's *Selection* was first published in 1787.

¹⁶² Ruhl, "Engaging the Heart," 100.

¹⁶³ One should be careful to distinguish the language of "affections" and "passions" in Fuller's day and that of "emotions" in our own, as the two categories are often confused. Keith

singing" will be recalled: "The intent of singing is by a musical pronunciation of affecting truth to render it still more affecting." Fuller's favorite hymnodist, Isaac Watts, saw singing psalms as a means whereby "spiritual Affections are excited within us."[164] Perhaps more influential for Fuller, though, was the judgment of his mentor in all things relating to the affections, Jonathan Edwards:[165]

> And the duty of singing praises to God seems to be appointed wholly to excite and express religious affections. No other reason can be assigned, why we should express ourselves to God in verse, rather than in prose, and do it with music, but only, that such is our nature and frame, that these things have a tendency to move our affections.[166]

While Fuller's church music—like his preaching—was plain, evangelical, and mindful of the affections, perhaps its most striking characteristic was its emphasis on the biblical text. While Fuller spoke of his love for hymns, he also indicated that, ideally, he would prefer the Scriptural text itself to be sung in church. Whatever detracted from a hymn's capacity to clearly communicate its biblical (or biblically-based) text—whether the use of instruments, unnecessary repetition, excessive musical ornamentation that obscured the words, or a style that drew undue attention to the musician—was to be eliminated.

A number of possible directions for further study may here be suggested. One might engage the Lutheran stream of church music, comparing the

---

Grant notes that Fuller in speaking of his pastoral ministry used the language of the affections "precisely because it married deep feelings and considered doctrine," *Andrew Fuller and the Evangelical Revival of Pastoral Theology*, 99. On the category shift from affections/passions to emotions, see Thomas Dixon, *From Passions to Emotions: The Creation of a Secular Psychological Category* (Cambridge: Cambridge University Press, 2003); Ryan J. Martin, *Understanding Affections in the Theology of Jonathan Edwards: "The High Exercises of Divine Love"* (London: T&T Clark, 2019).

[164] Watts, Preface to *Hymns and Spiritual Songs*, in David W. Music, *Hymnology: A Collection of Source Readings* (Lanham, MD: Scarecrow, 1996), 116.

[165] The influence of Edwards, and particularly of *Religious Affections*, upon Fuller is well known. Note Fuller's journal entries for 16 August 1780; 11 September 1780; 3 February 1781. See Thomas J. Nettles, "The Influence of Jonathan Edwards on Andrew Fuller," *Eusebia* 9 (2008): 91-116; Chris Chun, "'Sense of the Heart': Jonathan Edwards' Legacy in the Writings of Andrew Fuller," *Eusebia* 9 (2008): 117-134; and more fully, idem, *The Legacy of Jonathan Edwards in the Theology of Andrew Fuller*, SHCT (Leiden: Brill, 2012).

[166] Jonathan Edwards, *Religious Affections*, ed. Paul Ramsey, Works of Jonathan Edwards 2 (New Haven: Yale University Press, 1959), 115. Elsewhere, though doubtless beyond Fuller's access, Edwards noted, "Music, especially sacred music, has a powerful efficacy to soften the heart into tenderness, to harmonize the affections, and to give the mind a relish for objects of a superior character." J. Edwards to W. Pepperell, 28 November 1751, in Serano Edwards Dwight, *The Life of President Edwards* (New York: G. & C. & H. Carvill, 1830), 478.

theological underpinning of Fuller's "plainness" in music, on the one hand, with that of the polyphony that Martin Luther and J.S. Bach gloried in, on the other hand.[167] The present exploration of Fuller's church music might be correlated with other aspects of his theology of worship, or with his ecclesiology more broadly. Fuller's notion of music as rendering "affecting truth ... more affecting" could be considered in light of his engagement of the affections in his other writings,[168] and/or with other studies of music and the affections in the eighteenth and early nineteenth centuries.[169] Finally, and perhaps most notably, studies could be done on the church music of other Particular Baptist pastors, and the results combined with the present study to better understand Particular Baptist church music and worship as a whole.[170]

TABLE 1
HYMNS USED BY ANDREW FULLER

Compiled mainly from Fuller's *Works* and his *Diary*, the following list makes no claim to be exhaustive, but is an attempt to gather the various hymns (including metricized psalms) which Fuller references or which evidence indicates he knew. Unquestionably, he knew and could have quoted many more. Fuller's own verse is not referenced here, and his citation of Samuel Pearce's hymnic/poetic work as recorded in Pearce's memoirs is not listed here unless a particular piece is also contained in a hymnal. An asterisk (*) indicates Fuller is recording Samuel Pearce quoting from a hymn (except for "We walk a narrow path and rough," in which case, John Sutcliff is in view).

Note that for the entry "("Our God, our help in ages past"?)," Fuller's journal merely notes that he "sang Psa. xc." Given his partiality for Watts,

---

[167] Note in this regard the recent work by Miikka E. Anttila, *Luther's Theology of Music: Spiritual Beauty and Pleasure*, Theologische Bibliothek Töpelmann 161 (Berlin: de Gruyter, 2013).

[168] An excellent starting point here would be Keith Grant's discussion of "the language of the affections in Fuller's evangelical pastoral theology" in *Andrew Fuller and the Evangelical Renewal of Pastoral Theology*, 9-15.

[169] Chasing this question of musical aesthetics would involve interaction with the work of Charles Avison and others, for which see Edward A. Lippman, ed., *Musical Aesthetics: A Historical Reader, Volume 1, From Antiquity to the Eighteenth Century* (New York: Pendragon Press, 1986); Pierre Dubois, ed., *Charles Avison's Essay on Musical Expression: With Related Writings by William Hayes and Charles Avison* (Hants, UK: Ashgate, 2004). In his recent dissertation, Martin V. Clarke pursues this avenue of research as regards the musical thought of John Wesley. See Clarke, "John Wesley and Methodist Music," esp. his fifth chapter, "John Wesley's Writings on Music," and most specifically, 138-141.

[170] Temperley, "The Music of Dissent," is very helpful in this regard, but focuses on Dissenters more broadly, not Particular Baptists specifically.

though, we may assume the author. Watts wrote five pieces based on Psalm 90, however, and Fuller may have in mind one of the other four.

Hymn	Author	Source
* "A debtor to mercy alone"	Augustus Toplady	*Works*, 763
"Ah Lord, ah Lord, what have I done"	John Mason	*Works*, 875–876
* "Amazing grace! how sweet the sound"	John Newton	*Works*, 763
"Awake! sweet gratitude and sing"	Augustus Toplady	*Works*, 616
"Blest be the tie that binds"	John Fawcett	Letter to T. Steevens (1793)
* "Come, thou found of every blessing"	Robert Robinson	*Works*, 780, 782
* "Dear Lord, and will thy pardoning love"	John Fellows	*Works*, 763
"Election, sovereign and free"	Isaac Watts	*Works*, 168
"Ere the blue heavens were stretch'd abroad"	Isaac Watts	*Works*, 942
"God, my supporter and my hope"	Isaac Watts	*Works*, lxxxiv
"Hush, my dear; lie still and slumber"	Isaac Watts	*Diary*, 10 Feb 1785
"'I lift my banner,' saith the Lord"	Isaac Watts	*Works*, 474
"In the floods of tribulation"	Samuel Pearce	*Works*, 795
"Jesus is gone above the skies"	Isaac Watts	*Works*, lxxxiii
"Let others boast how strong they be"	Isaac Watts	*Works*, 669
* "Let the old heathens tune their song"	Isaac Watts	*Works*, 782
"Lord, teach a little child to pray"	John Ryland, Jr.	*Works*, 1
"Naked as from the earth we came"	Isaac Watts	A.G. Fuller, *Andrew Fuller*, 79
"Now from the roaring lion's rage"	Isaac Watts	*Works*, 466
"Now to the Lord a noble song"	Isaac Watts	*Diary*, 31 Dec 1784
"O for this love, let rocks and hills"	Isaac Watts	*Diary*, 31 Oct 1784
* "O the delights, the heavenly joys"	Isaac Watts	*Works*, 779
"O'er the gloomy hills of darkness"	William Williams	*Works*, 767
"Oh for a closer walk with God"	William Cowper	*Works*, 357
* "Oh, the sweet wonders of the cross"	Isaac Watts	*Works*, 791
("Our God, our help in ages past"?)	Isaac Watts	*Diary*, 27 & 31 Oct 1784
"Sweet is the work, my God, my King"	Isaac Watts	*Works*, 860
"Thus far my God hath led me on"	John Fawcett	Letter to T. Steevens (1793)
* "We walk a narrow path, and rough"	John Cennick	*Works*, 642
"Why does your face, ye humble souls"	Isaac Watts	*Diary*, 1 July 1780
* "Why is my heart so far from thee"	Isaac Watts	*Works*, 763
* "Why should we start and fear to die"	Isaac Watts	*Works*, 787

6
Christ as the Criterion for Preaching: Andrew Fuller and the Abrahamic Narrative

David G. Norman, Jr.

Preachers must derive their convictions from Holy Writ. However, when those convictions are attested and demonstrated by voices from the past, it is to the preacher's benefit to study the manner in which those same convictions were applied in that day. In light of the contemporary discussion regarding Christ-centered preaching, especially from Old Testament texts, it is helpful to look to the past for appropriate models.[1] Those who advocate proclaiming Christ responsibly from the Old Testament find a steadfast example in the person of eighteenth-century Particular Baptist, Andrew Fuller.

Standing before clerical students in the Bristol Education Society, the self-educated pastor charged them to preach Christ, stating, "However ingenious our sermons may be, unless they bear on Christ, and lead the mind to Christ, we do not preach the faith of the gospel."[2] In his *Thoughts on Preaching*, Fuller states it more emphatically: "Every sermon should contain a portion of the doctrine of salvation by the death of Christ."[3] This chapter considers Fuller's Christ-centered preaching, presents examples of his expositions from the Abrahamic narrative, and evaluates his model before presenting Fuller as an example to follow.

Andrew Fuller's Christ-Centered Emphasis

Born February 5, 1754 in Wicken, Cambridgeshire, England to Baptist parents, Andrew Fuller was baptized and joined the Baptist church in Soham in 1770.

---

[1] Greidanus writes, "It is well for us to take some distance from the contemporary scene and search for stability for our method of interpretation in a long-range, historical perspective." Sidney Greidanus, *Preaching Christ from the Old Testament: A Contemporary Hermeneutical Method* (Grand Rapids: Eerdmans, 1999), 69.

[2] Andrew Fuller, "Faith in the Gospel a Necessary Prerequisite to Preaching It," *The Complete Works of the Rev. Andrew Fuller*, vol. 1, ed. Joseph Belcher (1845 ed.; reprint, Harrisonburg, VA: Sprinkle Publications, 1988), 516. Hereafter *FW*.

[3] Andrew Fuller, "Thoughts on Preaching," in *FW*, 1:716.

The Soham congregation was high Calvinist in doctrine and had accepted Antinomian teachings as well.[4] Fuller described the pastor in Soham, John Eve, as "tinged with false Calvinism," and having "little or nothing to say to the unconverted."[5] The events surrounding the departure of Eve in 1771 are worthy of consideration as they have a direct influence on Fuller's preaching.

A member of the church had become a drunkard. Upon discovery, Fuller confronted the man and urged him to cease from his sin, but the man answered that he could not keep himself from it, revealing his Antinomian persuasion. Fuller recalled, "I therefore told him that he *could* keep himself from such sins as these, and that his way of talking was merely to excuse what was inexcusable."[6] Fuller then told his pastor of the man's sin and excuse. Eve "distinguished between internal and external power," and believed that "men had no power of themselves to perform any thing spiritually good; but contended that they could yield external obedience, and keep themselves from open acts of sin."[7] This distinction between internal and external power put Eve at odds with his Antinomian congregation. Whereas Eve believed that men were capable of exercising moral restraint, and as such, should be charged with doing so, the congregation maintained that if immoral acts were to be restrained or conquered, "it was altogether to be ascribed to God, and not to us."[8] These events forced Fuller to consider early in his ministry to what extent a person is able and responsible to do the will of God.

Eve did not remain in Soham long after these events and in 1775 Fuller became the pastor of the church. Upon his call to pastor, Fuller continued along the high Calvinist path set before him, refusing to trouble the church with any further theological conflict on this matter until he was certain that Scripture warrants calling the lost to repentance and faith.[9] In his search, he devoted himself to a careful study of the Scriptures, reading John Bunyan and, at the suggestion of like-minded pastors such as John Sutcliff and Robert Hall,

---

[4] Peter J. Morden, *Offering Christ to the World: Andrew Fuller (1754–1815) and the Revival of Eighteenth Century Particular Baptist Life*, SBHT (Carlisle, UK: Paternoster, 2013), 29. This chapter follows the usage of Andrew Fuller and utilizes the designations "high Calvinism" and "hyper Calvinism" interchangeably. Fuller does not equate high Calvinism with Antinomianism, but describes it as "bordering on Antinomianism." Andrew Gunton Fuller, "Memoir," in *FW*, 1:77.

[5] Fuller, "Memoir," in *FW*, 1:2.
[6] Fuller, "Memoir," in *FW*, 1:8.
[7] Fuller, "Memoir," in *FW*, 1:9.
[8] Fuller, "Memoir," in *FW*, 1:9.
[9] Fuller, "Memoir," in *FW*, 1:18.

Jonathan Edwards.[10] Fuller's studies resulted in his abandonment of high Calvinism in 1779 and his espousal of an evangelical Calvinism that "made direct appeals to the unconverted."[11]

The search that Fuller began in 1775 culminated in the publication of his most significant work, *The Gospel of Christ Worthy of All Acceptation: or The Obligations of Men Fully to Credit, and Cordially to Approve, Whatever God Makes Known. Wherein is Considered the Nature of Faith in Christ, and the Duty of Those Where the Gospel Comes in That Matter* in 1785, wherein Fuller writes that the Gospel "warrants every sinner to believe in Christ for salvation," and that "trusting in Christ ... is the *duty* of every sinner."[12] This theological conviction that sinners be called to repentance and faith completely revolutionized Fuller's preaching.

For Fuller, the cross was "the centre of Christianity."[13] He believed that the death of Christ held such a prominent place that without it,

> the sacrifices and prophecies of the Old Testament would be nearly void of meaning, and the other great facts recorded in the New Testament divested of importance. It is not so much a member of the body of Christian doctrine as the life-blood that runs through the whole of it. The doctrine of the cross is the Christian doctrine. ... There is not an important truth, but what is presupposed by it, included in it, or arises out of it; nor any part of practical religion but what hangs upon it.[14]

---

[10] Phil Roberts, "Andrew Fuller," in *Theologians of the Baptist Tradition*, rev. ed., eds. Timothy George and David S. Dockery (Nashville: B&H Academic, 2001), 36.

[11] Peter J. Morden, *The Life and Thought of Andrew Fuller (1754-1815)*, SEHT (Milton Keyes, UK: Paternoster, 2015), 43.

[12] Andrew Fuller, "The Gospel Worthy of All Acceptation," in *FW*, 2:335-336, 342. The 1801 revised edition of *The Gospel Worthy of All Acceptation* is printed in the three-volume set published by Sprinkle. All quotations come from this second edition. While there is considerable development from the first edition to the second, the nature of such development concerns the nature of the atonement (Phil R. Roberts, *Continuity and Change, London Calvinistic Baptists and the Evangelical Revival, 1760-1820* [Wheaton: Richard Owen Roberts, 1989], 171). Both editions present the argument that it is the duty of all men to trust in Christ for salvation. The first edition argues that limited atonement does not hinder the free offer of salvation, while the second edition presents a view of the atonement more influenced by the governmental understanding of the New England divines.

[13] Andrew Fuller, "Letters on Systematic Divinity," in *FW*, 1:690.

[14] Andrew Fuller, "Conformity to the Death of Christ," in *FW*, 1:310.

Just as Christ's cross is the center of all Christian doctrine, Fuller taught that it was the very criterion for Christian preaching.[15] He wrote, "A sermon ... in which this doctrine has not a place, and I might add, a prominent place, cannot be a *gospel sermon*."[16] Fuller did not believe that this conviction limited preaching texts to the passion narrative, for as "there is a rich variety in the sacred writings ... there ought to be in our ministrations."[17] Instead he believed that every biblical text has an inherent connection to the cross and "if we would introduce them in a truly evangelical manner, it requires to be *in that relation*."[18] Elsewhere he explained that Christ is the substance of all Christian preaching, for "his person and work are rich in fullness. Every Divine attribute is seen in him. All the types prefigure him. The prophecies point to him. Every truth bears relation to him. The law itself must be so explained and enforced as to lead to him."[19]

Thus, Christian preaching demands that every sermon demonstrate the text's connection to the person and work of Christ. Fuller's commitment to preaching Christ from the entirety of Scripture exists as an example for preachers to follow. However, as Sidney Greidanus notes, "Horror stories abound of preachers twisting an Old Testament text in order to land miraculously at Calvary."[20] Further, objections are made by homileticians arguing that Christ-centered preaching inadvertently "fail[s] to honor God the Father as he ought to be honored."[21] In light of these and other criticisms, one must consider Andrew Fuller's expositions critically. In doing so, however, the reader will discern Fuller's careful and responsible Christ-centered preaching of the Old Testament text.

---

[15] The phrase, "Christ as the criterion for preaching," is drawn from the author's description of Fuller's conviction in Keith S. Grant, *Andrew Fuller and the Evangelical Renewal of Pastoral Theology*, SEHT (Eugene, OR: Wipf & Stock, 2013), 91.

[16] Fuller, "Thoughts on Preaching," in *FW*, 1:716.

[17] Fuller, "Thoughts on Preaching," in *FW*, 1:716.

[18] Fuller, "Thoughts on Preaching," in *FW*, 1:716.

[19] Andrew Fuller, "Preaching Christ," in *FW*, 1:503. Prince elaborates on this idea, writing, "Ignoring the Christ-centered canonical context of Scripture is no less reductionistic and problematic than ignoring the immediate context of the human author." David Edward Prince, "The Necessity of a Christocentric, Kingdom-Focused Model of Expository Preaching" (Ph.D. diss., Southern Baptist Theological Seminary, 2011), 147.

[20] Greidanus, *Preaching Christ from the Old Testament*, 2.

[21] Ken Langley, "When Christ Replaces God at the Center of Preaching," *JEHS* 9.1 (2009): 56.

DAVID G. NORMAN, JR.

Preaching Christ from the Abrahamic Narrative

In describing his pastoral practice, Fuller preferred "to appropriate one part of every Lord's day to the *exposition* of a chapter, or part of a chapter, in the sacred writings."[22] In so doing, he believed he and his congregation were able "to take a more connected view of the Scriptures than could be obtained merely by sermons on particular passages."[23] His expositions from Genesis and Revelation are printed in his *Complete Works*. Three expositions from the Abrahamic narrative will suffice to demonstrate the responsible manner in which Andrew Fuller preached Christ from Old Testament texts.

Fuller practiced careful and unforced exposition of Old Testament texts. For example, Melchizedek's blessing of Abraham in Genesis 14 has led to much discussion.[24] In verse 18, the biblical author writes, "Melchizedek king of Salem brought out bread and wine. (He was priest of God Most High.)"[25] The difficulty of this portion of Scripture is that "in a book given over to genealogies, this man appeared on the scene without any such notice."[26] Melchizedek is given no introduction. This lack of material has forced scholars to consider several major questions. Kenneth A. Mathews demonstrates these questions resulting from this text:

> What individual could be greater than Father Abraham? In addition, his priesthood antedated that of the Levitical order, apparently functioning independently of the traditional priesthood of Israel. Melchizedek, moreover, appears and disappears in the text without mention of his parentage, his priestly accession, or death. What was the nature of his priesthood? Since he worshipped the same God as Abram, how did Melchizedek also know of the Lord? And, as the king of "Salem" (=Jerusalem), which became the center of Israel's political and religious life, what was the relationship of his priesthood and the royal house of

---

[22] Fuller, "Thoughts on Preaching," in *FW*, 1:712. Grant demonstrates that Fuller "follow[ed] the general categories used by Claude and others," and "distinguished between *expositions* ... and *sermons*." Grant, *Andrew Fuller and the Evangelical Renewal of Pastoral Theology*, 84. Indeed, Fuller's friend and biographer, John Webster Morris wrote, "one of the first books that Mr. Fuller read, after entering on the ministry, and which he frequently recommended to others, was CLAUDE's ESSAY on the composition of Sermon." John Webster Morris, *Memoirs of the Life and Death of the Rev. Andrew Fuller* (High Wycombe: n.p., 1816), 69.

[23] Andrew Fuller, "Expository Discourses in the Book of Genesis," in *FW*, 3:1.

[24] For a helpful discussion on Melchizedek, see Kenneth A. Mathews, *Genesis 11:27–50:26*. The New American Commentary, vol. 1b (Nashville: B&H, 2005), 151–156.

[25] Unless otherwise noted, all Scripture references are from the English Standard Version.

[26] Allen P. Ross, *Creation and Blessing: A Guide to the Study and Exposition of Genesis* (Grand Rapids: Baker Academic, 1996), 300.

David? These and related mysteries provided interpreters opportunities for speculation ... about his identity and role and the significance of his name as well as his city's name.[27]

Fuller, however, refused to enter into such speculation. For him, Melchizedek does not represent an opportunity to construct hypotheses, but rather to explore that which the biblical author describes. Fuller recognized that Melchizedek is presented as "a type of the Messiah" in Psalm 110 and Hebrews 7.[28] With the insight provided by these additional texts, Fuller directed his congregation to understand that Melchizedek was one "in whom were united the kingly and priestly offices; and, as such, he was a type of Messiah, and greater than Abram himself."[29]

Fuller observed that "though as a man [Melchizedek] was born like other men ... he derived his office from no predecessor."[30] In this sense, Fuller explains "he was 'made like unto the Son of God;' who also was a priest, not after the manner of the sons of Aaron, by descent from their predecessors ... but ... by an immediate Divine constitution."[31] Rather than speculating on Melchizedek's history and priesthood, Fuller restricted himself only to that which the Scriptures reveal—that Melchizedek is a *type* of Messiah. In doing so, he demonstrated a pastoral maturity in his willingness to resist forcing an interpretation upon the text and a preference to refrain from following any path to which the Bible does not direct.

This reliance upon the Scriptures to cast light upon the Old Testament is further demonstrated by Fuller's consideration of the Abrahamic blessing in Genesis 12, "I will make of you a great nation, and I will bless you and make your name great, so that you will be a blessing. I will bless those who bless you, and him who dishonors you I will curse, and in you all the families of the earth shall be blessed" (Gen. 12:2-3). Fuller wrote that this blessing declares "that [Abram] should not only be blessed himself, but that all others should be blessed or cursed as they respected or injured him."[32] As the result of this blessing, Abram and his posterity became the medium through which God would bless the nations of the earth. Fuller demonstrated this point when he

---

[27] Mathews, *Genesis 11:27–50:26*, 151.
[28] Fuller, "Expository Discourses in the Book of Genesis," in *FW*, 3:59.
[29] Fuller, "Expository Discourses in the Book of Genesis," in *FW*, 3:59.
[30] Fuller, "Expository Discourses in the Book of Genesis," in *FW*, 3:59.
[31] Fuller, "Expository Discourses in the Book of Genesis," in *FW*, 3:59.
[32] Fuller, "Expository Discourses in the Book of Genesis," in *FW*, 3:52.

revealed, "All the true blessedness which the world is now, or shall hereafter be, possessed of, is owing to Abram and his posterity. Through them we have a Bible, a Saviour, and a gospel."[33] Everything good that the earth has received since this moment in biblical history has come through the person and posterity of Abram. Yet, Fuller did not offer this haphazardly, but rather did so reliant upon that which is taught explicitly by New Testament authors.

He wrote that this blessing would "be bestowed through [Abram] and his posterity, as the medium."[34] Referring to Galatians 3:8, wherein it says, "And the Scripture, foreseeing that God would justify the Gentiles by faith, preached the gospel beforehand to Abraham, saying, 'In you shall all the nations be blessed,'" Fuller wrote, "Paul applies this to Christ, and the believing Gentiles being blessed in him."[35]

Further, he paraphrased Peter's sermon in Acts 3:

> You are descended from one who posterity were to be blessed above all nations, and made a blessing. And the time to favour the nations being now at hand, God sent his Son *first* to you, to bless you, and to prepare you for blessing them; as though it were yours to be a nation of ministers, or missionaries to the world. But how if, instead of blessing others, you should continue accursed yourselves? You must first be blessed, ere you can, as the true seed of Abraham, bless the kindreds of the earth, and that by every one of you being turned from his iniquities.[36]

Fuller's point is the very same as the New Testament authors: the blessing that belonged to the people of Israel as the result of God's blessing of Abram and was intended to flow through them to bless the nations culminates in the person and work of Christ Jesus. Fuller read the Old Testament text in light of the whole of Christian Scripture, and as the result, did not need to force Christ into the text, but rather explained and expressed only that which is made explicit by the New Testament authors. Once again, Fuller's pastoral maturity and interpretive responsibility are demonstrated.

In Fuller's exposition of Genesis 22, he decided from the outset to "deviate from [his] usual practice of expounding verse by verse," and to take a more

---

[33] Fuller, "Expository Discourses in the Book of Genesis," in *FW*, 3:52.
[34] Fuller, "Expository Discourses in the Book of Genesis," in *FW*, 3:52.
[35] Fuller, "Expository Discourses in the Book of Genesis," in *FW*, 3:52.
[36] Fuller, "Expository Discourses in the Book of Genesis," in *FW*, 3:52.

comprehensive consideration of the passage.³⁷ First he considered the nature of the testing of Abraham. He demonstrated the shock of God's command:

> The command is worded in a manner as if it were designed to harrow up all his feelings as a father: "Take now thy son, thine only son (of promise)—Isaac, whom thou lovest."—Or, as some read it, "Take now that son ... that only one of thine ... whom thou lovest ... that Isaac"—and what? Deliver him to some other hand to sacrifice him? No: be thou thyself the priest; go, "offer him up for a burnt-offering!"³⁸

Then Fuller pressed his hearers to consider the obedience shown by Abraham in the midst of the trial. Fuller observed, "we see no opposition," and "no sooner had the father of the faithful received the heavenly mandate than, without further delay, he prepares for the journey."³⁹ Fuller revealed Abraham's absolute obedience and faith in God's power, for Fuller pointed out that according to Hebrews 11:17, "Abraham from the first believed that the lad would in some way be restored to him because God had said, 'in Isaac shall thy seed be called.'"⁴⁰ Fuller emphasized the obedience and faith of Abraham: "He expected no other than that he should have to slay him, and that he would be burnt to ashes; but if so it were, he was persuaded that he should receive him again."⁴¹

Fuller then directed his congregation to consider the reward bestowed upon Abraham in light of his obedience. These blessings were very similar to those which were promised in Genesis 12, but as Fuller explains, "they are more than a mere repetition. The terms are stronger than had ever been used on any former occasion."⁴²

After considering Abraham's testing, obedience, and reward, Fuller made a shift in the discussion. He explained that God could have asserted his right as sovereign Creator to demand human sacrifice, yet he "never accepted but one human sacrifice; and blood in that case was not shed at his command, but by the wicked hands of men."⁴³ Without mentioning the name of Christ, Fuller demonstrated the great mercy of God in that the only human offering to have

---

³⁷ Fuller, "Expository Discourses in the Book of Genesis," in *FW*, 3:87.
³⁸ Fuller, "Expository Discourses in the Book of Genesis," in *FW*, 3:88.
³⁹ Fuller, "Expository Discourses in the Book of Genesis," in *FW*, *3:88*.
⁴⁰ Fuller, "Expository Discourses in the Book of Genesis," in *FW*, 3:89.
⁴¹ Fuller, "Expository Discourses in the Book of Genesis," in *FW*, 3:89.
⁴² Fuller, "Expository Discourses in the Book of Genesis," in *FW*, 3:89.
⁴³ Fuller, "Expository Discourses in the Book of Genesis," in *FW*, 3:90.

been received by God in the place of sinful man was Christ Jesus. Further, God's goodness is manifested in that he accepted the blood of Christ that was spilled by sinners. In one subtle sentence, Fuller drew a clear line from Genesis 22 to the cross.

He then demonstrated the biblical significance of the mountain upon which God had provided a substitution for Isaac:

> The very place of it, called "the mount of the Lord," seems to have been marked out as the scene of great events; and of that kind too in which a substitutional sacrifice was offered and accepted. Here it was that David offered burnt-offerings and peace-offerings, and called upon the Lord; and he answered him from heaven by fire upon the altar of burnt-offering, and commanded the angel of death to put up his sword. 1 Chron. xxi. 26, 27). It was upon the same mountain that Solomon was afterwards directed to build the temple, 2 Chron. iii. 1.) And, if it were not at the very spot, it could not be far distant that the Saviour of the world was crucified.[44]

Fuller explained that on the very same mountain upon which Abraham was commanded in Genesis 22:2 to "Take your son, your only son Isaac, whom you love," "God's own Son, his only Son, whom he loved, and in whom all the nations of the earth were to be blessed," was led.[45] The importance of the similarity is not to be missed. But, unlike the ram that would be provided as the substitute for Isaac's beloved son, God's Son was not "spared at the awful crisis by means of a substitute, but was himself freely delivered up as the substitute of others."[46]

Though Fuller does not use the typological terminology in his exposition of this text, it is clear that he envisioned Christ to be the greater and complete Isaac, for Christ did not require a substitute, but was himself the substitute. Christ is the greater and more complete "son of promise," for in him as the seed of Abraham the whole earth is blessed. Christ is the greater and more complete substitutional sacrifice, for in him the Father is well-pleased and the wrath of God has been expiated. But Fuller provided one further observation in the text—God the Father is the greater and complete Abraham, for "one

---

[44] Fuller, "Expository Discourses in the Book of Genesis," in *FW*, 3:90.
[45] Fuller, "Expository Discourses in the Book of Genesis," in *FW*, 3:90.
[46] Fuller, "Expository Discourses in the Book of Genesis," in *FW*, 3:90.

reason of the high approbation which God expressed of Abraham's conduct might be its affording some faint likeness of what would shortly be his own."[47]

These three examples from Genesis 12, 14, and 22 demonstrate the responsible manner in which Andrew Fuller preached Christ from Old Testament texts. His practice of unforced and consistent exposition of the Old Testament text shows a pastoral maturity that understood the importance of long-term, comprehensive biblical teaching. Rather than responding to a need to force Christ into the text, Fuller patiently and carefully allowed the New Testament text to cast light upon the Old Testament. Fuller is careful to venture only where the New Testament provides a more complete understanding of the text, and Fuller's biblical understanding is demonstrated in his willingness and ability to explain deep doctrinal connections to his congregation. He desired that his congregation would walk away from his expositions with a more complete understanding as the result of his efforts. He wrote to other preachers, "If the hearer, when you have done, understand no more of that part of Scripture than he did before, your labour is lost."[48]

Evaluating and Endorsing Fuller's Model: Systematic Exposition
In order to appreciate Fuller's preaching, one must place it in its context. Fuller maintained that consistent, verse-by-verse exposition enabled him to focus on the long-term health and understanding of his congregation. In doing so, the church in Kettering, where he spent the vast majority of his ministry from 1782 until his death in 1815, "maintained steady growth ... throughout his ministry."[49] During his pastorate, the membership "more than doubled," but this does not account for the number of non-members that grew to "well over a thousand, requiring several additions to the sanctuary."[50]

This verse-by-verse preaching, otherwise known as *systematic exposition*, is, according to contemporary authors Jerry Vines and Jim Shaddix, "the best preaching you can do. ... Such an approach will ensure the keenest interpretation and the best use of context."[51] They define it as, "the consecutive and

---

[47] Fuller, "Expository Discourses in the Book of Genesis," in *FW*, 3:90.
[48] Fuller, "Thoughts on Preaching," in *FW*, 1:712.
[49] Thomas R. McKibbens, Jr., *The Forgotten Heritage: A Lineage of Great Baptist Preaching* (Macon, GA: Mercer, 1986), 48.
[50] Thomas R. McKibbens, Jr., "Disseminating Biblical Doctrine Through Preaching," *BHH* 19.3 (1984): 45.
[51] Jerry Vines and Jim Shaddix, *Power in the Pulpit: How to Prepare and Deliver Expository Sermons* (Chicago: Moody, 1999), 32.

exhaustive treatment of a book of the Bible or extended portions thereof."[52] William Taylor assumes systematic exposition in the very definition of expository preaching when he writes that it "consists in the consecutive interpretation, and practical enforcement, of a book of the sacred truth."[53] It is notable that Shaddix lists Fuller as one of the rare exceptions to the predominate model of topical preaching of his day.[54]

Fuller believed that this model of exposition helped pastors in their understanding of the Scriptures, which prepared them to convey that meaning to their congregations. Preaching systematically through the whole counsel of God provided Fuller with a biblical awareness with which to approach each individual text and that comprehensive understanding was shared with his congregation. Systematic exposition, then, was "advantageous to a people that what they hear should come directly from the word of God, and that they should be led to see the scope and connexion of the sacred writers."[55]

While maintaining such a scope may tempt some to compress the variety of the Scriptures and reduce its meaning to a single core truth, Fuller sought to interpret each passage responsibly in its own context before bringing the entirety of biblical insight to the text. Concerning sermon preparation, he wrote, "It is necessary to read it in connexion with the context, and endeavor by your own judgment to gain a clear idea of its genuine meaning."[56] Elsewhere he wrote,

> It may seem to be a very easy thing, with the Bible in our hands, to learn the truth, clear of all impure mixtures, and to make it the subject of our ministry. But it is not so. ... I mention these things ... to inculcate the necessity of prayer for Divine guidance, and a close adherence to the Scriptures.[57]

Fuller did not attempt to impress any predetermined meaning upon the text. In his instruction on sermon preparation, he wrote, "Be satisfied ... that you have the mind of the Holy Spirit before you proceed."[58] Thus, while it is

---

[52] Vines and Shaddix, *Power in the Pulpit*, 94.

[53] William M. Taylor, *The Ministry of the Word* (Grand Rapids: Baker Book House, 1975), 155.

[54] Jim Shaddix, "A History of Text Driven Preaching," in *Text-Driven Preaching: God's Word at the Heart of Every Sermon*, eds. Daniel L. Akin, David L. Allen, and Ned L. Matthews (Nashville: B&H Academic, 2010), 46.

[55] Fuller, "Thoughts on Preaching," in *FW*, 1:712.

[56] Fuller, "Thoughts on Preaching," in *FW*, 1:718.

[57] Fuller, "Thoughts on Preaching," in *FW*, 1:714.

[58] Fuller, "Thoughts on Preaching," in *FW*, 1:718.

true that, "as he expounded the scriptures to believers, a concern for the spread of the gospel was never far from the surface," his concern did not provide the impetus for the interpretation, but instead, led him to emphasize the connection between the text and the person and work of Christ.[59] Andrew Blackwood professed a similar conviction in his instruction that, "while one should preach 'from the Bible,' the heart of the message should be about God in Christ."[60]

Paths to the Center of Christianity
Fuller's emphasis that the death of Christ is not merely "a member of the body of Christian doctrine," but is rather, "the life-blood that runs through the whole of it," led him to emphasize the connection of the Old Testament text to Christ.[61] In this effort, Fuller utilized biblical theology and allowed the New Testament to illuminate the Old Testament text. James M. Hamilton writes that such use of biblical theology "boils down to reading the Bible in context—not just the near context of the phrase, sentence, paragraph, the wider passage, or the individual book but also the context of the whole canon."[62] The careful reader can discern several methods of Christ-centered interpretation in Fuller's expositions. In the three examples above, Fuller's use of typology, analogy, longitudinal themes, promise-fulfillment, and New Testament references can be clearly demonstrated.

In Genesis 14, Fuller's treatment of Melchizedek is explicitly typological. Fuller went so far as to state clearly, "[Melchizedek] was a type of the Messiah."[63] Greidanus provides four characteristics of types, in that genuine types are historical, theocentric, they exhibit "a specific analogy with its antitype," and the relation with its antitype "is marked by escalation."[64] In evaluating Fuller's use of typology, one notes that each of these characteristics is evident in the person of Melchizedek. In Genesis 14, Melchizedek is presented as a historical person whose behavior provides the author of Hebrews justification to present him as a type of Messiah. Indeed, the presentation of Melchizedek

---

[59] Morden, *Offering Christ to the World*, 115. This is the manner of responsible Christ-centered preaching advocated by Edmund Clowney who wrote, "You must preach Christ as the text presents him." Edmund P. Clowney, *Preaching Christ in All of Scripture* (Wheaton: Crossway, 2003), 11.
[60] Andrew W. Blackwood, *Preaching from the Bible* (Nashville: Abingdon, 1941), 38.
[61] Andrew Fuller, "Conformity to the Death of Christ," in *FW*, 1:310.
[62] James M. Hamilton Jr., "Biblical Theology and Preaching," in *Text-Driven Preaching*, 198.
[63] Fuller, "Expository Discourses in the Book of Genesis," in *FW*, 3:59.
[64] Greidanus, *Preaching Christ from the Old Testament*, 255–256.

in Psalm 110 and Hebrews 7 demonstrates the analogy with the Messiah and marks it in its escalation. The Lord to whom David refers in Psalm 110 as "a priest forever after the order of Melchizedek" is identified as Jesus in Hebrews 7.

In Fuller's treatment of Genesis 22, his use of analogy is evident as he marks the similarity of God's description of Isaac with that of Christ Jesus. The description of Isaac as Abraham's "son, [his] only son Isaac, whom [Abraham] loves," in Genesis 22:2 echoes throughout the New Testament description of Jesus as "the Father's Son," "his only Son," "in whom [the Father] is well-pleased" (2 John 1:3; John 3:16; Matt. 3:17). Just as Abraham led his son up the mountain in order to offer him as a sacrificial offering, "hither then was led God's own Son, his only Son, whom he loved, and in whom all nations of the earth were to be blessed."[65]

In his exposition of Genesis 22, Fuller also used the longitudinal themes to direct his hearers to Christ. Specifically, Fuller identified the location of Abraham's testing—to present his son as a sacrificial offering—and the site of Isaac's substitution as the very same mount upon which David would offer burnt-offerings and peace-offerings, the same mount upon which Solomon would build the temple, and the very site upon which Christ's sacrifice would appease the wrath of God.[66] In so doing, Fuller traced the theme of a substitute through the entirety of the Bible in order to demonstrate the vast biblical importance of the sacrificial ram.

Fuller demonstrated the manner in which the promise made to Abram in Genesis 12:3 is fulfilled in Christ. The promise to Abram that in him "all the families of the earth shall be blessed," is fulfilled ultimately, according to Paul's description in Galatians and Peter's sermon in Acts, in the person and work of Christ. Utilizing New Testament references, Paul demonstrated how this Old Testament promise is fulfilled in Jesus.

In light of these examples, the responsible manner in which Fuller preached Christ from the Old Testament is evident. He did not stretch the text's meaning in an effort to get at the cross. He considered any artificial manner in which to get from the text to Christ inherently dangerous and as having potentially eternal consequences. In describing the abuse of allegory, he wrote,

---

[65] Fuller, "Expository Discourses in the Book of Genesis," in *FW*, 3:90.
[66] Fuller, "Expository Discourses in the Book of Genesis," in *FW*, 3:90.

If an unbeliever come into your assembly, and find you arraying Christianity in this fancy dress, is it likely he should be convinced of all—and, the secrets of his heart being made manifest, fall down and worship God, and report that God is among you, and that of a truth? If he hear you treat of the historical parts of Scripture as meaning something very different from what they appear to mean, will he not say you are mad, and be furnished with a handle for representing religion itself as void of truth and good sense?[67]

Insights from Fuller's Model

In light of his conviction that every sermon should direct his hearers to the cross and in light of the responsible manner in which he accomplished this, the modern preacher can draw several lessons from the expositions of Andrew Fuller. In following his pattern, the preacher can confidently preach Old Testament narratives responsibly while ensuring that the Gospel of Jesus Christ is proclaimed.

First, Fuller instructed that every sermon has a thesis, or to use Fuller's term, "an errand," from the text. "Every sermon," he wrote, "should have an errand; and one of such importance that if it be received or complied with it will issue in eternal salvation."[68] One cannot communicate the genuine meaning of the text, nor ensure that the sermon directs the congregation to Christ without careful study and consideration of the text. Fuller warned against the practice of those "who profess to go into the pulpit without an errand, and [who] depend on the Holy Spirit to furnish the with one at the time."[69] Without an errand, the preacher has no target to which to direct his aim. The target demands a bullet, which is the very imagery provided by Haddon Robinson in his description of a sermon's main idea.[70] Fuller insisted that preaching "should be plain and simple so that its central content—the Gospel of Jesus Christ—could be clearly communicated."[71]

Second, it is incumbent that every sermon points the hearer to the cross, the center of Christianity. Fuller wrote that cross-centeredness is that which distinguishes *preaching* from preaching the *Gospel*, for he wrote, "If I have any other end in view than, by convincing him of his lost condition, to make him

---

[67] Fuller, "Thoughts on Preaching," in *FW*, 1:727.
[68] Fuller, "Thoughts on Preaching," in *FW*, 1:715.
[69] Fuller, "Thoughts on Preaching," in *FW*, 1:715.
[70] Haddon Robinson, *Biblical Preaching: The Development and Delivery of Expository Messages*, 2nd ed. (Grand Rapids: Baker Academic, 2001), 35.
[71] Grant, *Andrew Fuller and the Evangelical Renewal of Pastoral Theology*, 82.

feel the need of the Saviour, I cannot be said to have preached *the gospel*."[72] Fuller saw this as so critical to the role of the pastor that he considered this the very substance of Christian preaching. He wrote,

> Unless the subject-matter of your preaching be truly evangelical, you had better be any thing than a minister. When the apostle speaks of a necessity being laid upon him to preach the gospel, he might mean that he was not at liberty to relinquish his work in favour of ease, or honour, or any other worldly object; but he was not bound the preach merely, but to preach that doctrine which had been delivered to him. The same may be said of us; woe unto us if we preach not the gospel![73]

Third, he warned preachers to beware the temptation to "imitate the orator, whose attention is taken up with his performance," and instead urged them to imitate the herald, "whose object is to publish, or proclaim, good tidings."[74] His concern that hearers are presented with the Gospel of Jesus Christ upholds the seriousness of the preaching task. Elsewhere he beckoned his reader, "If we must play, let it be with things of less consequence than the word of the eternal God!"[75] Fuller went so far as to argue against the use of fanciful oration, writing,

> I do not think a minister of Jesus Christ should aim at fine composition in the pulpit. We ought to use sound speech, and good sense; but if we aspire after great elegance of expression, or become very exact in the formation of our periods, though we may amuse and please the ears of a few, we shall not profit the many, and consequently shall not answer the great end of our ministry.[76]

Finally, Fuller urged that pastors should press the invitation upon their hearers. In his description of Fuller's preaching, Baptist historian Thomas McKibbens wrote that Fuller was "heart and soul a preacher of God's invitation for all to repent and come to faith in Christ."[77] This invitation stands at the center of Fuller's theology, and marks his preaching as a decisive shift

---

[72] Fuller, "Thoughts on Preaching," in *FW*, 1:716.
[73] Fuller, "Thoughts on Preaching," in *FW*, 1:714.
[74] Fuller, "Thoughts on Preaching," in *FW*, 1:716.
[75] Fuller, "Thoughts on Preaching," in *FW*, 1:726.
[76] Fuller, "Thoughts on Preaching," in *FW*, 1:717.
[77] McKibbens, "Disseminating Biblical Doctrine Through Preaching," 45.

within the British Particular Baptists of the eighteenth century.[78] According to Fuller, "it belongs to the work of the ministry, not merely to declare that truth, but to accompany it with earnest calls, and pressing invitations, to sinners to receive it."[79] One example of the manner in which Fuller made such an invitation illustrates the passion with which he called sinners to repentance and faith:

> My dear hearers! consider your condition without delay. God says to you, *To-day*, if ye will hear his voice, harden not your hearts. *To-day* may be the only day you have to live. Go home, enter the closet, and shut the door; confess your sins; implore mercy through our Lord Jesus Christ; "Kiss the Son, lest he be angry, and ye perish from the way, when his wrath is kindled but a little. Blessed are all they that put their trust in him."[80]

Conclusion

Andrew Fuller's theological shift from the constraints of high Calvinism to the promiscuous offer of the Gospel is demonstrated in his emphatic Christ-centered proclamation. His expositions stand as a model for contemporary preachers to follow in that they exemplify a responsible handling of God's Word and a pastoral maturity that comprehends the weight and importance of the preaching task.

In his expositions from the Abrahamic narrative, students of Christ-centered preaching can identify his use of typology, analogy, longitudinal themes, promise-fulfillment, and New Testament references in the responsible manner in which he connects Abraham, Isaac, and Melchizedek to the person and work of Christ. Fuller's conviction that "the preaching of Christ will answer every end of preaching," drove him to make the connection from his text to the cross because

> this is the doctrine which God owns to conversion, to the leading of awakened sinners to peace, and to the comfort of true Christians. If the doctrine of the cross be no comfort to us, it is a sign we have no right to comfort. This doctrine is calculated to quicken the indolent, to draw

---

[78] Morden, *Offering Christ to the World*, 118.
[79] Fuller, "Thoughts on Preaching," in *FW*, 1:717.
[80] Andrew Fuller, "Instances, Evil, and Tendency of Delay, in the Concerns of Religion," in *FW*, 1:151.

forth every Christian grace, and to recover the backslider. This is the universal remedy for all the moral diseases of mankind.[81]

Contemporary preachers should follow the model set forth by Andrew Fuller in establishing Christ as the criterion for Christian proclamation. That is a topic taken up in David Prince's chapter in this volume.

---

[81] Andrew Fuller, "Preaching Christ," in *FW*, 1:504.

7
What Contemporary Pastors Can Learn from Andrew Fuller

David E. Prince

Charles Haddon Spurgeon said of Andrew Fuller, he was "the greatest theologian" of his century.[1] Over two hundred years after his death, the shadow of the great English Baptist pastor and missionary-theologian still casts wide, and I pray it will loom larger still in the days ahead.

Andrew Fuller provided the theological foundation upon which the modern missionary movement was launched. Indeed, it is doubtful William Carey, the famed missions pioneer, would have ever been sent to India apart from Fuller's work. William Carey's great grandson and biographer, S. Pearce Carey wrote of Andrew Fuller, "More than anyone else he had rescued the churches from fatalism which had smothered all Christian sense of obligation to carry the Gospel to the unreached world. His sledge hammer had broken the cold reasoning of hyper-Calvinism. He had saved the day, too, at Nottingham, and was to prove to be the unrivaled home captain of the missionary cause."[2]

No non-biblical author has influenced my thinking as significantly as Andrew Fuller. In his sermons and written works, Fuller addressed every topic with the Christ-centered, sober-minded clarity of a working pastor. He spent forty years in pastoral ministry, thirty-two of those years at the Baptist Church of Kettering in Northamptonshire. And in his work as a theologian, apologist, and missionary, Fuller never lost sight of Jesus, the church, or the gospel. Despite treating an incredible number of issues (theology, apologetics, missiology, ecclesiology), Fuller never failed to consider the concrete implications for week-by-week gospel preaching, congregational worship, pastoral care, and church governance surrounding his topic.

---

[1] As cited in Gilbert Laws, *Andrew Fuller: Pastor, Theologian, Ropeholder* (London: Carey Press, 1942), 127.

[2] S. Pearce Carey, *William Carey* (London: Wakeman Trust, 1993), 81–82.

Andrew Fuller

He was consistently concerned about the danger of an empty ceremonial ministry that possessed the outward appearance of godliness but in practice denied its gospel power (2 Tim. 3:5). In a sermon from 2 Corinthians 4:13 to students at the Bristol Education Society, Fuller exhorted, "We must taste of truth as Christians, before we preach it. Studying it merely as ministers will never do. Believing belongs to us as Christians."[3] In assessing the state of Baptist church in Northamptonshire in 1814 Fuller warned,

> We are apt to think, that if we have but made up our minds on the leading points of controversy afloat in the world, and taken the side of truth, we are safe; but it is not so. If we walk not with God, we shall almost be certain in some way to get aside from the gospel, and then the work of God will not prosper in our hands. Ingenious discourses may be delivered, and nothing advanced inconsistent with the gospel, while yet the gospel itself is not preached. We may preach *about* Christ himself, and yet not "preach Christ." We may pride ourselves in our orthodoxy, and yet be far from the doctrine of the New Testament; may hold with exhortations and invitations to the unconverted, and yet not "persuade men;" may plead for sound doctrine, and yet overlook the things that "become sound doctrine." Finally, we may advocate the cause of holiness, while we ourselves are unholy.[4]

Andrew Fuller's writings have been my daily companion for about a decade now. Reading a portion of the Fuller corpus almost every day has rescued me from error, encouraged me to faithfulness, and directed me back to the gospel when I had lost a cruciform focus. I pray my own ministry might offer a fraction of the help that I have found in Andrew Fuller. I long for other pastors to drink from the well of Fuller's gospel-saturated wisdom.

The Truth as It Is in Jesus

When I first read through *Andrew Fuller's Complete Works*, I was struck by a recurring phrase. I believe the phrase to be an excellent way of summarizing the distinctiveness of Fuller's life and ministry: "the truth as it is in Jesus."[5]

---

[3] Andrew Fuller, "Faith in the Gospel a Necessary Prerequisite to Preaching It," in *The Complete Works of the Rev. Andrew Fuller*, vol. 1, ed. Joseph Belcher (1845 ed.; reprint, Harrisonburg, VA: Sprinkle Publications, 1988), 517. Hereafter *FW*.

[4] Andrew Fuller, "State of the Baptist churches in Northamptonshire [1814]," in *FW*, 3:483.

[5] Much of this chapter is taken from David E. Prince, *Preaching the truth as it is Jesus: A reader on Andrew Fuller* (Peterborough, ON: H&E Publishing, 2022). Used with permission.

Fuller explained the textual basis of the phrase and its significance for ordering Christianity as a system:

> With the idea of all Divine truth bearing an intimate relation to Christ agrees that notable phrase in Eph. 4:21, "The truth as it is in Jesus." To believe the truth concerning Jesus is to believe the whole doctrine of the Scriptures. Hence it is that in all the brief summaries of Christian doctrine the person and work of Christ are prominent.[6]

Fuller listed several examples of doctrinal summary statements, noting that each of them focuses on the truth as it is in Jesus (1 Cor. 15:1–4, 1 Tim. 3:16, 1 Tim. 1:15, 1 John 5:4, 11). He wrote, "Fully aware that this golden link would draw along with it the whole chain of evangelical truth, the sacred writers seem careful for nothing in comparison of it. It is on this ground that faith in Christ is represented as essential to spiritual life."[7] Fuller contended for the necessity of a Christ-centered approach to the Scripture:

> It is on this ground that error concerning the person and work of Christ is of such importance as frequently to become death to the party. We may err on other subjects and survive, though it be in a maimed state; but to err in this is to contract a disease in the vitals, the ordinary effect of which is death. When Peter confessed him to be the Son of the living God, Jesus answered, "Upon this rock will I build my church, and the gates of hell shall not prevail against it." Upon this principle, as a foundation, Christianity rests; and it is remarkable that, to this day, deviation concerning the person and work of Christ is followed by a dereliction of almost every other evangelical doctrine, and of the spirit of Christianity. How should it be otherwise? If the foundation be removed, the building must fall.[8]

The truth as it is in Jesus was Fuller's commitment in life and ministry. In expounding this theme, he echoed the apostle Paul. Contrasting the Christian's life with the unbeliever's life in his letter to the Ephesians, Paul adopted schoolroom language, "But that is not the way you learned Christ!" (Eph. 4:20), you "were taught in him, as the truth is in Jesus" (Eph. 4:21). In other words, the foundational content of the teaching is Christ, and all other truths are rightly understood only when their meaning and application is mediated

---

[6] Andrew Fuller, "Plan Proposed to Be Pursued," in *FW*, 1:690.
[7] Fuller, "Plan Proposed to Be Pursued," in *FW*, 1:691.
[8] Fuller, "Plan Proposed to Be Pursued," in *FW*, 1:691–692.

through him. Instruction in Christian living begins with Christ, ongoing instruction focuses on Christ, and the end point of the instruction is to learn Christ. Christians are to be pupils of Christ who never graduate. On August 21, 1784, Fuller wrote in his diary, "Oh that I might be led into Divine truth! 'Christ and his cross be all my theme.' I love his name, and wish to make it the centre in which all the lines of my ministry should meet!"[9]

Fuller was gospel-centered and missional well before that verbiage became vogue in evangelicalism. Michael Haykin observes, "Even where the atoning work of Christ is believed and embraced, Fuller was convinced that the failure to be crucicentric will have its baneful effects."[10] For Fuller, understanding the truth as it is in Jesus meant "every disciple of Jesus should consider himself as a missionary."[11] His commitment to this understanding enabled him to challenge biblical-theological, ecclesial, and missiological errors from all directions. In 1780, he covenanted before the Lord, "Thou hast given me a determination to take up no principle at second-hand; but to search for every thing at the pure fountain of thy word."[12] He opposed the errors of his day not as an end, but as a means, to the end of honoring Jesus and summing up all things in Christ (Eph. 1:10).

Fuller's missional Christ-centeredness led him to vigorously rebut both the man-centered Arminian theology and the anti-missions High Calvinism of his day.[13] He also defended the faith against those who denied the essential elements of Christianity including the full deity of Christ, penal substitutionary atonement, the moral inability of man to convert himself (Socinianism), that saving faith reduces to mere intellectual assent (Sandemanianism), and that Christians are under no obligation to obey the laws of ethics and morality (Antinomianism). It is worth noting that each of these theological errors have contemporary heirs.

According to Fuller, the truth as it is in Jesus is how the entire Bible should be understood. One must not pit the words of Christ against other parts of the Bible; doing so would constitute a rejection of the authority of Jesus who

---

[9] Andrew Gunton Fuller, "Memoir of Mr. Fuller," in *FW*, 1:42.

[10] Michael A.G. Haykin, ed. *The Armies of the Lamb: The Spirituality of Andrew Fuller*, PRS (Dundas, ON: Joshua Press, 2001), 39.

[11] Andrew Fuller, "Conformity to the Death of Christ," in *FW*, 1:315.

[12] Fuller, "Memoir," in *FW*, 1:20.

[13] Andrew Fuller, "Calvinism," in *FW*, 2:711. Fuller argued that what the false Calvinists called Calvinism was not Calvinism. As for Calvin, Fuller wrote, "I never met with a single passage in the writings of Calvin on this subject that clashed with my own views."

taught "Scripture cannot be broken" (John 10:35). Fuller explained, "Every Divine truth bears a relation to him: hence the doctrine of the gospel is called 'the truth as it is in Jesus.' In the face of Jesus Christ we see the glory of the Divine character in such a manner as we see it nowhere else."[14] This truth is foundational to every aspect of Fuller's biblical-theological vision and ministry practice.[15]

Preaching Christ

Historian Peter J. Morden described Andrew Fuller's seminal book, *The Gospel Worthy of All Acceptation* (1785), as the "theological motor" of the Baptist Missionary Society (1792), which launched the modern missionary movement.[16] It seems that Fuller's plea in *The Gospel Worthy* was the theological center of his life and ministry, especially his pulpit ministry. His convictions expressed in *The Gospel Worthy* were a rejection of his formative church influences:

> My father and mother were Dissenters, of the Calvinistic persuasion, and were in the habit of hearing Mr. Eve, a Baptist minister, who being what is here termed *high* in his sentiments, or tinged with false Calvinism, had little or nothing to say to the unconverted. I therefore never considered myself as any way concerned in what I heard from the pulpit.[17]

Fuller had heard sermons that explained the sovereignty of God in a way that minimized human responsibility, teaching that human depravity was so complete that no one had a duty to believe in Christ. There could be no sincere,

---

[14] Andrew Fuller, "The Uniform Bearing of the Scriptures on the Person and Work of Christ," in *FW*, 1:704.

[15] Here are some places the Fuller uses the phrase "the truth as it is in Jesus" in relation to a variety of disciplines: Preaching ("The Christian Ministry a Great Work," in *FW*, 1:515; "Faith in the Gospel a Necessary Prerequisite to Preaching It," in *FW*, 1:516); doctrine ("Ministers and Churches Exhorted to Serve One Another in Love," in *FW*, 1:544; "An Essay on Truth," in *FW*, 3:525–526); apologetics ("The Gospel Worthy of All Acceptation," in *FW*, 2:354; "An Essay on Truth," in *FW*, 3:537; "Remarks on Two Sermons by W.W. Horne of Yarmouth," in *FW*, 3:583; "The Gospel Its Own Witness," in *FW*, 2:8); Christian living ("Letter XIII," in *FW*, 2:560; "Strictures on Sandemanianism," in *FW*, 2:587; "On Antinomianism," in *FW*, 2:741; "Memoir of Mr. Fuller," in *FW*, 1:19); missions ("An Apology for Christian Missions," in *FW*, 2:826–827; "On Antinomianism," in *FW*, 2:741).

[16] Peter J. Morden, "Andrew Fuller and The Gospel Worthy of All Acceptation," in *Pulpit and People: Studies in Eighteenth-Century Baptist Life and Thought*, SBHT (Eugene, OR: Wipf and Stock Publishers, 2009), 129.

[17] Fuller, "Memoir," in *FW*, 1:2.

Andrew Fuller

free offer of the gospel to sinners because only the elect were destined for grace. Thus, the focus in preaching was directed toward individual introspection to determine if one was elect rather than promiscuous gospel proclamation. Fuller explained his thinking at the time: "I was not then aware that *any* poor sinner had a warrant to believe in Christ for the salvation of his soul; but supposed there must be some kind of qualification to entitle him to do it; yet I was aware that I had no qualifications."[18] Nevertheless, as he fixated more on Christ, he noted, "My mind was more and more fixed on him, my guilt and fears were gradually and insensibly removed."[19] He further explained, "I now found a rest for my troubled soul, and I reckon that I should've found it sooner, if I had not entertained the notion of my having no warrant to come to Christ, without some previous qualification. This notion was a bar that kept me back for a time, though, through divine drawings, I was enabled to overleap it."[20]

Describing the joy of his conversion, Fuller wrote, "But, having found rest for my soul in the cross of Christ, I was now conscious of my being the subject of repentance, faith, and love."[21] Andrew Fuller was baptized by pastor Eve on April 1770, becoming a member of the church in Soham. By 1775, Fuller became the pastor of the Soham church and the church joined the Northamptonshire Association of Particular Baptist churches. During his pastorate Fuller slowly began to publically move away from false Calvinism and to make direct gospel appeals to the unconverted. He wrote, "But as I perceived this reasoning would affect the whole tenor of my preaching, I moved on with slow and trembling steps; and, having to feel my way out of a labyrinth, I was a long time ere I felt satisfied."[22]

In 1782, Fuller became the pastor of the Baptist church at Kettering. He continued as the pastor until his death in 1815. Tracing Fuller's spiritual biography is necessary to understand his uncompromising commitment to preach Christ in every sermon and to call all sinners, in all places, to faith and repentance. In assuming his duties at the church in Kettering, Fuller provided a personal statement of his principles, including his conviction to preach Christ:

---

[18] John Webster Morris, *Memoirs of the Life and Writings of the Rev. Andrew Fuller* (Boston: Lincoln and Edmands, 1830), 19–20.

[19] Morris, *Memoirs*, 19–20.

[20] Morris, *Memoirs*, 19–20.

[21] John Ryland, *The Work of Faith, the Labor of Love, and the Patience of Hope Illustrated in the Life and Death of the Rev. Andrew Fuller* (London: Button and Son, 1818), 19–20.

[22] Fuller, "Memoir," in *FW*, 1:13.

I believe, it is the duty of every minister of Christ plainly and faithfully to preach the gospel to all who will hear it; and, as I believe the inability of men to spiritual things to be wholly of the *moral*, and, therefore, of the *criminal* kind,—and that it is their duty to love the Lord Jesus Christ, and trust him for salvation, though they do not; I, therefore, believe free and solemn addresses, invitations, calls, and warnings to them, to be not only *consistent*, but directly *adapted*, as means, in the hand of the Spirit of God, to bring them to Christ. I consider it as a part of my duty, which I could not omit without being guilty of the blood of souls.[23]

In *The Gospel Worthy*, Fuller explained, "The proper object of saving faith is not our being interested in Christ, but the glorious gospel of the ever-blessed God, (which is true, whether we believe it or not,) a contrary inference must be drawn; for it is admitted, on all hands, that it is the duty of every man to believe what God reveals."[24] Fuller continued, "The gospel is a *feast freely provided*, and sinners of mankind are *freely invited* to partake of it."[25] His commitment to the truth as it is in Jesus birthed Fuller's conviction to preach Christ in every sermon: "Let Christ be not only the theme of my remaining ministry, but the exaltation of him and the enlargement of his kingdom the great end of my life! If I forget Thee, O my Saviour, let my right hand forget; if I do not remember Thee, let my tongue cleave to the roof my mouth!"[26]

He argued that a sermon in which the cross of Christ does not have a prominent place "cannot be *a gospel sermon*. It may be ingenious, it may be eloquent; but a want of the doctrine of the cross is a defect which no pulpit excellence can supply."[27] But Fuller was not content to preach Christ in every sermon himself; he also believed that he had a responsibility to define and promote Christ-centered preaching to all within his sphere of influence. Fuller taught, "Preach Christ, or you had better be anything than a preacher."[28]

Preparing Sermons to Preach Christ

Andrew Fuller was foremost a pastor and a preacher. His activities as a theologian, apologist, itinerant evangelist, missions advocate, and administrator were all derivative of his primary calling as a shepherd of a local church.

---

[23] Fuller, "Memoir," in *FW*, 1:68.
[24] Fuller, "The Gospel Worthy of All Acceptation," in *FW*, 2:333.
[25] Fuller, "The Gospel Worthy of All Acceptation," in *FW*, 2:338.
[26] Fuller, "Preaching Christ," in *FW*, 1:504.
[27] Andrew Fuller, "Sermons—Subject-matter of Them," in *FW*, 1:716.
[28] Fuller, "Preaching Christ," in *FW*, 1:503.

Regarding Andrew Fuller's pastoral ministry, Keith S. Grant rightly contends, "Evangelical renewal did not take place *alongside* the local church, but especially in congregational ecclesiology, there was a transformation *within* the existing pastoral office, as it became in the words of a Kettering deacon and diarist, 'very affecting and evangelical.'"[29] Fuller exhorted, "The true churches of Jesus Christ travail in birth for the salvation of men. They are the armies of the Lamb, the grand object of whose existence is to extend the Redeemer's kingdom."[30]

Passionate Sermons that Equip the Army of the Lamb for Spiritual Battle
Fuller was convinced preaching was an act of spiritual war, and consequently he was deeply concerned with the process of preparing sermons. To young ministers, Fuller said, "It is a work *to which you may expect great opposition.—* Satan will dispute every inch of ground with you, and his opposition will be varied."[31] He believed the gospel mission of the church mandated willing sacrifice and suffering. He wrote, "The very existence of Christian churches is in subserviency to the preaching of the gospel."[32] Suggesting the early church as a model, Fuller wrote, "They spoke the truth; but it was in love: they observed discipline; but, like an army of chosen men, it was that they might attack the kingdom of Satan to greater advantage."[33]

Fuller believed a pastor's preaching should clearly demonstrate his awareness that eternity hangs in the balance. In his diary on February 5, 1781, Fuller expressed his understanding of the weight of the preaching task, "A pulpit seems an awful place!—An opportunity for addressing a company of immortals on their eternal interests—Oh how important! We preach for eternity."[34]

In an ordination charge Fuller exhorted, "You may preach even the gospel dryly. It must be preached faithfully, firmly, earnestly, affectionately. The apostle *so* spoke that many believed. Manner is a means of conveying truth. A

---

[29] Keith S. Grant, *Andrew Fuller and the Evangelical Renewal of Pastoral Theology*, SEHT (Milton Keynes, UK: Paternoster, 2013), 2–3.

[30] Andrew Fuller, "The Promise of the Spirit the Grand Encouragement in Promoting the Gospel," in *FW*, 3:359.

[31] Andrew Fuller, "The Christian Ministry a Great Work," in *FW*, 1:514.

[32] Andrew Fuller, "The Pastor's Address to His Christian Hearers, Entreating Their Assistance in Promoting the Interest of Christ," in *FW*, 3:345.

[33] Fuller, "The Pastor's Address to His Christian Hearers," in *FW*, 3:346.

[34] Fuller, "Memoirs," in *FW*, 1:25.

cold manner disgraces important truth."[35] Fuller warned about the danger of preaching an "unfelt gospel":[36]

> When we are thinking or preaching, we need to *burn*, as well as shine. When we study, we may rack our brains, and form plans; but unless "our hearts burn within us," all will be mere skeleton—our thoughts mere bones; whatever be their number, they will all be dry—very dry; and if we do not feel what we say, our preaching will be poor dead work. Affected zeal will not do. A gilded fire may shine, but it will not warm. We may smite with the hand, and stamp with the foot, and throw ourselves into violent agitations; but if we feel not, it is not likely the people will—unless, indeed, it be a feeling of disgust.[37]

Contemporary preachers would do well to envision the preaching task as stepping to the center of a spiritual war and passionately preaching a felt gospel.

Expository Preaching and Biblical Theology
Fuller was committed to practical, expository preaching that was rooted in Christ-centered biblical theology. Biographer J.W. Morris says of Fuller's commitment to systematic biblical exposition, "Had his life been continued, he would, in all probability, have completed his exposition of the sacred volume."[38] And Fuller's own counsel reflects this concern: "I would advise that one service of every Sabbath consist of a well-digested exposition, that your hearers may become Bible Christians. Be concerned to understand and to teach the doctrine of Christianity—'the truth as it is in Jesus.'"[39]

After preaching for twenty-two years at the Baptist Church in Kettering, Fuller wrote in the dedicatory preface to his *Expository Discourses on the Book of Genesis* "I acknowledge that, as I have proceeded, the work of exposition has become more and more interesting to my heart."[40] He explained the benefit to both the preacher and the congregation of a steady diet of expository sermons:

---

[35] Andrew Fuller, "Affectionate Concern of a Minister for the Salvation of His Hearers," in *FW*, 1:510.
[36] Andrew Fuller, "Ministers Should Be Concerned Not to Be Despised," in *FW*, 1:489.
[37] Andrew Fuller, "Knowledge and Love Essential to the Ministry," in *FW*, 1:480.
[38] Morris, *Memoirs of the Life and Writings of the Rev. Andrew Fuller*, 72.
[39] Andrew Fuller, "Ministers and Churches Exhorted to Serve One Another in Love," in *FW*, 1:544.
[40] Andrew Fuller, "Expository Discourses on the Book of Genesis," in *FW*, 3:1.

> I have found it not a little useful, both to myself and to the people, to appropriate one part of every Lord's day to the *exposition* of a chapter, or part of a chapter, in the sacred writings. In this way, during the last eighteen years, I have gone over the greater part of the Old Testament, and some books in the New. It is advantageous to a minister to feel himself necessitated, as it were, to understand every part of Scripture, in order to explain it to the people. It is also advantageous to a people that what they hear should come directly from the word of God, and that they should be led to see the scope and connexion of the sacred writers.[41]

As to his method, Fuller was committed to understanding each passage of Scripture in its immediate context and also within the larger canonical context. According to Fuller, "The great thing necessary for expounding the Scriptures is *to enter into their true meaning*."[42] He often used the language "true meaning" or "true system" to signify his belief that no particular text or truth is rightly understood when it is abstracted from the Christ-centered, biblical storyline; to do so would inevitably lead to a false meaning. He warned,

> I shall attempt to show the importance of a *true* system; and to prove that truth itself, by being displaced from those connexions which it occupies in the Scriptures, may be perverted, and prove injurious to those that hold it. No system can be supposed to be *wholly* erroneous; but if a considerable part of it be false, the whole will be vitiated, and that which is true will be divested of its salutary influence.[43]

Fuller continued in his letter "The Importance of a True System" to argue that when true ideas are incorporated into a false system, the result is delusion. No particular scriptural truth is meant to be understood apart from its larger scriptural connections. He illustrated this point with reference to Israel:

> The Jews, in the time of our Saviour, professed the same creed, in the main, as their forefathers; they reckoned themselves to believe Moses; but, holding with Moses to the exclusion of Christ, their faith was rendered void. "If ye believed Moses," said our Lord, "ye would believe me; for he wrote of me." Thus it is with us: if we hold the law of Moses to the exclusion of Christ, or any otherwise than as subservient to the

---

[41] Andrew Fuller, "Expounding the Scriptures," in *FW*, 1:712.
[42] Fuller, "Expounding the Scriptures," in *FW*, 1:712.
[43] Andrew Fuller, "The Importance of a True System," in *FW*, 1:685.

gospel, or Christ and the gospel to the exclusion of the law of Moses, neither the one nor the other will profit us.[44]

Fuller was critical of any approach to expository preaching that ignores the larger biblical scope, connections, and canonical meaning of the text, in favor of myopic textual concerns or proof-texting. Fuller explained, "The scope of the sacred writers is of greater importance in understanding the Scriptures than the most critical examination of terms, or the most laborious comparison of the use of them in different places."[45]

According to Fuller, expositors need to be so familiar with the biblical testimony in the pursuit of "the true meaning of the Scriptures" that they "drink into the spirit of the writers." He was not suggesting a mystical, revelatory inspiration apart from the Scriptures, but rather "a spiritual frame of mind," or "unction from the Holy One," by which "he can understand more of the Scriptures in an hour than he can at other times, with the utmost application, in a week."[46] Fuller's commitment to the absolute sufficiency of Scripture is demonstrated in these words from a letter he wrote to a church member: "We ought not look for any new revelation of the mind of God, but to rest satisfied with what has been revealed already, in his word."[47]

Fuller contended it is only after the preacher becomes personally conversant with a portion of Scripture by prayerfully reading and pondering the text as a Christian, and not simply as a preacher or student, that the he should consult commentaries. He wrote, "But to go first to expositors is to preclude the exercise of your own judgment; and, after all, that which is furnished by the labours of another, though equally good in itself, will be far less interesting to us than that which is the result of our own application."[48]

In "Reading the Scriptures," Fuller explained why the preacher should not turn to commentaries too soon for help in sermon preparation:

> If I read them *instead* of reading the Scriptures, I may indeed derive some knowledge; but my mind will not be stored with the best riches; nor will the word "dwell richly in me in all wisdom and spiritual understanding." If, on the other hand, I read the Scriptures, and exercise my

---

[44] Fuller, "The Importance of a True System," in *FW*, 1:685.
[45] Fuller, "Expounding the Scriptures," in *FW*, 1:713.
[46] Fuller, "Expounding the Scriptures," in *FW*, 1:713.
[47] Fuller, as quoted in Ryland, *The Work of Faith, the Labor of Love and the Patience of Hope*, 376.
[48] Fuller, "Expounding the Scriptures," in *FW*, 1:714.

own mind on their meaning, only using the helps with which I am furnished when I particularly need them, such knowledge will avail me more than any other; for, having felt and laboured at the difficulty myself, what I obtain from others towards the solution of it becomes more interesting and abiding than if I had read it without any such previous efforts. And as to my own thoughts, though they may not be superior nor equal to those of others, in themselves considered, yet, if they be just, their having been the result of pleasing toil renders them of superior value to me. A small portion obtained by our own labour is sweeter than a large inheritance bequeathed by our predecessors. Knowledge thus obtained will not only be always accumulating, but of special use in times of trial; not like the cumbrous armour which does not fit us, but like the sling and the stone, which, though less brilliant, will be more efficacious.[49]

In approaching the Scriptures, Fuller contended that God did not reveal himself to us in an abstract and hyper-systematized fashion, but in the context of particular examples in redemptive history. He described biblical truth as being introduced "incidentally." He was not rejecting God's purposeful intention in biblical revelation, but rather was noting that God's revelation of doctrinal truth is embedded in his historical interaction with his image bearers.[50] Thus, as we hear and learn the Bible on its own terms, we gradually gain a better understanding and commitment to biblical doctrine and principles without even recognizing them as such.

Sermon Preparation, Delivery, and Notes

Fuller's advice on preparation for the pulpit combined a commitment to hard, diligent, exegetical work and an utter dependence on the supernatural grace of God. In a letter on sermon preparation, Fuller wrote, "Though we must think for ourselves, we must not depend on ourselves, but, as little children, learn at the feet of the Saviour."[51] Fuller warned about using divine favor as an excuse for inadequate preparation: "It is a shameful abuse of the doctrine of Divine influence to allege it as a reason for neglecting diligent study for the pulpit."[52] In Fuller's biography of Samuel Pearce, he included a letter from Pearce to a

---

[49] Andrew Fuller, "Reading the Scriptures," in *FW*, 3:788–789.
[50] Andrew Fuller, "Thoughts on the Manner Which Divine Truth Is Communicated in the Holy Scriptures," in *FW*, 3:537.
[51] Fuller, "Sermons—Subject-matter of Them," in *FW*, 1:714.
[52] Andrew Fuller, "Habitual Devotedness to the Ministry," in *FW*, 1:506.

young minister that explained well Fuller's approach to sermon preparation: "I would [prepare] as though I expected no help from the Lord, whilst I would depend upon the Lord for assistance as though I had never made any preparation at all."[53]

Elsewhere, Fuller asserted bluntly, "To preach the gospel as we ought to preach it requires, not the subtilty of the metaphysician, but the simplicity of the Christian."[54] And he explained his commitment to urgently prepare and deliver gospel sermons with eternity in view:

> It is possible there may be in the audience a poor miserable creature, labouring under the load of a guilty conscience. If he depart without being told how to obtain rest for his soul, what may be the consequence? ... Possibly some one of my constant hearers may die in the following week; and is there nothing I should wish to say to him before his departure? It may be that I myself may die before another Lord's day: this may be the last time that I shall ascend the pulpit; and have I no important testimony to leave with the people of my care?[55]

Biographer J.W. Morris explained of Fuller, "He was all intent on searching out its riches, sounding its depth, comparing it with the analogy of faith, pointing out its application, and deducing consequences, seldom obvious to the hearer, but meeting his judgment in all their force, and carrying conviction to the heart."[56]

Fuller also believed that the preparation to preach effectively included a study of the people to whom you preach. According to Fuller, the preacher must be aware of the way his listeners viewed the world and the ways in which they struggle so he might effectively press and apply the gospel at their point of greatest need. Frustrated with his own failings in this area Fuller confessed in his diary on July 29, 1780,

> Surely I do not study the cases of the people enough in my preaching. I find by conversation today, with one seemingly in dying circumstances, that but little of my preaching has been suited to her case. Visiting the sick, and conversing sometimes even with the unconverted part of my

---

[53] Samuel Pearce as quoted in Fuller, "To a Young Minister, Mr. Cave, of Leicester, on Preparation for the Pulpit," in *FW*, 3:442.

[54] Andrew Fuller, "The Nature of the Gospel, and the Manner in Which It Ought to be Preached," in *FW*, 1:496.

[55] Andrew Fuller, "Letter II - The Composition of a Sermon," in *FW*, 1:715-716.

[56] Morris, *Memoirs*, 72.

hearers about their souls, and especially with the godly, would have a tendency to make my preaching more experimental."[57]

He urged the preacher not to think of himself as a formally trained and polished orator performing for his listeners, but rather as a "herald, *whose object is to publish, or proclaim good tidings.*"[58] His preaching style was direct, simple, and urgent. Biographer J.W. Morris explained of Fuller's sermon delivery, "His presence in the pulpit was imposing, grave, and manly; tending to inspire awe, rather than conciliate esteem."[59] Morris also asserted that Fuller "was not the model of an orator," which is interesting in light of the fact Fuller directly stated, "In preaching the gospel, we must not imitate the orator whose attention is taken up with his performance, but rather the herald."[60] Fuller also said in an ordination sermon, "I abhor the spirit that shall send for an orator, merely for the purpose of gathering a respectable congregation."[61]

He was committed to sermonic plainness of speech: "There are many sermons that cannot fairly be charged with untruth, which yet have a tendency to lead off the mind from the simplicity of the gospel."[62] Fuller noted, "Illiterate hearers may be very poor *judges* of preaching; yet the effect which it produces upon them is the best criterion of its real excellence."[63] He was committed to preparing sermons with orality in mind because the sermon is what is said and not what is written down by the preacher.

Below is a list where I have enumerated some of Fuller's advice on sermon notes and delivery from "Letter IV, The Composition of a Sermon":

1. "Do not overload your memory with words."
2. "Write down a few leading things for the sake of arrangement and assistance of memory; but not a great deal. Memory must not be

---

[57] By "experimental preaching," Fuller means preaching that is direct and applicable in ways that penetrate the affections of the heart. See Fuller, "Memoirs," in *FW*, 1:23.

[58] Fuller, "Sermons—Subject-matter of Them," in *FW*, 1:717.

[59] Morris, *Memoirs*, 68–69.

[60] Fuller, "Sermons—Subject-matter of Them," in *FW*, 1:716.

[61] Fuller, "The Work and Encouragements of a Christian Minister," in *FW*, 1:499. Fuller's writings were in concert with the words of his friend Samuel Pearce who urged a young minister, "Divest yourself of all fear. If you should break the rules of grammar, or put in or leave out a word, and recollect at the end of the sentence the impropriety, unless it makes nonsense, or bad divinity, never try to mend it, but let it pass." Samuel Pearce as quoted in Fuller, "To a Young Minister, Mr. Cave," in *FW*, 3:443.

[62] Andrew Fuller, "The Qualifications and Encouragement of a Faithful Minister Illustrated by the Character and Success of Barnabas," in *FW*, 1:140.

[63] Fuller, "Letter III - The Composition of a Sermon," in *FW*, 1:717.

overburdened."

3. "Never carry what you write into the pulpit."
4. "Avoid vulgar expressions: do not affect finical ones, nor words out of common use."
5. "As to division and arrangement, it barely respects the assortment of your materials. You must endeavor to understand and feel your subject, or the manner in which you divide it will signify but little."
6. "But if both these may be taken for granted, then I should say much depends, as to your being heard with pleasure and profit, on a proper discussion and management of the subject. At all events avoid a multiplying of *heads* and particulars. A few well-chosen thoughts, matured, proved, and improved, are abundantly more acceptable than when the whole is chopped, as it were, into mince-meat."[64]

Fuller urged that after the preacher had recruited his leading truths and thoughts from his study of the text, he must then "*arrange* them in order, or to give each thought that place in your discourse which it will occupy to the greatest advantage."[65] He believed sermons must be marked by a unity of design:

Many sermons are a *mob* of ideas; they contain very good sentiments, but they have no object in view; so that the hearer is continually answering the preacher, Very true, very true; but what then? What is it you are aiming at? What is this to the purpose? A preacher, then, if he would interest a judicious hearer, must have an object at which he aims, and must never lose sight of it throughout his discourse. This is what writers on these subjects call *a unity of design*; and this is a matter of far greater importance than studying well-turned periods, or forming pretty expressions.[66]

Below I enumerate Fuller's reasons for advocating that sermons have a clear unity of design and connectedness:

1. "The human mind is so formed as to delight in unity."[67]
2. "It has been said, and I think justly, that *evidence* should constitute the body or substance of every doctrinal discourse."[68]

---

[64] Fuller, "Letter IV – The Composition of a Sermon," in *FW*, 1:724.
[65] Fuller, "Letter III – The Composition of a Sermon," in *FW*, 1:719.
[66] Fuller, "Letter III – The Composition of a Sermon," in *FW*, 1:719.
[67] Fuller, "Letter III – The Composition of a Sermon," in *FW*, 1:719.
[68] Fuller, "Letter III – The Composition of a Sermon," in *FW*, 1:720.

3. "It is greatly assisting to *memory*, both with respect to the preacher and the hearer. Memory is exercised by the *relation* of one thing to another."[69]
4. "I cannot so well satisfy my *conscience* unless I have some interesting truth to communicate, or some important duty to enforce."[70]

Fuller illustrated the power of sermonic unity of design with a helpful and vivid illustration:

> Were you to attempt to remember seven different objects which bore no manner of relation to each other, such as *water, time, wisdom, fruit, contentment, fowls*, and *revenues*, you would find it almost impossible; but take seven objects which, though different in nature, yet possess some point of unity, which associates them in the mind, and the work is easy. Thus, *sun, moon, stars, earth, air, fire*, and *water*, are readily remembered, being so many principal parts of the *one creation*.[71]

For Fuller, unity of design is essential in sermons because faithful sermons are always on a gospel errand to which the preacher is calling all of his listeners to respond. The purpose of the sermon is never merely to inform, but to cultivate gospel transformation. Fuller was committed to being a persistent, courageous gospel agitator in the pulpit and he encouraged this kind of dangerous heart-preaching in other ministers as well:

> You must not calculate consequences as they respect this life. If you would preach the gospel as you ought to preach it, the approbation of *God* must be your main object. What if you *were* to lose your friends and diminish your income; nay, what if you lose your liberty, or even your life—what would this all be, compared with the loss of the favour and friendship of *God?* Woe unto us, if we shun to declare any part of the counsel of God! He that is afraid or ashamed to preach the whole of the gospel, in all its implications and bearings, let him stand aside; he is utterly unworthy of being a soldier of Jesus Christ.[72]

---

[69] Fuller, "Letter III – The Composition of a Sermon," in *FW*, 1:720.
[70] Fuller, "Letter III – The Composition of a Sermon," in *FW*, 1:720.
[71] Fuller, "Letter III – The Composition of a Sermon," in *FW*, 1:720.
[72] Fuller, "The Nature of the Gospel," in *WF*, 1:495.

Fuller believed that "there are two main objects to be attained in the work of the Christian ministry—*enlightening the minds* and *affecting the hearts* of the people."[73] He understood that the heart and the mind are inseparable, constituent parts of a life surrendered to the glory of God in Christ. For Fuller, the goal of preaching is to affect the whole person, producing godly affection and spiritual knowledge. Mere assent to a fact as true can only produce an opinion or theory, only a sense perception of a truth can produce true knowledge and virtue.[74]

The preacher must not preach an unfelt gospel. He must not be satisfied with his listeners assenting to an unfelt gospel. In an ordination sermon, Fuller charged the pastor regarding his congregation, "You could never expect to do them good, unless you were interested in their affections."[75] Unapologetically, Fuller preached to move the feelings and affections of his hearers, but he was burdened to do so with gospel truth, and not apart from it. The goal of preaching was not moralism or emotionalism but true virtue, the obedience of faith motivated by the gospel—clear and felt.[76]

Conclusion

Andrew Fuller's combination of a keen mind, love for the church, pastoral heart, global gospel-burden, clarity of insight, gospel-centered practicality, intensity of affections, power of expression, and commitment to spiritual friendships, were all rooted in his commitment to pursuing the truth as it is in Jesus. His ministry practice and vision has captivated my mind, stirred my affections, and spurred me on in gospel ministry. I thank God for Andrew Fuller and for leading me to his writings. He has become a vital and constant conversation partner for me in life and ministry and I have written in hopes that he will become one to you as well.

---

[73] Andrew Fuller, "Spiritual Knowledge and Love Necessary for the Ministry," in *FW*, 1:479.

[74] Andrew Fuller, "The Connexion between Knowledge and Disposition," in *FW*, 2:603-604. See Chris Chun, *The Legacy of Jonathan Edwards in the Theology of Andrew Fuller*, SHT (Leiden: Brill, 2012) for an excellent treatment on Andrew Fuller's theological indebtedness to Jonathan Edwards.

[75] Fuller, "The Work and Encouragements of the Christian Minister," in *FW*, 1:497.

[76] Fuller, "The Gospel Worthy of All Acceptation," in *FW*, 2:390-391. Fuller approvingly quotes John Owen, "It is the duty of ministers to plead with men about their sins; but always remember that it be done with that which is the proper end of law and gospel; that is, that they make use of the sin they speak against to the discovery of the *state* and *condition* wherein the sinner is, otherwise, haply, they may work men to formality and hypocrisy, but little of the true end of preaching the gospel will be brought about.

Since Fuller believed that the person and work of Christ was the central thread that runs throughout Scripture and gives life to all other facts, truths, and redemptive history, his teachings do not have an expiration date. Since Fuller never bypassed Christ and the church when addressing any subject, the working pastor-theologian has in his writings a gospel goldmine to be scoured for the sake of practical ministry. Fuller reminds us that all ministry (in every generation) is a pursuit of the truth as it is in Jesus. He also reminds us that the truth as it is in Jesus calls us to preach Christ to all people, in all places, to the ends of the earth. Finally, Fuller offers the contemporary preacher a wealth of wisdom in preparing sermons that effectively preach Christ. May we follow in the footsteps of the elephant of Kettering as we lead armies of the Lamb toward the truth as it is in Jesus.

8
C. H. Spurgeon: A Fullerite?[1]

Steve Weaver

Andrew Gunton Fuller (1799–1884), the son of the Andrew Fuller (1754–1815), lived to the age of eighty-five. In 1831, he gathered together his father's writings and published them in five volumes. This set was later revised by Joseph Belcher and published in three volumes by the American Baptist Publication Society in 1845. Both these sets included a biographical memoir of Fuller by A.G. Fuller. In 1882, near the end of his own life, he published a biography of his father in the "Men Worth Remembering" series published by Hodder & Stoughton.[2] He apparently sent a copy to the most famous Baptist English preacher of the latter half of the nineteenth century, Charles Haddon Spurgeon (1834–1892). Spurgeon responded with a "thank you letter" that survives.[3] It is an important piece as it reveals how highly Spurgeon regarded Andrew Fuller as a theologian.

> Venerable Friend,
> I thank you for sending me your *Andrew Fuller*. If you had lived for a long time for nothing else but to produce this volume, you have lived to good purpose.
> I have long considered your father to be the greatest theologian of the century, and I do not know that your pages have made me think more highly of him as a *divine* than I had thought before. But I now see him within doors far more accurately, and see about the Christian man a soft radiance of tender love which had never been revealed to me either by former biographies or by his writings.

---

[1] An earlier version of this essay appeared as "C.H. Spurgeon—A Fullerite?" in *The Journal of Baptist Studies* 8 (2016): 99–117. It is reprinted here with permission of the journal.

[2] Andrew Gunton Fuller, *Andrew Fuller*. Men Worth Remembering (London: Hodder and Stoughton, 1882).

[3] It was used in advertisements for the Fuller volume in subsequent publications by Hodder and Stoughton. See William Mackergo Taylor, *John Knox* (London: Hodder and Stoughton, 1884), 215.

You have added moss to the rose, and removed some of the thorns in the process.

Yours most respectfully,
C.H. Spurgeon[4]

Even if this letter had not survived, there would still be ample evidence to demonstrate Spurgeon's appreciation for Fuller. The purpose of this chapter is to explore this evidence and to demonstrate that Spurgeon not only read and appreciated Fuller throughout his ministry, but also consciously identified himself as a Fullerite. The chapter will have three sections. In the first section, Spurgeon's use of anecdotes from Fuller's life in his preaching and teaching will be catalogued. In the second section, Spurgeon's knowledge of the writings of Fuller will be demonstrated. In the third section, the question of whether Spurgeon identified himself as a Fullerite will be explored.

Spurgeon's Use of Fuller Anecdotes

Spurgeon clearly admired Fuller and read books both by and about him. From time to time in his sermons, Spurgeon alludes to an incident from Fuller's life as an illustration of some biblical truth. In what follows, I have provided some examples for how Spurgeon used Fuller anecdotally in his preaching, teaching, and writing ministries.

On July 19, 1863, Spurgeon was preaching from Romans 10:10 on "Confession with the Mouth" at the Metropolitan Tabernacle in London. During the sermon he reflected on his previous day's reading of "the life of good Andrew Fuller."

> I was noting when reading yesterday the life of good Andrew Fuller, after he had been baptized, some of the young men in the village were wont to mock him, asking him how he liked being dipped? and such like questions which are common enough now-a-days. I could but notice that the scoff of a hundred years ago is just the scoff of to-day.[5]

---

[4] Cited in Gilbert Laws, *Andrew Fuller: Pastor, Theologian, Ropeholder* (London: The Carey Press, 1942), 127.

[5] C.H. Spurgeon, *The Metropolitan Tabernacle Pulpit Sermons*, vol. 9 (London: Passmore & Alabaster, 1863), 401. Hereafter, *MTPS*. Spurgeon described this reading in almost identical words in his autobiography: "I was noting, when reading the life of good Andrew Fuller, that, after he had been baptized, some of the young men in the village were wont to mock him, asking him how he liked being dipped, and such like questions which are common enough nowadays. I could but

This is likely a reference to Fuller's account in the memoir of his early life compiled from two series of letters written to friends. This memoir formed the basis of the nineteenth-century biographies of Fuller by his son Andrew Gunton Fuller, John Morris, and John Ryland, Jr. Fuller had written,

> Within a day or two after I had been baptized, as I was riding through the fields, I met a company of young men. One of them especially, on my having passed them, called after me in very abusive language, and cursed me for having been "dipped." My heart instantly rose in a way of resentment; but though the fire burned, I held my peace; for before I uttered a word I was checked with this passage, which occurred to my mind, "In the world ye *shall* have tribulation." I wept, and entreated the Lord to pardon me; feeling quite willing to bear the ridicule of the wicked, and to go even through great tribulation, if at last I might but enter the kingdom.[6]

Spurgeon's familiarity with the life of Fuller and the popular stories about him that were circulating in the nineteenth century served him well for illustration purposes throughout his ministry.

Another example of Spurgeon's use of Fuller comes in a December 29, 1867, sermon preached at the Metropolitan Tabernacle from Psalm 136 titled "A Song, A Solace, A Sermon, and A Summons." Near the end of the sermon, Spurgeon referred to an occasion when Fuller preached in Scotland from a text very dear to Spurgeon's heart—Isaiah 45:22 "Look unto me, and be ye saved, all the ends of the earth."[7]

> When that man of God, Mr. Andrew Fuller, was once preaching in Scotland, the place was very crowded, and numbers were outside. A woman, the worst woman in the town, seeing the crowd, thought she would push into the Kirk to listen to the English minister. He was preaching from the text, "Look unto me, and be ye saved, all the ends of the earth." "Ah," said she, "I have gone far, but I have not gone over the ends of the earth, at any rate, and if God says, 'Look, and be saved, all the ends

---

notice that the scoff of a hundred years ago is just the scoff of to-day." Spurgeon, *The Autobiography of Charles H. Spurgeon*, vol. 1 (Nashville: M.E. Church South, 1900), 1:149-150.

[6] Andrew Gunton Fuller, "Memoir," in *FW*, 1:7. This was originally from a letter written by Fuller to a friend in Liverpool in January, 1815. See Michael A.G. Haykin, *The Armies of the Lamb: The Spirituality of Andrew Fuller*, PRS (Dundas, ON: Joshua Press, 2001), 77-78.

[7] This is the text from which the layman was preaching when Spurgeon was converted on January 6, 1850. For Spurgeon's own account of this, see Spurgeon, *Autobiography*, 1:105-108.

of the earth,' he must mean me." She did look, and became afterwards an honourable woman in that parish, converted by the grace of God.[8]

Another illustration from the life of Fuller comes in a June 6, 1869, sermon titled "The Overflowing Cup." In this message from Psalm 23:5, Spurgeon warned of the danger of allowing the goods of the world to become idols of the heart. He told of Andrew Fuller going to a gold bullion merchant's shop and having been shown a mass of gold, took it in his hand and said, "How much better it is to hold it in your hand than to have it in your heart!" Spurgeon commented, "Goods in the hand will not hurt you, but the goods in the heart will destroy you."[9]

Spurgeon used another illustration from Fuller's life in a May 14, 1885, sermon delivered on a Thursday evening at the Metropolitan Tabernacle on behalf of the British and Foreign Bible Society. Spurgeon expressed his admiration of the ingenuity of Fuller and friends in creatively finding ways to spread the gospel.

> I admire the enterprise of Andrew Fuller, and some others long ago, who printed hymns upon papers which were to be used in the sale of cottons and other small wares. They gave those papers to tradesmen that they might do their goods up in them. So long as the truth does but travel, it does not matter how.[10]

Spurgeon drove home his point with the forceful question: "How is he a Christian who in some shape or other does not spread this matchless Word?"[11]

Spurgeon preached an undated sermon at the Metropolitan Tabernacle titled "Work for Jesus" from Matthew 21:28, "Son, go work to-day in my vineyard." Spurgeon urged that the text said, "Go and Work," not "go and criticize." He then cited an uncomfortable encounter that Fuller had with some Scottish Baptists about the "discipline" (i.e., polity) of the English churches. The Scots had given Fuller severe lecture on the topic, when Fuller replied, "You say that your discipline is so much better than ours. Very well, but discipline is meant to make good soldiers. Now, my soldiers fight better than

---

[8] Spurgeon, *MTPS*, 13:719.
[9] Spurgeon, *MTPS*, 15:318.
[10] Spurgeon, *MTPS*, 58:248. This incident was recorded in the previously mentioned 1882 volume by Andrew Gunton Fuller which Spurgeon had read a few years earlier. Fuller, *Andrew Fuller*, 88.
[11] Spurgeon, *MTPS*, 58:248.

yours, and I think therefore that you ought not to say much about my discipline."[12] Spurgeon concluded in a manner that seems to have been Fuller's inclination as well,

> So the real thing is not to be for ever calculating about modes of church government, and methods of management and plans to be adopted and rules to be laid down, which it shall be accounted a serious breach to violate. All well in their place, for order is good in its way. But come, now, let us go to work. Let us have something done.[13]

In another undated sermon preached at the Metropolitan Tabernacle titled "Christ the Tree of Life" from Revelation 22:2, Spurgeon used an incident in the life of Fuller as an illustration of the nature of saving faith.[14]

> When Mr. Andrew Fuller was going to preach before an Association, he rode to the meeting on his horse. There had been a good deal of rain, and the rivers were very much swollen. He got to one river which he had to cross. He looked at it, and he was half afraid of the strong current, as he did not know the depth. A farmer, who happened to be standing by, said, "It is all right, Mr. Fuller; you will get through it all right, sir; the horse will keep its feet." Mr. Fuller went in, and the water got up to the girth, and then up to the saddle, and he began to get uncomfortably wet. Mr. Fuller thought he had better turn round, and he was going to do so when the same farmer shouted, "Go on, Mr. Fuller; go on; I know it is all right;" and Mr. Fuller said, "Then I will go on; I will go by faith." Now, sinner, it is very like that with you. You think that your sins are so deep that Christ will never be able to carry you over them; but I say to you,—It is all right, sinner; trust Jesus, and he will carry you through hell itself, if that is needful. If you had all the sins of all the men that have ever lived, and they were all yours, if you could trust him, Jesus Christ would carry you through the current of all that sin. It is all right, man! Only trust Christ. The river may be deep, but Christ's love is deeper still. It is all right, man! Do not let the devil make you doubt my Lord and Master. He is a liar from the beginning, and the father of lies, but my Master is faithful and true. Rest on him, and all will be well. The waves may roll, the river may seem to be deeper than you thought it to be,—and rest assured it is much deeper than you know it to be;—but

---

[12] Spurgeon, *MTPS*, 23:89.
[13] Spurgeon, *MTPS*, 23:89–90.
[14] The incident is recorded in a footnote from the editor of Andrew Fuller, "The Nature and Importance of Walking by Faith," in *FW*, 1:117.

Andrew Fuller

the almighty arm of Jesus—that strong arm that can shake the heavens and the earth, and move the pillars thereof as Samson moved the pillars of Gaza's gates,—that strong arm can hold you up, and bear you safely through, if you do but cling to it, and rest on it. O soul, rest in Jesus, and you are saved![15]

According to Joseph Belcher, this incident occurred when Fuller was on his way to preach at Nottingham to the Northamptonshire Association on June 2, 1784. The encounter brought to his mind the text of 2 Corinthians 5:7, "We walk by faith, not by sight." which Fuller then decided to preach at the meeting. Upon the request of the brethren present, it became his first published sermon, "The Nature and Importance of Walking By Faith." This background information was only included in the 1845 American edition, indicating that Spurgeon must have owned this edition.

Spurgeon also used Fuller in his lectures to the students of his Pastors' College. In a lecture titled "Attention!", Spurgeon cited Andrew Fuller on the importance of a preacher keeping the attention of his hearers. He told of a time when Andrew Fuller had just begun his sermon and already the people were going asleep. Fuller reportedly said, "Friends, friends, friends, this won't do. I have thought sometimes when you were asleep that it was my fault, but now you are asleep before I begin, and it must be your fault. Pray wake up and give me an opportunity of doing you some good."[16]

In 1889, Spurgeon published a two-volume collection of proverbs arranged topically, which he titled *The Salt Cellars*.[17] In the second volume, under the heading "Praise little, dispraise less," Spurgeon added the following "homely note" coupled with an anecdote from Fuller's life:

Let your expressions be well weighed, so that value may be attached to them. He who is constantly expressing his hasty opinions will find that little regard is paid to him. Andrew Fuller tells of one, who, being much

---

[15] Spurgeon, *MTPS*, 57:247–248.

[16] C.H. Spurgeon, *Lectures to My Students: A Selection from Addresses Delivered to the Students of the Pastors' College, Metropolitan Tabernacle*, vol. 1 (London: Passmore and Alabaster, 1875), 149. Although it is uncertain where Spurgeon read this, the anecdote had been cited in the July 1853 issue of *The Church*: "Andrew Fuller, one Sunday afternoon, saw the people, during the singing of the hymn before sermon, composing themselves for a comfortable nap; and, taking the Bible, he beat it against the side of the pulpit, making a great noise. Attention being excited, he said, 'I am often afraid that I preach you to sleep; but it can't be my fault to-day, for you are asleep before I have begun.'" *The Church* 7 (July 1853): 188.

[17] C.H. Spurgeon, *The Salt Cellar. Being a Collection of Proverbs, Together with Homely Notes Thereon*, 2 vols. (London: Passmore and Alabaster, 1889).

edified by the discourse of a popular minister, met him at the pulpit stairs with, "I really must not say what I think of your sermon, it might do you harm." "Not at all, my friend," was the rejoinder, "speak out, for I do not attach much importance to your opinion." More frank than flattering.[18]

Spurgeon's use of Fuller was not always positive; he used him as a negative example on at least two occasions—once in a sermon and once in the pages of *The Sword and the Trowel*. In a Thursday evening sermon preached at the Metropolitan Tabernacle on July 5, 1883, Spurgeon admonished his hearers to use a delicate hand when giving necessary rebukes. He cites Fuller as one who did not do this. "It was said of good Andrew Fuller that frequently he gave a rebuke so severely that it reminded you of one who saw a fly upon his brother's forehead and seized a sledge hammer to knock it off."[19] Spurgeon perhaps had in mind the incident to which he had referred in a February 1865 article in *The Sword and the Trowel*. There Spurgeon was similarly urging gentleness to his readers, when he cites almost verbatim a passage from John Morris' memoir of Fuller:

> It is written of Andrew Fuller, that he could rarely be faithful without being severe; and, in giving reproof, he was often betrayed into intemperate zeal. Once, at a meeting of ministers, he took occasion to correct an erroneous opinion delivered by one of his brethren, and he laid on his censure so heavily that Ryland called out vehemently, in his own peculiar tone of voice, "Brother Fuller! brother Fuller! you can never admonish a mistaken friend, but you must take up a sledge hammer and knock his brains out."[20]

Spurgeon's Knowledge of Fuller's Writings

Spurgeon was not merely knowledgeable of the life of Fuller and the various anecdotes that were popularly circulated in his day; he also knew the writings of Fuller. In Spurgeon's library which is preserved in part at Midwestern Baptist Theological Seminary there are only two books authored by Fuller, but we

---

[18] Spurgeon, *Salt Cellar*, 2:101.
[19] Spurgeon, *MTPS*, 29:392. Joseph Belcher provides a couple examples of Fuller's severity in a footnote in Andrew Gunton Fuller, "Memoir," in *FW*, 1:112.
[20] C.H. Spurgeon, *The Sword and Trowel* (London: Passmore & Alabaster, 1865), 42. Cf. John Morris, *Memoirs of the Life and Writings of the Rev. Andrew Fuller, Pastor of the Baptist Church at Kettering, and Secretary to the Baptist Missionary Society* (London: Wightman and Cramp, 1826), 369.

know that Spurgeon likely owned more than these.[21] There is evidence that he was very familiar with Fuller's writings. That evidence will now be explored.

On May 3, 1850, the recently converted fifteen-year-old Charles Haddon Spurgeon was immersed as a believer at the Isleham Ferry on the River Lark. Baptized with Spurgeon that day was Eunice Fuller, a descendant of Andrew Fuller's oldest brother, Robert.[22] The first baptism at this spot had occurred a little more than fifty years before when on September 13, 1798, Andrew Fuller baptized a father and his son and three others.[23] The month before fully identifying with the Baptists through baptism, Spurgeon had read from the Baptist theologian Andrew Fuller. In his diary for April 17, 1850, Spurgeon wrote, "Read some of 'Fuller upon Antinomianism.' My God, what a gulf is near me! I think I can say that I hate this religion [i.e., Antinomianism]; I would desire to love God, and to be as holy as my Father-God Himself."[24] This reading of Fuller would continue throughout the rest of his life.

In 1876, Spurgeon published *Commenting and Commentaries*.[25] In this work, he provided an annotated list of commentaries. Spurgeon's comments are often entertaining in their candor. Fuller's *Expository Discourses* on the books of Genesis and Revelation are included in his list of commentaries. Also included is a commentary on Genesis by George Bush (1796–1859), professor of Hebrew and Oriental Literature at New York University from 1832–1846. Spurgeon strongly denounced the blatant plagiarism he had discovered in Bush's work.

> *Bush* has in the most barefaced manner taken copious verbatim extracts from *Andrew Fuller*, without acknowledgment, and he has also plagiarized *Lawson* on *Joseph* by wholesale, without even mentioning his name. For such a scholar to be guilty of wholesale plunder is inexcusable. It is one of the worst cases of robbery we have ever met with, and

---

[21] The list of items in the Spurgeon Collection at Midwestern Library is currently being revised. The online records are not exhaustive at this point. The two volumes by Fuller which are listed are: Andrew Fuller, *Memoirs of the Rev. Samuel Pearce A.M.* (London: G. Wightman, 1831); and Andrew Fuller, *Strictures on Sandemanianism: in twelve letters to a friend* (Nottingham: C. Sutton, 1810).

[22] Laws, *Andrew Fuller*, 12.

[23] Spurgeon, *Autobiography*, 1:151–152.

[24] Spurgeon, *Autobiography*, 1:131.

[25] C.H. Spurgeon, *Commenting and Commentaries; Lectures Addressed to the Students of the Pastors' College, Metropolitan Tabernacle* (New York: Sheldon & Company, 1876).

deserves a far stronger denunciation than our gentle pen and slender space will permit.[26]

A few entries later, Spurgeon commends Fuller's *Expository Discourses on Genesis* as "Weighty, judicious, and full of Gospel truth. One of the very best series of discourses extant upon Genesis, as Bush also thought."[27] Spurgeon also gave a positive blurb to Fuller's *Expository Discourses on the Apocalypse* with only slightly less humor. "Fuller is too judicious to run into speculations. The work is both condensed and clear. Fuller called Faber "the Fortune-teller of the Church," and there are others who deserve the name."[28] There is a hint at his disgust for many commentators on the book of Revelation. Spurgeon had tipped his hand at his view of some of the commentators on apocalyptic literature. "We reverence the teaching of the prophets, and the Apocalypse, but for many of the professed expounders of those inspired books we entertain another feeling."[29] In one of his lectures to the students of the Pastors' College, Spurgeon had put it more forcefully,

> Blessed are they who read and hear the words of the prophecy of the Revelation, but the like blessing has evidently not fallen on those who pretend to expound it, for generation after generation of them have been proved to be in error by the mere lapse of time, and the present race will follow to the same inglorious sepulchre.[30]

Spurgeon quoted widely from Fuller in his "magnum opus," *The Treasury of David*—a seven-volume exposition of the book of Psalms completed in 1885. Spurgeon referenced Fuller by name sixteen times—three times in his "Hints to Preachers" and thirteen times in his "Explanatory Notes and Quaint Sayings." These citations indicate a broad reading of Fuller's sermons and other writings.

Spurgeon: the Fullerite

What is a Fullerite? Scientifically, according to the Moscow Institute of Physics and Technology, a Fullerite is a polymer composed of fullerenes, or spherical molecules made of carbon atoms. It has become first on the list of ultra-

---

[26] Spurgeon, *Commenting and Commentaries*, 81.
[27] Spurgeon, *Commenting and Commentaries*, 82.
[28] Spurgeon, *Commenting and Commentaries*, 280.
[29] Spurgeon, *Commenting and Commentaries*, 62.
[30] Spurgeon, *Lectures to My Students*, 1:83.

hard materials (harder than diamond), with values that range from 150 to 300 GPa (gigapascals). But that is not the kind of Fullerite that this chapter is considering. According to Michael A.G. Haykin, "A Fullerite is a Calvinist who is committed to the free offer of the gospel since it highlights the reality of moral obligation and human responsibility alongside the divine sovereignty of salvation."[31] In short, a Fullerite is a Calvinist who answers the Modern Question—is faith a duty for all people?—with a resounding yes.[32]

Throughout his ministry, Spurgeon was accused of being a Fullerite, a badge he wore with honor. In his expansive treatment of the theology of Spurgeon, Tom Nettles expresses a similar understanding as Haykin for what it meant to be a Fullerite. Nettles assesses that Spurgeon "would agree with the confessional commitment of Andrew Fuller." He cites from a sermon in which Spurgeon said he did not consider a man "faithful to his own conscience, who can preach simply the doctrine of sovereignty, and neglect to insist upon the doctrine of responsibility."[33]

In his book on the spirituality of Spurgeon, Peter J. Morden references one of the unpublished sermon manuscripts from the Waterbeach days where Spurgeon preached from Isaiah 1:18. As he continued to do until his dying day, the young Spurgeon "insisted that 'none' were 'excluded' from the gospel invitation to come to Christ and trust in him except those who excluded themselves. The invitation was to 'all sinners.'"[34] Not all were happy with this kind of preaching. In his autobiography, Spurgeon tells the story of how he was accused of being a Fullerite, likely for the first time.

> Another of those worthy brethren, a dear old Christian man, said to me, one day, when I was at his house to dinner, "My dear sir, I wish you would not preach those *invitation sermons.* You are too general in your appeals; you seem to press the people so much to come to Christ. I do not like it; for it is not at all consistent with my doctrinal views." "Well," I replied, "what would you have me preach?" "Well, sir," he said, "though I don't like such preaching, yet it is evident that the Lord does; for my son-in-law was converted to God under one of those

---

[31] Michael A.G. Haykin, e-mail message to author, February 4, 2015.

[32] For an exploration of how Fuller's work can be seen as a response to the Modern Question, see Gerald L. Priest, "Andrew Fuller's Response to the 'Modern Question'—A Reappraisal of *The Gospel Worthy of All Acceptation*" in *DBSJ* 6 (Fall 2001): 45–73.

[33] Tom Nettles, *Living By Revealed Truth: The Life and Pastoral Theology of Charles Haddon Spurgeon* (Fearn, Scotland: Mentor, 2013), 279–280.

[34] Peter J. Morden, *"Communion with Christ and His People": The Spirituality of C.H. Spurgeon,* CBHHS (Oxford: Regent's Park College, 2010), 65.

sermons; and when I came home, the other Sunday, so angry with you *for being such a Fullerite*, there was my daughter crying fit to break her heart; so," he added, "don't you take any notice of an old man like me. As long as God blesses you, you go on in your own way." I said to him, "But, my dear brother, don't you think, if God approves of this kind of preaching, that you ought to like it, too?" "Well," he answered, "perhaps I ought; but I am an old man, and I have always been brought up in those views. I am afraid I shall not get out of them; but don't you take the slighest notice of what I say." That was exactly what I had determined in my own mind that I would do, so we agreed after all.[35]

Spurgeon does not deny the charge of being a Fullerite and affirms that he purposed to continue in this style of preaching.

On another occasion early in his ministry, Spurgeon preached that God heard the prayers of the unregenerate. He was strongly rebuked by some of "the brethren" who "were of the 'very sound' sort." As he said of them elsewhere, "They believed in Calvinistic doctrine, not as I do, reckoning sixteen ounces to the pound, but allowing eighteen or nineteen ounces, and those extra ounces were not good for the people to feed upon."[36]

> Possibly, you doubt whether natural cries are heard by God; let me assure you that they are. I remember saying something on this subject on one occasion in a certain Ultra-Calvinistic place of worship. At that time I was preaching to children, and was exhorting them to pray, and I happened to say that long before any actual conversion I had prayed for common mercies, and that God had heard my prayers. This did not suit my good brethren of the superfine school; and afterwards they all came round me professedly to know what I meant, but really to cavil and carp according to their nature and wont. "They compassed me about like bees; yea, like bees they compassed me about!" After awhile, as I expected, they fell to their usual amusement of calling names. They began to say what rank Arminianism this was; and *another expression they were pleased to honour with the title of "Fullerism;" a title, by the way, so honourable that I could heartily have thanked them for appending it to what I had advanced*. But to say that God should hear the prayer of natural men

---

[35] Spurgeon, *Autobiography*, 1:256–257.

[36] Spurgeon, *MTPS*, 51:415. Spurgeon told this story with slight variation two times. The first time was in a sermon titled "The Ravens' Cry" preached at the Metropolitan Tabernacle on Sunday evening, January 14, 1866. The second time was in a sermon titled "True and Not True" preached at the Metropolitan Tabernacle on Sunday evening, May 23, 1875. In the latter sermon, Spurgeon says, "They considered me to be as bad as Andrew Fuller, and to them he was, doctrinally, about the most horrible person that could be." Spurgeon, *MTPS*, 51:415.

was something worse than Arminianism, if indeed anything could be worse to them.[37]

Spurgeon considered "Fullerism" to be an honorable title and something for which he would thank his opponents for attributing to him.

The esteem with which Spurgeon held Fuller can be further demonstrated by the company in which he included him. In an 1871 article in *The Sword and the Trowel*, Spurgeon reacted vehemently against the intellectual elites of his day and those who praised the sophisticated audiences of preachers with liberal theology. He stated his preference with sanctified sarcasm: "Those superficial beings, the Puritans, and those unintelligent persons of the type of Jonathan Edwards and Andrew Fuller, are, to our mind, far better models than the intellectual dandies who have been in fashion."[38] Instead of the intelligentsia of his day, Spurgeon declared his preference for the Puritans, Jonathan Edwards, and Andrew Fuller. These, he regards as "better models" than the latest fashionable preachers. I would argue that these three who most quickly came to his mind are the major influences in his theology.

So, it is clear that Spurgeon identified himself favorably with the terms "Fullerite" and "Fullerism," but how did his Fullerism manifest itself in his preaching ministry? The first work by Fuller which the young Spurgeon read would have been Fuller's *Antinomianism Contrasted with the Religion Taught and Exemplified in Holy Scriptures* that he read a few weeks before his baptism in 1850. In this book, Fuller emphasized the importance of holy living as a duty for a Christian. Fuller argued that human beings were responsible before God for their actions by distinguishing between moral and natural (or physical) ability/inability:

> It is undoubtedly true that the Scriptures represent man by nature as unable to do any good thing; that is, they declare that an evil tree cannot bring forth good fruit; that they who are evil cannot speak good things; that they whose eyes are full of adultery cannot cease from sin; that they who are in the flesh cannot please God; finally, that they whose hearts are attached to their idols, or to the mammon of this world, cannot serve the Lord. This doctrine, if properly understood, is of great account in true religion. Hence arises the necessity of our being created anew in Christ Jesus ere we can perform good works; and of our being

---

[37] Spurgeon, *MTPS*, 12:56, emphasis added.
[38] C.H. Spurgeon, *The Sword and Trowel: 1871* (London: Passmore & Alabaster, 1871), 52.

continually kept from falling by the power of God. He that has the greatest sense of his own weakness and insufficiency to do any thing as he ought, will be most earnest in crying to the strong for strength, and most watchful against the temptations of the world. It is thus that "when we are weak, then are we strong." But if this doctrine be confounded with *physical inability*, and understood to excuse the sinner in his sins, it is utterly perverted. If the connexion of the above passages were consulted, they would be found to be the language of the most cutting reproach; *manifestly proving that the inability of the parties arose from the evil dispositions of their own minds, and therefore had not the least tendency to render them less accountable to God, or more excusable in their sins*; yet such, in spite of Scripture, conscience, and common sense, is the construction put upon it by Antinomianism.[39]

Fuller learned this distinction through his reading of Jonathan Edwards' philosophical and theological masterpiece, *Freedom of the Will*.[40] Fuller would make use of this distinction to argue against two characteristics of the hyper-Calvinism of his day—antinomianism and the denial of the free offer of the gospel.

In Fuller's most influential work, *The Gospel Worthy of All Acceptation*, which was subtitled in its second edition: *The Duty of Sinners to Believe in Jesus Christ*, Fuller used the Edwardsean distinction to argue that the inability of sinners to come to Christ is not because of a "physical" or "natural inability," but because of a "moral inability." This means that sinners do not lack the physical ability to respond to the gospel, but the desire to do so. Therefore, they are morally responsible and culpable if they fail to do so. All sinners have a duty to believe in Jesus Christ and therefore Christians have a responsibility to declare the gospel to everyone indiscriminately. Spurgeon, who learned to hate antinomianism as a new Christian by reading Fuller, would employ the distinction widely in his preaching. He would do so, just as Fuller had, both against antinomianism and to stress the duty of sinners to respond to the

---

[39] Andrew Fuller, "Antinomianism Contrasted with the Religion Taught and Exemplified in Holy Scriptures," in *FW*, 2:745, emphasis added.

[40] Jonathan Edwards, *A Careful and Strict Enquiry into the Modern Prevailing Notions of That Freedom of Will, Which is Supposed to be Essential to Moral Agency, Virtue and Vice, Reward and Punishment, Praise and Blame* (Boston: S. Kneeland, 1754). For a careful study of Edwards' influence upon Fuller, see Chris Chun, *The Legacy of Jonathan Edwards in the Theology of Andrew Fuller*, SHT (Leiden: Brill, 2012).

gospel message. In what follows, some examples of Spurgeon's use of the distinction between moral and natural ability/inability are shown.[41]

On October 23, 1881, in a Sunday morning sermon on "Without Christ-Nothing" from John 15:5, Spurgeon simply declared that the doctrine of moral inability of the unregenerate was a "doctrine I most firmly believe."[42] On July 3, 1864, Spurgeon had gone into more detail on the distinction between moral and natural inability in a sermon titled, "A Bad Excuse is Worse Than None" from Luke 14:18, "And they all with one consent began to make excuse."

> "Well," says one, "I cannot trust Christ, I cannot believe him." You talk Latin, brother; you talk Latin. "No," you say, "I do not talk Latin." Yes, you do. I will translate that word into the English for you. It means, "I will not." When you say, "I cannot," it means, "I will not;" and understand, whenever the minister says, "You cannot," he means, "you will not;" for he does not mean that you have any *natural inability, but that you have a moral inability caused by your love of sin—a wilful inability.* "I cannot," is the Latin, but "I will not," is the English of it.[43]

Spurgeon went on to illustrate the difference between the two kinds of inability:

> A man once sent his servant to a certain town to fetch some goods; and he came back without them. "Well, sir, why did you not go there?" "Well, when I got to a certain place, I came to a river, sir, a very deep river: I cannot swim, and I had no boat; so I could not get over." A good excuse, was it not? It looked so, but it happened to be a very bad one, for the master said, "Is there not a ferry there?" "Yes, sir." "Did you ask the man to take you over?" "No, sir." Surely the excuse was a mere fiction! So there are many things with regard to our salvation which we cannot do. Granted, but then there is a ferry there! There is the Holy Spirit who is able to do all things, and you remember the text, "If ye then, being evil, know how to give good gifts unto your children, how much more shall your Father which is in heaven give good things to them that ask him?" It is true you cannot make yourself a new heart, but did you ask for a new heart with sincerity and truth? Did you seek

---

[41] Although Spurgeon read and benefited directly from the writings of Jonathan Edwards, his use of the Edwardsean distinction between moral and natural ability/inability seems to be mediated through Fuller as he applies it to their common areas of concern in Baptist life in the nineteenth century—Antinomianism and the refusal to offer the gospel indiscriminately to all.

[42] Spurgeon, *MTPS*, 27:593.

[43] Spurgeon, *MTPS*, 10:386, emphasis added.

Christ? If you say, "Yes, I did sincerely seek Christ, and Christ would not save me," why then you are excused; but there never was a soul who could in truth say that. There never was a sinner yet who perished seeking Christ, and there never will be; and if thy heart's sincere desire is after the salvation which is treasured in Christ Jesus, then heaven and earth may pass away, but Christ will never cast you out while his own word stands, "Him that cometh to me I will in no wise cast out." "Still," you say, "I cannot trust Christ." Now, I am at issue with you here—I am at issue with every awakened sinner. I agree with you, if you will let me give my own translation of the word cannot—that you *will not*, but if it is to stand as the word is generally used, I am at issue with you.[44]

In a March 5, 1871, sermon on "Faith and Regeneration" from 1 John 5:1, Spurgeon used the distinction between moral and physical ability to argue for the sinner's responsibility to believe the gospel message:

Inasmuch as the gospel command, "Believe in the Lord Jesus Christ and thou shalt be saved," is addressed by divine authority to every creature, it is the duty of every man so to do. What saith John: "This is his commandment, That we should believe on the name of his Son Jesus Christ," and our Lord himself assures us, "He that believeth on him is not condemned: but he that believeth not is condemned already, because he hath not believed in the name of the only-begotten Son of God." I know there are some who will deny this, and deny it upon the ground that man has not the spiritual ability to believe in Jesus, to which I reply that it is altogether an error to imagine that the measure of the sinner's moral ability is the measure of his duty. There are many things which men ought to do which they have now lost the moral and spiritual, though not the physical, power to do. A man ought to be chaste, but if he has been so long immoral that he cannot restrain his passions, he is not thereby free from the obligation. It is the duty of a debtor to pay his debts, but if he has been such a spendthrift that he has brought himself into hopeless poverty, he is not exonerated from his debts thereby. Every man ought to believe that which is true, but if his mind has become so depraved that he loves a lie and will not receive the truth, is he thereby excused? If the law of God is to be lowered according to the moral condition of sinners, you would have a law graduated upon a sliding-scale to suit the degrees of human sinfulness; in fact, the worst man would then be under the least law, and become consequently the least

---

[44] Spurgeon, *MTPS*, 10:386.

guilty. God's requirements would be a variable quantity, and, in truth, we should be under no rule at all. The command of Christ stands good however bad men may be, and when he commands all men everywhere to repent, they are bound to repent, whether their sinfulness renders it impossible for them to be willing to do so or not. In every case it is man's duty to do what God bids him.[45]

Spurgeon not only used the distinction between moral and natural ability to argue for the duty of sinners to repent and believe the gospel, he also used the distinction to refute an antinomian view of the law. In a Sunday morning sermon on "The Perpetuity of the Law of God" from Matthew 5:18 preached at the Metropolitan Tabernacle on May 21, 1882, Spurgeon used the Fuller/Edwards distinction between moral and physical inability to show that men are not free from their responsibility to obey the law of God:

It has been said that man's moral inability to keep the perfect law exempts him from the duty of doing so. This is very specious, but it is utterly false. Man's inability is not of the kind which removes responsibility: it is moral, not physical. Never fall into the error that moral inability will be an excuse for sin. What, when a man becomes such a liar that he cannot speak the truth, is he thereby exempted from the duty of truthfulness? If your servant owes you a day's labour, is he free from the duty because he has made himself so drunk that he cannot serve you? Is a man freed from a debt by the fact that he has squandered the money, and therefore cannot pay it? Is a lustful man free to indulge his passions because he cannot understand the beauty of chastity? This is dangerous doctrine. The law is a just one, and man is bound by it though his sin has rendered him incapable of doing so.[46]

In another Sunday morning sermon preached on August 25, 1889, from Colossians 2:13 titled "Life and Pardon," Spurgeon used the distinction to show that humans are responsible for their sin against God:

One point must be noticed here, which makes this spiritual death the more terrible: they are dead, but yet responsible. If men were literally dead, then they were incapable of sin; but the kind of death of which we speak involves a responsibility none the less, but all the greater. If I say of a man that he is such a liar that he cannot speak the truth, do you

---

[45] Spurgeon, *MTPS*, 17:136–137.
[46] Spurgeon, *MTPS*, 28:283.

therefore think him blameless? No; but you judge him to be all the more worthy of condemnation because he has lost the very sense which discerns between a truth and a lie. If we say of a certain man, as we have had to do, "He is a rogue ingrained; he is so tricky that he cannot deal honestly, but must always be cheating"; do you therefore excuse his fraud, and pity him? Far from it. *His inability is not physical, but moral inability, and is the consequence of his own persistence in evil.* The law is as much binding upon the morally incapable as upon the most sanctified in nature. If, through a man's own perversity, he wills to reject good and love evil, the blame is with himself.[47]

This evidence can be multiplied many times over from Spurgeon's voluminous sermons. There is ample evidence to demonstrate that Spurgeon thought as a Fullerite. He not only proudly identified himself as such, he utilized the same distinction between moral and natural ability/inability made by Fuller to argue as Fuller had for the duty of sinners to respond to the gospel message in repentance and faith and to refute any sense of antinomianism.

Conclusion

On June 3, 1801, Andrew Fuller preached a sermon on Jude 3 to an "Association of Baptist Ministers and Churches at Oakham." In the sermon, titled "The Common Salvation," Fuller gave four aspects of the "common salvation":

> There are, I conceive, four things which essentially belong to the "common salvation;" its *necessity*, its *vicarious medium*, its *freeness* to the chief of sinners, and its *holy efficacy*. If we doubt whether we stand in need of salvation, or overlook the atonement, or hope for an interest in it any otherwise than as unworthy, or rest in a mere speculative opinion, which has no effectual influence on our spirit and conduct, we are at present unbelievers, and have every thing to learn.[48]

Fuller did not expound any further on these four aspects in his sermon, but nearly eighty years later on April 10, 1881, Spurgeon quoted Fuller in his own sermon on Jude 3 also titled, "The Common Salvation." Spurgeon believed that the four aspects mentioned by Fuller could and should unite all

---

[47] Spurgeon, *MTPS*, 35:459, emphasis added.
[48] Andrew Fuller, "The Common Salvation," in *FW*, 1:411.

Christians, even those who differed on the perennially divisive five points of Calvinism. After quoting Fuller, Spurgeon declared,

> We may differ on the "five points," but we are agreed upon these four points. ... there is an agreement upon their need of a Saviour, their faith in his death, the freeness of his grace, and the change of heart which it produces. All believers in Christ have a common delight in a common salvation.[49]

Just as Spurgeon expressed a belief that true Christians were united around the four essentials of common salvation espoused by Fuller, could modern-day Baptists be united through a recovery of the theological vision of Andrew Fuller? Could the divisions between Calvinists and non-Calvinists be overcome, if Baptists on both sides of the issue understood the distinction between moral and natural ability? This distinction enabled Fuller and Spurgeon to hold both a high view of divine sovereignty and a strong view of human responsibility. The legacy of Andrew Fuller is that his theological emphases not only fueled the Modern Missionary movement, it also underlay the evangelistic preaching ministry of Charles Haddon Spurgeon. Perhaps a recovery of the theology of Andrew Fuller can motivate similar movements and ministries today.

---

[49] Spurgeon, *MTPS*, 27:198.

A Chronology of Andrew Fuller's Life

Nathan A. Finn

1754	Born on February 6 in the village of Wicken, Cambridgeshire
1761	Family moves to Soham, Cambridgeshire
1769	Converted in November after several years of wrestling with spiritual matters on account of his exposure to High Calvinist theology
1770	Baptized by Pastor John Eve and becomes a member of Soham Baptist Church in April
1774	Called to preach by Soham Baptist Church in January
1775	Ordained as the pastor of Soham Baptist Church in May; Robert Hall Sr. preaches for the occasion
	Soham Baptist Church joins the Northamptonshire Association, which had been formed in 1769
1776	Becomes friends with John Sutcliff and John Ryland Jr.
	Marries Sarah Gardiner
1777	Introduced to Jonathan Edwards's *Freedom of the Will* by Robert Hall Sr.
1781	Writes the first draft of *The Gospel of Christ Worthy of All Acceptation*

1782	Moves to Kettering, Northamptonshire in October to become pastor of Kettering Baptist Church
	Writes "The Excellence and Utility of Hope," the circular letter to the Northamptonshire Association
1783	Formally installed as the pastor of Kettering Baptist Church in October; Robert Hall Sr. and John Ryland Jr. preaches for the occasion
	Presents his Confession of Faith to Kettering Baptist Church
1784	John Sutcliff issues the "Prayer Call" to the churches of the Northamtonshire Association
	Publishes the sermon *The Nature and Importance of Walking by Faith*
1785	Writes "Causes of Declension in Religion, and Means of Revival," the circular letter to the Northamptonshire Association
	Publishes the first edition of *The Gospel of Christ Worthy of All Acceptation*
1787	Publishes *A Defence of a Treatise Entitled, The Gospel Worthy of All Acceptation: Containing a Reply to Mr. Button's Remarks, and Observations of Philanthropos*, defending his views against critiques from High Calvinist William Button and Arminian Daniel Taylor (as "Philanthropos")
1788	Publishes *Letters Relative to Mr. Martin's Publication on The Duty Faith in Christ*, defending his views against critique from High Calvinist John Martin
1790	Publishes (as "Agnostos") *The Reality and Efficacy of Divine Grace, with the Certain Success of Christ's Kingdom, Considered in a Series of Letters*, further engaging with Arminian pastor Daniel Taylor

1791	Publishes the sermon *The Pernicious Consequences of Delay in Religious Concerns*
1792	William Carey publishes *An Enquiry into the Obligations of Christians to Use Means in the Conversion of the Heathen*, at the urging of Fuller and others
	Helps found the Particular Baptist Missionary Society (BMS) and appointed as secretary of the BMS
	Sarah Fuller dies in August
1793	Publishes *The Calvinistic and Socinian Systems Examined and Compared as to Their Moral Tendency*
	William Carey and John Thomas embark for India as BMS Missionaries
	Suffers a stroke and temporary facial paralysis
1793–1795	Publishes *Dialogues and Letters between Crispus and Gaius* on various theological topics in the *Evangelical Magazine*
1794	Marries Ann Coles
1795	Writes "Why Christians in the Present Day Possess Less Joy than the Primitive Disciples," the circular letter to the Northamptonshire Association
1796	Engages in controversy with Abraham Booth over the nature of justification, imputation, and penal substitution
1797	Publishes *A Sermon the Importance of a Deep and Intimate Knowledge of Divine Truth*
1798	Awarded an honorary D.D by Princeton University (Fuller declines to accept the honor)
1799	Publishes *The Gospel Its Own Witness*, a critique of Thomas Paine's Deist tract *The Age of Reason*

	Writes "The Discipline of the Primitive Churches Illustrated and Enforced," the circular letter to the Northamptonshire Association
	First visit to Scotland on behalf of the BMS
1800	Publishes *Memoirs of the Late Rev. Samuel Pearce*
	Second visit to Scotland on behalf of the BMS
1801	Publishes second edition of *The Gospel Worthy of All Acceptation*, which included an appendix criticizing the Sandemanian view of faith
	Publishes *The Backslider: Or, An Enquiry into the Nature, Symptoms, and Effects of Religious Declension with the Means of Recovery*
1802	Publishes *Letters to Mr. Vidler on the Doctrine of Universal Salvation*, a critique of William Vidler's belief in universal Restoration
	Writes "The Practical Uses of Christian Baptism," the circular letter to the Northamptonshire Association
1803	Writes *Six Letters to Dr. Ryland Respecting the Controversy with Rev. A. Booth*, defending Fuller's view of justification and atonement
	Publishes *Three Conversations on Imputation, Substitution, and Particular Redemption*, which were related to the ongoing controversy with Booth
1804	Visit to Ireland on behalf of the BMS
1805	Kettering Baptist Church meeting house is enlarged
	Awarded an honorary D.D. by Yale University (Fuller declines to accept the honor)
	Third visit to Scotland on behalf of the BMS
1806	Publishes *Expository Discourses on the Book of Genesis*

	Writes "The Pastor's Address to His Christian Hearers, Entreating Their Assistance in Promoting the Interest of Christ," the circular letter to the Northamptonshire Association
1807	Writes "On Moral and Positive Obedience," the circular letter to the Northamptonshire Association
1808	Publishes *Apology for the Late Christian Missions to India*, defending BMS missionaries against the accusation that they provoked the Vellore uprising
	Fourth visit to Scotland on behalf of the BMS
1810	Publishes *Strictures on Sandemanianism in Twelve Letters to a Friend*, a more substantial critique of the Sandemanian view of faith
	Publishes "The Promise of the Spirit the Grand Encouragement in Promoting the Gospel," the circular letter to the Northamptonshire Association
1811	Publishes *Dialogues, Letters, and Essays on Various Subjects*
	John Keen Hall is appointed as Fuller's assistant pastor
1812	Visit to Wales on behalf of the BMS
1813	Fifth and final visit to Scotland on behalf of the BMS
1814	Begins writing *Letters on Systematic Divinity* to John Ryland Jr.; the project, which is never finished, is intended to be a complete systematic divinity
1815	Publishes *Expository Discourses on the Apocalypse*
	Publishes "The Situation of the Widows and Orphans of Christian Ministers"
	Dies at Kettering on May 8

Contributors

CHARLES J. BUMGARDNER completed a PhD in New Testament studies at Southeastern Baptist Theological Seminary in Wake Forest, NC

NATHAN A. FINN is Provost and Dean of the University Faculty in Tigerville, SC.

MATTHEW D. HASTE is Associate Professor of Biblical Spirituality and Biblical Counseling and Director of Professional Doctoral Studies at The Southern Baptist Theological Seminary in Louisville, KY and a Senior Fellow of the Andrew Fuller Center for Baptist Studies

MICHAEL A.G. HAYKIN is Professor of Church History and Biblical Spirituality and Director of the Andrew Fuller Center for Baptist Studies at The Southern Baptist Theological Seminary in Louisville, KY

DAVID G. NORMAN, JR. is Senior Pastor of University Baptist Church in San Antonio, TX and Vice President of Equip the Nations

DAVID E. PRINCE is Assistant Professor of Christian Preaching at The Southern Baptist Theological Seminary in Louisville, KY and Pastor of Preaching and Vision of Ashland Avenue Baptist Church in Lexington, KY

SHANE SHADDIX is Pastor of Discipleship at Imago Dei Church in Raleigh, NC

STEVE WEAVER is Senior Pastor of Farmdale Baptist Church in Frankfort, KY, State Minister at the Kentucky Capitol with Capitol Commission, and a Senior Fellow of the Andrew Fuller Center for Baptist Studies

Ryan West is the Founder and CEO of Paro Development and a Senior Fellow for the Andrew Fuller Center for Baptist Studies

Scripture Index

Old Testament

Genesis
- 1:26–27 51
- 2:18–25 46
- 11:27–50 106
- 19 46
- 22:2 109

1 Chronicles
- 21:26–27 109

2 Chronicles
- 3:1 109

Psalms
- 2:1 12
- 2:2 12
- 2:12 12
- 23:5 140
- 101:2 48

Isaiah
- 1:18 146
- 6:10 12
- 45:22 139

Ezekiel
- 16:1–5 55

New Testament

Matthew
- 5:18 152
- 21:28 140
- 28:19–20 11

Mark
- 16:15–16 11

Luke
- 14:18 150

John
- 3:16 113
- 5:23 13
- 6:26 12
- 6:27 12
- 6:28 13
- 6:29 .... 12, 13
- 6:36 12
- 10:35 123
- 12:36 12
- 12:37 12
- 12:40 12
- 12:46 12
- 15:5 150

Acts
- 4:27 12
- 12:24 33

Romans
- 10:10 138

1 Corinthians
- 6:16–17 54
- 8:13 91
- 15:1 121
- 15:1–4 121

Subject Index

2 Corinthians
    4:13 120
    5:7 142

Galatians
    3:8 107

Ephesians
    1:10 122
    4:20 121
    4:21 121
    5:25 55

Colossians
    2:13 152

2 Timothy
    3:5 120

Hebrews
    11:17 108

1 John
    5:1 151
    5:4 121
    5:11 121

2 John
    1:3 113

Revelation
    22:2 141

Subject Index

Activism, 17, 21, 31, 43
Adultery, 46, 148
Anabaptists, 90
Andrew Fuller Center for Baptist Studies, 1, 161
Anglicanism, 63, 90
Antinomianism, 102, 149, 153
Apostasy, 17
Arianism, 17
Arminianism, 8, 9, 14, 17, 19, 22, 23, 62, 63, 95, 122, 147, 156
Atonement, 3, 25, 26, 27, 29, 56, 103, 122, 153, 158
Bach, Johann Sebastian, 98
Baptism, 69, 144, 148
Baptist Missionary Society, 3, 6, 31, 32, 33, 36, 37, 38, 39, 40, 41, 42, 43, 72, 123, 157, 158, 159
Baptist renewal, 2
Barton, William, 65, 66
Baxter, Richard, 46, 52, 65
Beddome, Benjamin, 62, 73
Belcher, Joseph, 137, 142
Believer's baptism, 15
Biblicism, 17
Book printing, 11
Booth, Abraham, 1, 157
Brainerd, David, 21
Brine, John, 8, 9
Bristol Baptist Academy, 18, 68
Bristol Collection, 62, 65, 69, 75
Bristol Education Society, 101, 120
Buell, Samuel, 67
Bunyan, John, 7, 52, 102
Bush, George, 144

Calvin, John, 6, 14, 22, 61, 90, 122
Calvinism, 1, 5, 6, 7, 14, 15, 16, 20, 22, 30, 63, 96, 102, 103, 116, 119, 122, 123, 124, 149, 154
Carey, S. Pearce, 119
Carey, William, 1, 6, 14, 32, 37, 38, 40, 72, 119, 157
Children, 12, 48, 130, 147, 150
Church discipline, 59
Church of England, 62
Colchester Baptist Church, 13
Colman, Benjamin, 67
Congregational singing, 61, 63, 66, 76, 78, 83, 92
Conversionism, 17
Cox, Frank, 84
Crucicentrism, 17
Deism, 6, 15, 17
Dicey, Thomas, 11, 25
Dissenters, 8, 31, 52, 61, 79, 84, 98, 123
Diver, Joseph, 70
Doctrines of grace, 23
Doddridge, Philip, 63
Domestic duties, 48
Dundas, Robert, 32
East India Company, 31, 32
Ecclesiology, 59, 60, 98, 119, 126
Edwards, Jonathan, 7, 1, 16, 20, 21, 38, 56, 67, 68, 78, 97, 103, 148, 149, 152, 155
Enlightenment, 15
Erskine, Ralph, 7, 65, 68, 70, 71
Evangelical Awakening, 18, 21
Evangelical renewal movement, 1
Evangelical Revival, 62, 63

Subject Index

Evangelical Theological Society, 6, 2
Evangelicalism, 17, 18, 57, 63, 122
Evangelistic preaching, 29, 154
Eve, John, 7, 53, 102, 123, 124, 155
Family, i, 7, 11, 47, 48, 49, 50, 51, 72, 106, 113
Family worship, 51
Fawcett, John, 62, 64, 65, 68, 74, 99
Fornication, 46, 47
Free offer of the gospel, 15, 16, 20, 21, 23, 25, 27, 28, 29, 96, 103, 124, 146, 149
Friendship, i, ii, 14, 16, 18, 21, 41, 50, 51, 65, 69, 70, 73, 74, 78, 105, 132, 134, 139, 140, 142, 143, 144, 155
Fuller, Andrew Gunton, 6, 7, 64, 65, 67, 69, 71, 96, 102, 137, 139
Fuller, Robert, 6, 144
Fullerism, ii, 1, 2, 5, 14, 20, 63, 96, 147, 148
Fullerite, ii, 14, 138, 145, 146, 147, 148, 153
Gender roles, 50
General Baptist, 15, 17, 61
German Pietism, 17
Gill, John, 8, 9, 17, 18, 19, 57, 62, 79
Glas, John, 88
Glasgow Missionary Society, 35, 36, 39
Gouge, William, 49, 51
Grant, Charles, 32
Great Commission, 11
Grigg, Jacob, 36
Gunton, Philippa, 6
Hall Sr., Robert, 1, 155
Hall, John Keen, 79, 90, 159
Hall, Robert, 1, 70, 102, 155

Handel, George Frideric, 93, 96
Hastings, Selina, 73
Haykin, Michael, i, 2
Haykin, Michael A.G., 6
Henry, Matthew, 48, 49
Heresy, 15
High Calvinism, 1, 6, 8, 14, 16, 18, 19, 95, 96, 122
Hindus, 34
Holy Spirit, 7, 9, 10, 15, 20, 38, 61, 111, 114, 125, 150, 159
Homiletics, 2
Homosexuality, 46
Horsleydown Church, 17
Hupton, Job, 5, 6, 14
Husbands, 49, 50
Hussey, Joseph, 19
Hymnody, 60, 61, 62, 63, 64, 67, 69, 72, 73, 74, 75, 79, 89, 95
Idolatry, 35, 37, 40
Instrumental music, 90, 91
Jarman, Thomas, 84, 85
Johnson, John, 52
Justification, 54, 112, 157, 158
Keach, Benjamin, 61
Limited atonement, 25, 103
Long eighteenth century, 1
Lord's Supper, 59, 71, 72, 90
Luther, Martin, 1, 98
Lutherans, 90, 97
Mardon, Richard, 42
Marriage, 45, 46, 47, 49, 50, 51, 52, 53, 54, 55, 56, 57
Marshman, Joshua, 38
Mason, John, 65, 71, 99
Maurice, Matthias, 8
McLean, Alexander, 88
Milton, John, 64
Missions, 1, 3, 30, 32, 33, 36, 41, 42, 43, 63, 64, 119, 122, 123, 125
Modern missions movement, 1

Modern Question, 8, 9, 14, 18, 146
Moral ability, 16
Morris, J.W., 139, 143
Music, 59, 60, 62, 63, 64, 68, 69, 70, 74, 75, 78, 79, 80, 83, 84, 85, 86, 88, 89, 90, 91, 92, 93, 94, 95, 96, 97, 98
Natural ability, 16, 20, 150, 152, 153, 154
Natural revelation, 33, 34
New World, 17
Newton, John, 63, 73, 75, 99
Northampton Baptist Association, 38
Northamptonshire Association, 124, 142, 155, 156, 157, 158, 159
Owen, John, 8, 15, 16, 20, 21, 22, 23, 24, 25, 26, 27, 28, 29, 56, 135
Paine, Thomas, 6, 157
Parry, Edward, 32
Particular redemption, 11, 16, 23, 25, 27
Particular Redemption, 25
Pastoral theology, 15, 22, 59, 60, 95, 98
Pastors' College, 142, 144, 145
Pearce, Samuel, 32, 40, 41, 42, 43, 72, 98, 99, 130, 131, 132, 158
Persian Pamphlet, 32
Piety, 32, 33, 35, 36, 37, 40, 41, 42, 43
Plagiarism, 144
Poetry, 60, 64
Politics, 31, 32, 36, 38, 40, 105
Polygamy, 46, 47
Pope, Alexander, 64
Prayer, 3, 16, 38, 42, 47, 72, 75, 111, 147
Preaching, 8, 9, 13, 28, 41, 59, 95, 97, 101, 102, 103, 104, 110, 111, 112, 114, 115, 116, 119, 124, 125, 126, 127, 129, 131, 132, 134, 135, 138, 139, 146, 147, 148, 149
Priestley, Joseph, 8
Protestantism, 17, 90
Providence of God, 34
Psalmody, 61, 63, 67, 76, 78, 83, 92
Puritans, 1, 16, 21, 22, 29, 45, 46, 47, 48, 49, 50, 51, 56, 57, 148
Reformation, 15, 67, 90
Reformed theology, 23
Reformers, 15, 29
Revival, 16, 62, 63, 72
Rippon, John, 62, 63, 64, 65, 69, 74, 75, 77, 78, 79, 84, 96
Robinson, Haddon, 114
Robinson, Robert, 4, 62, 66, 99
Ryland Jr., John, 1, 5, 99, 139, 155, 156, 159
Sanctification, 53
Sandeman, Robert, 88, 89
Sandemanianism, 46, 86, 88, 89, 95, 122, 144, 159
Satan, 53, 126
Scotch Baptists, 88, 89, 140
Second London Confession, 46
Secret will of God, 26
Serampore, 32, 38, 42
Seventh-Day Baptists, 66
Silesian revivals, 17
Singing, 61, 62, 63, 66, 67, 71, 72, 74, 75, 76, 78, 79, 80, 83, 84, 85, 86, 88, 89, 90, 92, 95, 97, 142
Smith, Isaac, 83
Socinianism, 6, 19, 68, 95, 122, 157
Soteriology, 1, 22, 27, 29
Southern Baptist Theological Seminary, i, 10, 161
Special revelation, 34
Spirituality, 2, 28, 42, 45, 48, 146
Spurgeon Collection, 144

Subject Index

Spurgeon, Charles Haddon, ii, 11, 88, 119, 137, 138, 139, 140, 141, 142, 143, 144, 145, 146, 147, 148, 149, 150, 151, 152, 153, 154
Steele, Anne, 62, 73
Steevens, Thomas, 13, 14, 70, 74, 99
Stennett, Joseph, 65, 66
Stennett, Samuel, 47, 48, 62, 64, 65
Stonehouse, George, 5
Sutcliff, John, 14, 21, 38, 98, 102, 155, 156
Systematic theology, 35
Taylor, Abraham, 8, 9
Thomas, John, 37, 40, 157
Total Depravity, 18, 20
Trinity, 7
Unitarianism, 15, 17, 95
Unity, 36, 38, 133, 134
Universalism, 19
Wallis, Beeby, 70, 78
Wallis, Martha, 78
Ward, William, 32, 38
Warrant, 19, 124
Watts, Isaac, 61, 62, 65, 66, 67, 69, 70, 71, 72, 73, 75, 76, 77, 78, 95, 96, 97, 98, 99
Wesley, Charles, 62, 63, 73, 93
Wesley, John, 17, 62, 64, 79, 83, 93, 98
Whitefield, George, 17, 68, 73
Williams, William, 72, 99
Wives, 47, 49, 50
Women, 11, 12, 13, 19, 20, 23, 47, 49, 50, 51, 52, 55, 57, 78, 80, 139, 140
Young, Edward, 64
Zwingli, Ulrich, 90

www.ingramcontent.com/pod-product-compliance
Lightning Source LLC
Chambersburg PA
CBHW021425070526
44577CB00001B/68